SCOTTISH TRADE
with
COLONIAL CHARLESTON
1683 - 1783

David Dobson

CLEARFIELD

ISBN 9780806358598

SCOTTISH TRADE WITH
COLONIAL CHARLESTON, 1683-1783

INTRODUCTION

THE SEVENTEENTH CENTURY
ECONOMIC BACKGROUND

During the seventeenth century Scotland was a nation in transition. The Union of the Crowns in 1603 had transformed the political relationship that had existed between Scotland and England for centuries, and the old enmity, at least officially, had largely disappeared. The period of peace and harmony between the two countries, as well as with Ireland, was, however, short-lived, as the Wars of the Three Kingdoms 1638-51 demonstrated. The outbreak of these hostilities ended the period of peaceful economic expansion, particularly in the Scottish Lowlands, and during the period of the wars Scotland, in line with the rest of the British Isles, was divided in its attitude towards the House of Stuart. Military campaigns involved Scottish armies fighting at home, in England and in Ireland, and ended with the occupation of Scotland by the Parliamentary army. This period also saw the destruction of important resources, especially capital assets such as shipping, rural and urban buildings, and the plague which broke out towards the end of the period of war affected the numbers of skilled workers available, resulting in disrupted production and retarded the country's economic development.[1]

1 see Ian D Whyte, *Scotland before the Industrial Revolution, An Economic and Social History c1050-c1750*, London, 1995, pp.281-290

SCOTTISH TRADE WITH
COLONIAL CHARLESTON, 1683-1783

The Cromwellian or Commonwealth period following the years of unrest allowed the opening up of markets with both England and its colonies to Scottish trade, but for the reasons above, Scots were not in a position immediately to take full advantage of this economic opportunity.   In addition, much of the restricted range of Scottish marketable commodities, such as herring, cattle, hides and skins, linen and woollen cloth, coal and salt and available for export were also available from English sources, often of a higher standard or at lower cost.   Nevertheless, the evidence of the surviving Scottish port books reveal an expansion of trade with England, particularly London, and a corresponding contraction of business with its traditional trading partners of France and the Netherlands.[2]

Trade with the Netherlands did, however, continue until the period of the 1660s, but the Anglo-Dutch Wars of the 1660s and 1670, affected adversely commerce with the Netherlands, Scotland's hitherto most important European trading partner, and the later hostilities between England and France, together with internal unrest involving the Covenanter Risings, all contributed to Scotland's lack of economic growth into the 1680s.

Another problem with Scottish international trade, before the Union of 1707, was protection of mercantile shipping.   The Scots had no equivalent of England's Royal Navy, which was able to protect fleets of merchant ships from the attack by foreign privateers during intermittent periods of conflict between England, France and The Netherlands.   The only protection Scottish mercantile ships had were two frigates, authorised for this use in 1689 by the Scots Parliament,

2 For a recent concise analysis of the situation, see Richard J Finlay's article on the economy in Michael Lynch [ed.], *The Oxford Companion to Scottish History,* Oxford, 2005, pp.197-198
3 E J Graham, *A Maritime History of Scotland, 1650-1790,* East Linton, Scotland,2002, pp.65-87

SCOTTISH TRADE WITH
COLONIAL CHARLESTON, 1683-1783

but only in Scottish waters. By 1703 the Scots Navy amounted to three vessels, none of which were capable of protecting ships in the privateer-infested English Channel.[3] Although Scotland was duty bound to supply a quota of Scots for duty on English ships, they were not obliged to come to the aid of the Scottish mercantile fleet under attack. With political backing, however, Scotland's economy was just beginning a slow growth in the 1680s when, in the 1690s, it was hit by a succession of harvest failures due to extremely bad summer weather.

The benefits in matters of trade which were expected to occur by the union of Scotland and England at the time of James VI's accession to the English throne, did not reach the anticipated levels, though some clear benefits did occur. For example, before the outbreak of the Civil Wars, the salt-panning industry was stimulated by a rise in demand from England.[4] For a period, during the Interregnum, from 1651 – 1660, there had existed free trade between the countries, but within a few years of the accession of Charles II to the throne of England, there was introduced the first of the English Navigation Acts which imposed restrictions on all countries trading with England and its colonies. These Acts of the Parliament of England had the effect of officially eliminating direct trade between Scotland and the English colonies, and this consequently affected Scottish economic growth. The principal aims of the Navigation Acts were to strengthen the economy and maritime power of England and at the same time curtail the activities of the Dutch. They effectively stopped any direct trade, authorised by

---

[3] Eric J Graham, *A Maritime History of Scotland, 1650-1790,* East Linton, Scotland, 2002, pp.65-87

[4] T. C. Smout, 'The Anglo Scottish Union of 1707. The Economic Background', *Economic History Review, 2nd series, Volume XVI,* Utrecht, the Netherlands, 1964, p.455

SCOTTISH TRADE WITH
COLONIAL CHARLESTON, 1683-1783

England, between Scotland and England's American colonies. However, since the trading partners wished to continue to do business, they had to choose between obtaining Scotland's goods indirectly, via an English port, often Whitehaven in Cumberland, or engage in smuggling.   The mutual benefits of trade between the American colonists and the Scots merchants ensured that it continued to some degree,[5] and the scale of this 'clandestine' trade should not be underestimated.   In addition, the English Navigation Acts had no detrimental effect on trade between Scotland and England, and the export of linen and cattle grew during this period.[6]   These particular commodities were produced throughout Scotland and meant that this expansion in trade brought benefits to many parts of the country, but especially the areas of central and western Highlands for cattle and the eastern Lowlands for linen.

The country, however, remained generally poor in relation to England, Holland, and some other European countries and the living conditions harsh.   No doubt this factor was influential in the extremely high level of emigration during the seventeenth century.   Significant Scottish communities were to be found in most nearby European countries, especially in Scandinavia, the Baltic, the Netherlands, France, and particularly in Ireland.[7]   From a population reckoned to be around one

---

[5] Op.cit. Roy H. Campbell, 'The Anglo-Scottish Union of 1707: the Economic Consequences', *Economic History Review*, 2nd Series, Volume XVI, Utrecht, the Netherlands, 1964, p.468
[6] T. C. Smout, *Scottish Trade on Eve of Union, 1660-1707*, Edinburgh, Scotland, 1963, p.213; T. M. Devine, *Scotland's Empire, 1600-1815*, London, England, 2003, p. 31
[7] See Alexia Grosjean and Steve Murdoch, (eds) *Scottish Communities Abroad in the Early Modern Period*, Leiden, the Netherlands, 2005.

SCOTTISH TRADE WITH
COLONIAL CHARLESTON, 1683-1783

million at the end of the century, 30,000 Scots are believed to have moved to Poland and 100,000 to Ireland, and while no overall figure is available for the Netherlands it is known that there were around 1,000 Scots living in Rotterdam by the end of the seventeenth century. While some of these were religious or political refugees, and a few were scholars, the majority were economic migrants, many of whom, in the case of continental Europe, had originally left as soldiers-of-fortune and then settled abroad. Famine, notably in the early 1620s and the 1690s, was another factor motivating emigration from Scotland.[8]

From the Restoration period onwards, and especially after 1681, the Scottish government made various attempts to develop and diversify the economy. Between 1681 and 1707 over 60 manufacturing concerns were established in Scotland.[9] Certain of the products of these new industries were among the goods exported to overseas markets including Charleston and are dealt with in chapter 2. Despite the expansion of the industrial base by the late seventeenth century Scotland was facing mounting difficulties in traditional continental markets.[10] Corn imports were subject to high taxes in Norway from the 1680s; herring imports into France were banned from 1689; by the 1690s coal exports to The Netherlands were increasingly subject to competition from Newcastle; salt exports were falling due to French and Newcastle competition in the markets of Holland, Norway and the Baltic by the 1690s; and during the period between 1685 and 1695 the

---

[8] T M Devine, *Scotland's Empire 1600-1815,* London, England, 2003, p. 15;
Ian Whyte, *Agriculture and Society in Seventeenth Century Scotland,*
Edinburgh, Scotland, 1979, p. 251
[9] Whyte, *Scotland,* p. 289
[10] Devine, *Scotland's Empire,* p. 30

SCOTTISH TRADE WITH
COLONIAL CHARLESTON, 1683-1783

markets for Scottish rough woollen plaiding in France, Sweden and Holland diminished and were lost.[11]   Fishing, which could have developed into a major export trade was largely in the hands of the Dutch, leaving only a small area available for the Scots to exploit. Very much aware of the increasing problems being encountered in their traditional markets in Europe, the Scots began to give serious consideration to transatlantic opportunities.   By-passing the trading restrictions of the English Navigation Acts, a number of Scots merchants and shipmasters were already engaged in smuggling goods into the English colonies, encouraged by Scots and other settlers there.[12] Sir William Alexander, had in the 1620s been given the opportunity by King James VI to develop a Scottish colony in Nova Scotia. Had this been exploited, the Scots would have had a base from which they could have developed a trading post between the country and the colonies. For political reason, however, it was closed down before having a chance to become established.[13]

Possibly as many as seven thousand Scots had settled in the Americas during the seventeenth century, living in English, Swedish and Dutch colonies, from Surinam north to Hudson's Bay. Many of these settlers had arrived in the Americas involuntarily, as prisoners-of-war exiled there by Oliver Cromwell or the later Stuart monarchs, or as felons banished to the Plantations. Some arrived as indentured servants, transported through England, Scotland or the Netherlands, while others

[11] Smout, 'The Anglo-Scottish Union', p.457
[12] David Dobson, *Scottish Emigration to Colonial America, 1607-1785*, Athens, Georgia, 1994, p.60
[13] Op cit David Dobson, 'Seventeenth-century Scottish Communities in the Americas', Alexia Grosjean and Steve Murdoch, *Scottish Communities Abroad in the Early Modern Period*, Leiden, the Netherlands, 2005

SCOTTISH TRADE WITH
COLONIAL CHARLESTON, 1683-1783

were immigrants, attracted by the colony's commercial or agricultural opportunities. Scottish seafarers are known to have been familiar with the sea-routes to the Americas from an early period.[14] Shipping links between Scotland and Newfoundland were established around 1600 with the voyages of The Gift of God of Dundee[15]; with the West Indies from 1611 with the Janet of Leith[16]; with Nova Scotia in 1622 by an unknown reconnaissance ship sent by Sir William Alexander[17]; and with the Chesapeake from 1627 and the voyage of the Golden Lion of Dundee.[18] Scots mariners served aboard vessels from Denmark, Norway, Sweden, the Netherlands and England which sailed to the Americas during the seventeenth century, while over one hundred voyages directly from Scotland to the Americas before 1707 have been recorded. [19] The main concentrations of Scots were to be found around Boston, East New Jersey, the Chesapeake, and in the neighborhood of Charleston, and temporarily at Darien on the Isthmus of Panama.

14 National Records of Scotland, (hereafter NRS), GD90.SEC3/23, for example, describes the sea route to Nova Scotia in 1622
14 David Dobson, 'A Description of New England and the Sea Route to Nova Scotia, written by two Scottish Seafarers in 1622', *The New England Historical and Genealogical Register*, Volume 157, Boston, Massachusetts, April, 2003, pp.155-157; National Records Scotland: NRS.GD90.Sec3/23
[15] W. A. McNeill, 'Papers of a Dundee Shipping Dispute, 1600-1608', in *Miscellany of the Scottish History Society, Volume X,* Edinburgh, Scotland, 1965, p.68
[16] NRS.E71.29.6/22
[17] Dobson,'Seventeenth-century Scottish Communities in the Americas', ibid
[18] NRS.E190.31.1
[19] see David Dobson, *Ships from Scotland to America, 1628-1828, Volumes I, II, and III,* Baltimore, Maryland, 2002-2004; David Dobson, *Transatlantic Voyages, 1600-1699,* Baltimore, Maryland, 2004

SCOTTISH TRADE WITH
COLONIAL CHARLESTON, 1683-1783

With this drift westward, by 1680 Scots were eager to establish a colony
of their own. The Caribbean area was first considered, encompassing
the islands of Aruba, Trinidad, St Lucia, St Vincent, Jamaica, and the
Bahamas as well as Venezuela and Florida on the mainland. [20] Probably
the most detailed plan for a Scots settlement in the West Indies was a
project relating to St Vincent in 1678, where the intention was to
produce sugar.[21] Although nothing came of these deliberations, they
may have indirectly influenced the eventual disastrous choice of the
Darien on the Isthmus of Panama, in which a significant proportion of
the wealth of the nation was lost. In 1695 the Scots Parliament passed
an act which created "The Company of Scotland Trading to Africa and
the Indies."   The prime objective of the Company was the
establishment of a trading settlement at Darien, which was considered
to be strategically well placed to effect trade links with settlements of
both the Pacific and the Atlantic. An estimated one-sixth of the liquid
capital of Scotland was raised to support the venture and its collapse
within a few short years was likely to have severe impact on the nation's
economic health. It is ironic, however, that failure of the Darien
Scheme contributed towards the political union of Scotland and
England in 1707 which, among other things, opened up the English
colonial empire to the Scots.

At the close of the seventeenth century, therefore, Scotland was in an
unenviable economic state.   Scottish overseas expansion had gone
disastrously wrong; the country was unable, due to the English
Navigation Acts, to trade formally and officially with English colonies;

---

[20] P. Hume Brown, (ed) Register of the Privy Council of Scotland, (hereafter
RPCS), 3rd Series, Volume VII, p.664
[21] NRS. Society of Antiquaries of Scotland Collection, GD103.2.4.42

SCOTTISH TRADE WITH
COLONIAL CHARLESTON, 1683-1783

its traditional continental markets were gradually closing owing to protectionist policies and similar restrictions were making it increasingly difficult for it to trade with England.

The new century then saw Scotland as an economically backward country when compared with England or The Netherlands. But it was not alone in its poverty. Scotland's situation could be compared with other such north-western Europe countries as Ireland, Norway, Denmark, Poland and some of the German principalities. Its transformation from a poor and backward nation of Western Europe to becoming within a century the second most industrialised, achieving high rates of economic growth, was based on several factors. The most important of these was the Parliamentary Union with its more powerful neighbor, England in 1707. This Union removed the restrictions on Scotland of the Navigation Acts, and allowed free access to the rapidly developing American market, as well removing barriers which had latterly been imposed against free trade with the English domestic market. The potential of the West Indies was used by Scottish politicians in 1706 to support their argument in favor of the Union of Parliaments when they stated "...(the Union) may enable us to export beef and pork and butter to the West Indies and other foreign parts which will be a considerable branch of our trade after the Union".[22]

Scots particularly took advantage of the increasing demand for sugar. They were experienced in its refining in Scotland, and a removal of quota restrictions for import of the raw material would be economically extremely beneficial. Conditions in the islands of the West Indian

---

[22] Acts of the Parliaments of Scotland, (hereafter APS), 1706, Volume XL, Edinburgh, Scotland, 1824, p.337b

9

islands were perfect for the production of sugar, and the profits generated in Barbados alone are reckoned to exceed all the combined exports from the English mainland colonies. By the close of the seventeenth century four sugar refineries had been built in Glasgow to process the cargoes of sugar that were being brought from Barbados and elsewhere in the West Indies.[23] Tobacco was another American colonial product that found an expanding market throughout Western Europe and Scotland was no exception. The records of both national and local government increasing contain references to tobacco. Initially much of this was obtained from the Caribbean, both directly and indirectly, but soon the tobacco planters of the Chesapeake were supplying the Scottish consumers.[24] The first Scottish ship to sail to the Chesapeake was the Golden Lion of Dundee in 1627 which is likely to have returned with a cargo of tobacco. [25] Throughout the seventeenth century there are references to tobacco being imported into Scotland from a number of locations in Europe and America. David Peirson, master of the bark Allan brought tobacco from Bordeaux to Dundee in 1622.[26] John Hamilton of Boighall brought 100,000 weight of tobacco from the West Indies in 1643 and again in 1644. [27] The Antelope of Glasgow landed 20,000 lbs of Martinique tobacco at Dumbarton in 1647. [28] Six hundred weight of tobacco from Maryland was unloaded at Kirkcaldy in May 1673. [29] Tobacco was brought to Glasgow aboard

[23] T. M. Devine, *Scotland's Empire, 1600-1815,* London, England, 2003, p.
[24] See Eric J. Graham, *A Maritime History of Scotland, 1650-1790,* East Linton, Scotland, 2002, pp.37-51
[25] TNA.E190.31.1
[26] Dundee City Archives, *Dundee Shipping Register, 29 July 1622*
[27] APS.VI.i.228, Edinburgh, Scotland, 1870
[28] Fergus Roberts and I. M. M. McPhail, *Dumbarton Common Good Accounts, 1614-1660,* Dumbarton, Scotland, 1972, p. 266
[29] NRS.E72.9.8/2   30 APS.IX.31, Edinburgh, Scotland, 1822

SCOTTISH TRADE WITH
COLONIAL CHARLESTON, 1683-1783

the <u>George of Belfast</u> in 1689. [30] All of such consignments seem to have
been for domestic consumption but the experience of this trade laid the
foundations of what would be the most significant international trading
activity that was carried out in Scotland during the following century.
The English Navigation Acts of the 1660s had prohibited direct trade
between the American colonies and Scotland but the profits to be made
from importing tobacco resulted in smuggling. The degree to which
much of Scotland's transatlantic trade was dependant on smuggling is
dealt with in a later chapter. Had the Darien Company been
successfully established it would have had the right of access to the
Scottish market of tobacco and sugar produced in its own plantations,
however the colony had to be abandoned before such crops had been
produced.[31] Mercantile motivation was certainly there, but other factors
were also necessary to achieve success. These included the availability
of key raw materials in Scotland such as coal and iron, and technical
expertise in other industries.[32] Scotland was fortunate in that the
relatively few immigrants it attracted included those with advanced
skills. These were the Huguenots and Dutch who, in addition to
knowing how to refine sugar, were experienced in textile manufacture,
fishing and whaling, as well as some specialist crafts. Some English
entrepreneurs, attracted by opportunities in Scotland, arrived bringing
with them more skilled workers, modern technology and often capital.
The pre-conditions, therefore, of motivation, skilled labor, raw
materials, and enough capital were increasingly available at this period
of transition, and Scotland was ripe for an expansion of its economic
base when the access to English and English colonial markets presented

---

[30] APS.IX.31, Edinburgh, Scotland, 1822
[31] APS.IX Act for a Company Trading to Africa and the Indies
[32] C. A. Whatley, *Scottish Society, 1707-1830,* Manchester, England, 2000, pp26-31

11

SCOTTISH TRADE WITH
COLONIAL CHARLESTON, 1683-1783

itself. [33]   Over the following decades, Scotland gradually established a strong economic base enabling its entrepreneurs to flourish.

The eighteenth century saw the transformation of the economy and society of Scotland from being relatively primitive, compared to England and The Netherlands, to being one of the most developed European nations of the period.   At one point the economy of Ireland showed a greater potential than Scotland, being larger, more populous, more fertile, and having at least restricted access to the colonial market, but by the close of the eighteenth century it was evident that Scotland had overtaken Ireland.[34]   Despite having its own Parliament, Ireland could not operate an independent economic policy and was tied to England as a market for its agricultural produce and as a source of manufactured goods.   Ireland was not in a position, during the eighteenth century, of having unrestricted access to the American colonial markets, but had to import many colonial exports, such as tobacco and muscavado sugar, from Scotland.[35]

The profits made by Scots entrepreneurs in this trade directly contributed to the Scots ability to finance industrialisation and produce economic growth in excess of that being achieved in Ireland.[36]   As has been seen, several factors came together to create this situation, of which the single most important was Scotland's level of participation

33 Whatley, *Scottish Society, p.41*
[34] T. M. Devine, "The English Connection and Irish-Scottish Development in the Eighteenth Century", T. M. Devine and D. Dickson '*Ireland and Scotland, 1600-1850'*, Edinburgh, Scotland, 1983, p.19
[35] See L. E. Cochran, *Scottish Trade with Ireland in the Eighteenth Century,* Edinburgh, Scotland, 1985, passim
[36] T. M. Devine, 'The Union of 1707 and Scottish Development' in T.M.Devine,(ed.), *Exploring the Scottish Past,* East Linton, Scotland, 1995, p.48

SCOTTISH TRADE WITH
COLONIAL CHARLESTON, 1683-1783

in trans-Atlantic trade.   Raw materials were obtained from the American colonies, which allowed Scotland to process new items for trade, notably tobacco and timber.   Increasingly, also, benefits were got from the access to capital, technology and expertise from England, Holland and France, all feeding the industrial revolution in Scotland.

Scottish Trade with Charleston and its Significance
The most significant early commerce between Scotland and the colonies was undoubtedly the tobacco trade, and the profits from this lucrative trade introduced financial services, which in turn facilitated industrialisation, and the development of Glasgow and its environs in the eighteenth century.[37]   Other imported products, including timber, sugar, rice and latterly cotton must also have had an advantageous impact on the country, but their history has yet to be documented.

Throughout most of this period there existed thirteen mainland American colonies divided into four socio-economic regional groupings.   These were New England, centered on Boston; the Hudson Valley incorporating New York, east New Jersey, and Connecticut, whose main port was New York; the Delaware Valley containing Delaware, Pennsylvania and west New Jersey, their port being Philadelphia; the Chesapeake, comprising Virginia, Maryland, and northern North Carolina, with the port of Norfolk; and finally the American South, comprising the remainder of the Carolinas and Georgia, with the port of Charleston.   This study focuses on just one of these, trade with the colonial port of Charleston.

---

[37] See T. M. Devine, *The Tobacco Trade. A Study of the Tobacco Merchants of Glasgow and their Trading Activities c1740-90*, Edinburgh, Scotland, 1975

SCOTTISH TRADE WITH
COLONIAL CHARLESTON, 1683-1783

Charleston, or 'Charles Town' as it was then known, grew to dominate the commerce of the southern region comprising South Carolina, much of North Carolina and Georgia. This region had links with the West Indies, Africa, the lower Mississippi valley, and latterly Florida. It largely produced, processed, and exported all the major colonial raw materials, timber, furs, sugar, rice, indigo, and to a small extent tobacco, and is therefore ideal for a study of contemporary colonial trade.

Using both Scottish and Charleston historical records this study aims to identify Scots merchants doing business in Charleston as well the merchants in Scotland with whom they traded. This study will consider who were the Scottish merchants trading in Charleston during the colonial period, identify what products they were handling, the markets they participated in, and how the trade was organised within Charleston specifically and in South Carolina generally. It will look also to where Scots merchants were located in colonial South Carolina, if they were operating as international merchants based in Charleston or if they were Indian traders in the backwoods of the region. The particular occupations of those settling in South Carolina will be discussed and the activities of these factors, importers, exporters, wholesalers and retailers examined. Aspects such as marketing, finance and networking are examined

It will examine also the quantities and types of goods bought and sold, and trace the origin of items shipped from Scotland to the colonies. Also considered is the extent to which Scotland was an entrepot and whether the transatlantic trade stimulated the growth of the domestic manufacturing industry. The importance of family connections and networking will be shown to be an important factor in the success of trading ventures, both in financial terms and the wider commercial
14

SCOTTISH TRADE WITH
COLONIAL CHARLESTON, 1683-1783

activities generated. The evidence makes it clear that some merchants settled permanently in the colony of South Carolina, and others, often known as 'sojourners', went intentionally for a limited period of time in a speculative venture hoping to make good. Transatlantic trade, such as that between Charleston and Scotland, inevitably involved shipping, and this gives rise to a number of questions. Among these which are addressed here include the degree to which Scotland was self-sufficient in available ships, or the extent to which it was dependant on English or colonial vessels, crews, shipmasters and owners. The book will examine the size and type of ship, the proportion built in Scotland compared to those English-built or constructed in the colonies. The study also examines the matter of trade balance of payments in this example of invisible trade and whether this was in Scotland's favor or that of South Carolina. Ancillary trades will also be taken into account, examining the extent to which shipping impacted on not only the construction of ships, but trades such as sail-making or rope-spinning. The matter of emigrants will be addressed in terms of the extent to which Scots and Irish increased in numbers as the eighteenth century progressed, with particular emphasis on those settling in the American South and the manner of their recruitment.

The transport of people was a significant, if not the most important, commodity in the development of the American colonies, and the emigrant trade was at this time flourishing. During the eighteenth century, the largest ethnic groups settling within the Thirteen Colonies were the 'Scotch-Irish' and the Germans. While immigrants from Scotland were not as numerous as their cousins from Ulster, they too made a substantial contribution to the settlement of America during the colonial period. It is known that Scots, the Scotch-Irish and the Germans tended to settle in the South and the Middle Colonies during

SCOTTISH TRADE WITH
COLONIAL CHARLESTON, 1683-1783

much of this period. This study will look into the factors which
motivated potential Scottish emigrants to favor South Carolina and the
methods employed to attract potential emigrants either by the colonial
authorities or by private individuals. For a period of time, between
1614 and 1775, British courts, primarily English ones, used America
and the West Indies as places of punishment for political and religious
undesirables as well as felons. England is reckoned to have transported
around 50,000, while Ireland about 12,000, and Scotland fewer than
3,000, in total to the colonies before 1776. [38] This study will seek to
determine the extent to which South Carolina was used for the purpose
of involuntary emigration of Scots by the authorities in Scotland. It
also, addresses how substantial in number was voluntary emigration
from Scotland to South Carolina during the colonial period, whether it
was a mass movement, as happened to Canada during the Highland
Clearances, or a migration of individuals. It will examine the surviving
evidence concerning the details of settlement of Scots in South
Carolina, and whether the intention was permanent settlement as
occurred further north in North Carolina, or intended as an opportunity
to create personal wealth, but with no intention of permanent settlement
as was the situation of sojourners in the West Indies.

The slave trade was one of the most profitable activities in which to
engage, and British and colonial merchants and shipmasters of the
eighteenth century used the port Charleston for this purpose. As South
Carolina was unarguably an economy based on slavery, it was virtually
impossible for any resident there not to be either directly or indirectly
involved in the use of slave labor. Chapter Five examines the extent
to which Scots participated in the slave trade between Africa, the West

---

[38] See Peter Wilson Coldham, *British Emigrants in Bondage, 1614-1788,* Baltimore, Maryland,
2004

SCOTTISH TRADE WITH
COLONIAL CHARLESTON, 1683-1783

Indies, and South Carolina, and in which capacities. It considers the selection of slaves, their transportation, sale and eventual employment in the colony and the available evidence of the number of slaving voyages in which the Charleston Scots were involved, the numbers of slaves landed in Charleston, and the locations in Africa or the West Indies from which they came.

Another chapter deals with colonial produce exported by Scots merchants from Charleston bound for Scotland and Europe. It looks at the items despatched, either raw materials or semi-processed goods which Charleston was in a position to export, and the extent to which they were locally produced within South Carolina, or brought in from elsewhere in America, the colonies in and around the Caribbean, or even Africa. The chapter shows the markets that these merchants supplied, and how the restrictions of the Navigation Acts were set aside to enable commerce to expand, and discusses the impact of international rivalry and periods of hostilities on the Charleston trade. Also, he types and quantities of produce which was despatched directly to Scotland from South Carolina and where their market was; whether they were for domestic or industrial consumption, for despatch to England or onward transport to more distant markets.

Sources

Most of the material for original research was located in Charleston, London and Edinburgh. The main sources were the Library of the South Carolina Historical Society in Charleston, the National Archives (formerly the Public Record Office) in London and the National Records of Scotland in Edinburgh, (formerly the Scottish Record Office). The State Library in Raleigh, North Carolina, especially its massive British Colonial Records collection, was a major source of

SCOTTISH TRADE WITH
COLONIAL CHARLESTON, 1683-1783

information. The collection here, which had been built up over many years, contains copies of documents brought from all the main archives in Great Britain, in particular the National Archives in London. Other source libraries and archives included Charleston Public Library, Aberdeen University Library and its Department of Special Collections, Angus Archives and Museum in Montrose, Dundee University Library, Dundee City Archives, the library of the University of St Andrews, the Mitchell Library in Glasgow, and the National Library of Scotland.

None of the existing records were comprehensive. For example, although without doubt the most important sources of information were the contemporary port books of Charleston and of the various Scottish ports, in the case of the Scottish port books, housed in the National Archives of Scotland, those which provide detailed exports and imports only exist from 1742, while the equivalent records for Charleston, now in the National Archives in London, while dating from a generation earlier, do not contain the detail found in the Scottish sources. Business records of the period were particularly meagre, both in Charleston and in Scotland, although some detail can be found by examining extant records of court cases from the Court of Session[39] in Edinburgh and the High Court of the Admiralty of Scotland.[40] Possibly the best single published source for the economic and social history of Charleston and of South Carolina is the South Carolina Historical Magazine (1899-2004), the quarterly journal of the South Carolina Historical Society which was founded in 1855. The society's library in Charleston is undoubtedly the pre-eminent source for historical material in South Carolina. As far as can be established there is little, if anything, in print specifically concerning Scottish trade, or Scots merchants, with, or in,

---

[39] For example, NRS.CS228/Miscellaneous.27/2, re Francis Russell, a merchant in Leith, shipping a consignment of linen to South Carolina during the 1750s.
[40] For example, NRS.AC7.49.1293-1534, AC9.1591.7, re the merchant vessel the Elizabeth and Peggy and its cargo bound for South Carolina in 1750

SCOTTISH TRADE WITH
COLONIAL CHARLESTON, 1683-1783

South Carolina, apart from some articles on the Scottish settlement at Stuartstown, Port Royal, or some local family histories.   As a consequence, research for this study was largely original.

SCOTTISH TRADE WITH
COLONIAL CHARLESTON, 1683-1783

CHAPTER ONE

SCOTTISH EXPORTS TO COLONIAL CHARLESTON

The background against which the Scottish trade with Charleston began to flourish will be examined in the first section of this chapter. Records in Scotland, in particular the port books, have been examined carefully and these, together with other contemporary state documents, have revealed the extent of the export trade with Charleston and the goods produced for it. These are detailed in Section Two. In addition, these papers also occasionally identify the producers of goods and their location within the country. Trade between Scotland and the Chesapeake has been well researched, but until now the contemporary trade between Scotland and Charleston has not been examined. In Section Three a comparison between the two will be undertaken.

I - Background

In the late seventeenth century an increase in economic protectionism in Europe began to close some traditional markets open to Scottish exporters on the continent.[41] At this time the country which had arguably the most rapidly expanding market in Europe was England, which shared a common king with Scotland, but not a common parliament. This situation meant that Scottish trade with England and its colonies was subject to restrictions. In areas where a Scottish export trade was possible, Scottish manufacturers sometimes failed to compete with English entrepreneurs on the basis of price or quality. At the end of the seventeenth century the political masters of Scotland faced a dilemma, whether to remain a small, independent country, or to grasp

---

[41] T. M. Devine, *The Scottish Nation, 1700-2000,* London, 1999, pp. xxi-xxii; 51

21

SCOTTISH TRADE WITH
COLONIAL CHARLESTON, 1683-1783

the possible benefits of entering a political and economic union with England.   The former option meant that the Scots would have to overcome restrictions on trade both in Europe and America and especially with England.[42] The latter option opened up a legal trade with England and its colonial American market to the Scots.   One risk they faced if they chose the latter option was that the Scottish domestic market could be taken over by the more efficient English manufacturers.   In the event the second option was chosen, and the Scottish merchants seized on the benefits of the expansion of trade between Scotland and the American colonies.   This increase in transatlantic trade developed slowly, not becoming significant until the middle of the eighteenth century.   English manufacturing industries were more technologically advanced and their commercial skills and business networks were also more developed, but Scottish ports began to be used as entrepots, especially in trading colonial produce between the Americas and continental markets.

As has been shown, the Parliamentary Union of 1707 officially opened up the former English colonies in America and elsewhere to direct trade with Scotland.   With a few exceptions, before that date any trade that did occur between Scotland and the English colonies contravened the English Navigation Act of the 1660s and the Staple Act of 1663.   One of the few legal exceptions occurred around 1684 when the Scottish Carolina Company was authorised to establish a trading settlement at Port Royal, south of Charleston. The Scottish customs books of the period, while incomplete, record three shiploads of goods sent from Scotland to supply the colony at Port Royal.   As the Naval Officer's reports for Charleston do not begin until 1712 there is no record in Carolinian sources of imports arriving from Scotland before that date.

---

[42] Angus Calder, *Revolutionary Empire. The Rise of the English Speaking Empires from the Fifteenth Century to the 1780s,* London, p.377.

SCOTTISH TRADE WITH
COLONIAL CHARLESTON, 1683-1783

These first vessels were the James of Ayr,[43] the Charles of Glasgow,[44] and the Pelican of Glasgow[45] (renamed the Carolina Merchant), all of which sailed in the summer of 1684. The James of Ayr, which carried passengers from Belfast as well as cargo, was wrecked on the coast of Carolina. A later ship, the Rachel and John of London, which had loaded goods in London, sailed from Kelburn, near Largs, in March 1686 with settlers bound for Stuartstown, Port Royal. This last ship, however, stopped off in Antigua where the cargo was sold and by the time it reached its original destination the Scots colony there had been destroyed by Spanish military action.[46] These were the only merchant vessels known to have left Scotland bound for southern Carolina before the Act of Union, though it is not impossible that Scottish vessels bound north along the Carolina coast from the West Indies for Scotland engaged in landing goods illegally. While some Scottish trade with the colonies did exist via London and English outports, especially Whitehaven, there is no evidence of goods being despatched to Carolina this way. The cargoes of the first three ships are contained in the contemporary Scottish port books,[47] which have been analysed below. These cargoes were presumably the trading stock of the Scottish Carolina Company selected for commerce with the colonists and with the Indians. Early exports to Carolina comprised a limited range of goods which no doubt reflected the relatively undeveloped state of the Scottish economy at the time. They were predominantly textiles such as linen, pack-cloth, worsteds, thread, woollens, stockings, gloves, plaiding, ticking, hose, figrams, leather goods, particularly boots and

[43] NRS.E72.3.6/12
[44] NRS.E72.19.9
[45] NRS.E72.19.9; TNA.CO.5.287.126
[46] Tom Barclay and Eric J Graham, 'The Covenanters in Carolina, 1682-1686', in *History Scotland*, Volume 4, number 4, Edinburgh, 2003, p.26; Miscellaneous Bound Collections, W C Clements Library, Michigan
47 NRS.E72 series

shoes, metal-wares, aqua vitae and brandy, loaf sugar and coal. All these were to form the backbone of Scottish exports to Charleston during the colonial period. It should be kept in mind, however, that the surviving evidence may not necessarily reveal the complete picture regarding Scottish trade with the Carolinas in the seventeenth century.

Scots merchant skippers were ignoring the restrictions of the English Navigation Acts and are known to have been actively trading with the colonists in New England, the Chesapeake, and the Middle Colonies, as well as in the West Indies. So, an illicit trade, in English eyes, with the settlements in the Carolinas was not out of the question. On 27 June 1692 Edward Randolph reported to the customs commissioners noting the problems he was encountering in Maryland. In Somerset County, he found two vessels, the Providence of London and the Catherine of Londonderry, both loaded with goods manufactured in Scotland contrary to the Navigation Acts. However, when he attempted to take legal action the local sheriff, a Scotch-Irishman, selected a jury formed of Scots and their friends who decided in favor of the smugglers. He also mentioned that in that county, there were 'hundreds of Scotch and Irish families' who had set up a linen factory there, and that Scottish and Irish vessels were illegally shipping out cargoes of tobacco.[48] Scottish entrepreneurs, particularly from the Glasgow area, were early participants in the transportation of tobacco from the Chesapeake area, and in due course the profits they made were to become considerable. Scottish participation, however, was in direct contravention of the English Navigation Acts and could, therefore, only occur through smuggling, or at least through trade of dubious legality,

[48] *Calendar of State Papers, America and the West Indies, 1692* (No 2295),

orchestrated by Englishmen in Scottish ports and Scots based in English ones.[49]   While the exchange of colonial produce (mainly tobacco) for manufactured goods was of direct benefit to both the colonists and the entrepreneur, it was clearly contrary to government policy. In practice, it was condoned by many in authority in the region and the Scots even established a factory and community in Newfoundland around 1700 to aid their activities.[50]   An English Customs Committee report of 1695 states that for many years people had been trading directly from the sugar and tobacco plantations to Scotland in violation of the English Navigation Acts, and a Thomas Meach, formerly employed in the trade, claimed that in 1693 twelve ships had gone directly to Scotland with sugar and tobacco and that eight were then at sea engaged in the trade, particularly tobacco, between Virginia and Glasgow.[51]   Even Scots prominent in colonial society were involved, such as the Reverend James Blair, commissary of Virginia and president of the College of William and Mary, who was said to be engaged with smuggling tobacco from the James River to Scotland in 1695.[52]   As Scots traded with the Chesapeake to the north and the West Indies to the south, smuggling to the settlements along the Carolina coast is quite probable.

The most informative source for exports from Great Britain is to be found in the post-Union Customs and Excise records, but these do not exist in Scotland prior to 1742.   The equivalent records in contemporary Charleston were the Naval Officer's accounts which, although they begin as early as 1712, do not provide the necessary

[49] T C Smout, *Scottish Trade on the Eve of Union,* Edinburgh, Scotland,1963, pp. 80, 144, 178; T M Devine, *Scotland's Empire,* London, 2003, pp. 32-33
[50] T M Devine, *Scotland's Empire,* pp. 32-33
[51] L F Stock, (editor)., *Acts of the British Parliaments Relating to North America,* Volume II, Washington, DC, 1924, p. 104
52 J W Fortescue, *Calendar of State Papers, America and the West Indies, 1696-1697,* London, England, 1896, p. 329

SCOTTISH TRADE WITH
COLONIAL CHARLESTON, 1683-1783

detail, often referring to the cargoes as '*European wares*'. While this source does not analyse the Scottish or any other imports arriving in the colony, it does note the names of vessels arriving from Scotland, and therefore gives some idea of the volume of trade between the two locations.

These records were established because of the need of the English, later the British government, to maintain that some check be made on the volume of trade, both imports and exports, ships, ports of embarkation and destination, and a record maintained in colonial ports as had been kept in domestic ports for generations. The accounting system was formalised by the English Navigation Act of 1696 and operated within the American colonies until the War of Independence, and to a later date within other colonies. Every port of any consequence had a naval officer appointed whose task it was to maintain records ensuring that the laws were complied with, tariffs were paid, bills of lading were issued, and a record of shipping maintained. The records for Charleston are probably the most comprehensive for any American colonial port. In Scotland, also, there are almost completely comprehensive records, giving great detail, for every port or precinct from 1742. Before that date there are letter-books recording communications sent by the local Customs Collector to the Board of Customs in Edinburgh,[53] but these only record the names of ships arriving or departing, and give no information on their cargoes.

53 For example, NRS.CE53 for Dundee, and NRS.CE70 for Montrose

SCOTTISH TRADE WITH
COLONIAL CHARLESTON, 1683-1783

According to the Charleston Naval Office Shipping Lists,[54] from 1712 until 1742 when the Scottish Customs Records[55] began, only seventeen Scots vessels are noted as having used the port of Charleston. In these Lists their cargoes are referred to as '*European goods*' or as '*European goods and sundry household goods*', except when the vessel brought wine from Madeira when this is quantified.   For example, on 27 November 1735 the <u>Anslie of Leith</u>, eighty tons, six guns, with an eight man crew, built in Leith during 1727, and registered there on 14 August 1735, master John Hay, owned by George Anslie and John Hay, arrived in Charleston from Leith via Madeira with a cargo of twenty pipes of wine and European goods.[56] The <u>Anslie</u> left Charleston on 2 January 1736 with four-hundred and thirty barrels of rice, thirty barrels of pitch, eighty eight tons of Brazil wood, one hogshead of rum, and five pipes of Madeira wine, bound for Cowes on the Isle of Wight, a Channel port. The only specific reference to textiles aboard a Scots ship during the early eighteenth century occurred in August 1736 when the <u>Rebecca and Mary of Montrose</u>, master George Ouchterlonie, brought seven bales of linen and two boxes of thread. [57]   However, as his last port of call was Cork it is just possible that the cargo originated in Ireland rather than in Scotland.   Due to the lack of evidence in the Port Officer's Records it is not possible to identify the range and volume of imports arriving in Charleston from Scotland before 1742 and the commencement of the Customs Records in Scotland.   The local

54 TNA.CO5.508/509
55 NRS.E504 series
56 TNA.CO5.509
57 TNA.CO5.509

SCOTTISH TRADE WITH
COLONIAL CHARLESTON, 1683-1783

newspaper, the South Carolina Gazette, was first published in 1732 and its columns provide some insight into early trade with Scotland. The first such reference occurred in 1743 when the ship the Jerviswood, master Thomas Baillie, is reported to have arrived from Orkney via the Isle of Maia with a cargo of twelve servants together with forty tons of salt.[58]   The salt, however, was more likely to have been produced on the Isle of Maia, or elsewhere in the Cape Verde islands, rather than in the isles of Orkney, as the former was famed for the quality of its salt.

The phenomenal rise of transatlantic trade in the eighteenth century provided a real stimulus to the Scottish economy. The opening up of England and its colonies to Scottish traders and manufacturers expanded their markets and also their sources of raw materials. However, as far as can be established from the evidence available, trade between Scotland and Charleston was relatively small scale until the 1740s. From 1742 to 1776 it has been possible to analyse the range and quantities of products exported from Scotland bound for Charleston, and what this shows is a very wide range of goods being shipped, much of which was of Scots origin although there is evidence of Scotland acting as an entrepot for goods brought from other parts of the British Isles and Europe. An assumption that all this increase in trade originated on the Clyde and other Scottish locations facing the Atlantic, but the evidence of the Customs Records reveal that the east coast ports of the Forth and Dundee despatched about the same number of vessels and a similar range of goods. Some of the historical orthodoxy concerning Scotland and the transatlantic trade has to be modified in the light of that information.

---

[58] *South Carolina Gazette*, No 51, 6 January 1733

SCOTTISH TRADE WITH
COLONIAL CHARLESTON, 1683-1783

II – Raw Materials and Manufactured Goods
Coal

Evidence for this important trade comes from the Scottish Customs records.[59] Between 1742 and 1774 exports of coal from Scotland to South Carolina totalled thirty-two thousand, three hundred and fourteen tons.   At least one hundred and eleven consignments of coal left Scotland bound for Charleston in the colonial period.   The ports involved were Greenock, Glasgow, Dunbar, Leith, Dundee, Bo'ness, and to a far lesser extent Irvine, Alloa, and Kirkcaldy.   An analysis of the annual coal exports to South Carolina indicates a substantial rise in the quantity after 1763. Surprisingly the existence of a colonial market for Scottish coal is not mentioned in Baron Duckham's, A History of the Scottish Coal Industry [60] which is the standard work on the commodity.

Table 1/1
Coal Exports to Charleston by Port, 1743-1773 (in tons)

Glasgow	4,105
Bo'ness	3,164
Irvine	510
Kirkcaldy	121
Alloa	70
Dunbar	1,629
Greenock	19,002
Leith	3,489
Dundee	224
Totals	**32,314**

---

[59] NRS.E504 series
[60] Baron F Duckham, *A History of the Scottish Coal Industry,* Volume I, 1700-1815', Newton Abbot, England, 1970

SCOTTISH TRADE WITH
COLONIAL CHARLESTON, 1683-1783

Regional analysis	
East Coast	8,697
West Coast	23,617
Totals	**<u>32,314</u>**

As far as can be established the coal was exported in response to demand from the domestic market within Charleston, though it is possible that to some extent coal was shipped as ballast. Angus Calder claims that '*the better off in the port towns burnt coal sent from Britain as paying ballast in ships*'.[61] On arrival in Charleston the shipmaster, supercargo, or factor would advertise the availability of the coal. The following two advertisements appeared in the South Carolina Gazette.

> "Scotch coal at £4 per chalder available from the brigantine <u>Betty</u>, master Joseph Boyd, from Glasgow"[62]
> "<u>The Industry</u>, Andrew Cowan, from Leith, with coal etc – available from the skipper's shop on Beaton's wharf – merchandise and rice accepted in payment".[63]

The market in Charleston for Scottish coal was certainly important but only formed a small part of total coal exported from Scotland in the period. Exact figures are not easily available but Henry Hamilton reckoned that the average annual exports of coal between 1755 and 1757 did not exceed eighteen thousand tons, and that London, alone, took six thousand, three hundred and seventy-eight tons in 1765.[64]

---

[61] Angus Calder, *Revolutionary Empire, The Rise of the English-Speaking Empires from the Fifteenth Century to the 1780s*, London, 1981, p. 490
[62] South Carolina Gazette, (hereafter SCGaz), Issue No 80, 21 July 1733
[63] SCGaz, No 817, dated 8 January 1750
[64] H. Hamilton, *The Industrial Revolution in Scotland*, London, 1966, p. 169

SCOTTISH TRADE WITH
COLONIAL CHARLESTON, 1683-1783

Regrettably, the evidence of the Naval Officer's Records in Charleston does not provide a detailed analysis of imports, often just referring to them as *'European goods'*.[65]

The demand for coal in Charleston seems to have arisen through the lack of available firewood in the locality. Local firewood had been brought by river to Charleston during the late seventeenth and early eighteenth centuries but by the mid-eighteenth century the increase in demand for firewood greatly exceeded the local supply, pushing up the market price, until it reached such a level that it was more economic to import coal.[66] For this reason, cargoes of coal began to be shipped from Scotland. While it is possible that some coal was used for the process of making bricks, tanning, and for use by blacksmiths in and around the neighborhood of Charleston, the majority of the imported coal was used for heating houses.[67]

Salt

The production of salt had been established in Scotland since the medieval period and by the seventeenth century was an important export. [68] One of the more prominent figures active in the salt trade was Sir James Cockburn of that Ilk, who, in the 1670s, was exporting salt from Dysart and Cockenzie to Danzig, Holland, Norway and Ireland.[69]

---

[65] TNA.CO5.508-511, passim
[65] Op. cit. S. Max Edelson, 'Planting the Low Country: Agricultural and Economic Experience in the Lower South, 1695-1785', Ph.D. diss. The John Hopkins University, Baltimore, Maryland, 1998, pp. 326-328
[65] Ibid
[66] Op. cit. S. Max Edelson, 'Planting the Low Country: Agricultural and Economic Experience in the Lower South, 1695-1785', Ph.D. diss. The John Hopkins University, Baltimore, Maryland, 1998, pp. 326-328
[67] Ibid
68 C A Whatley, *The Scottish Salt Industry, 1570-1850*, Aberdeen, Scotland, 1987, pp.33-43

SCOTTISH TRADE WITH
COLONIAL CHARLESTON, 1683-1783

Saltpans were developed using peat, charcoal and latterly coal to boil seawater to produce salt. The availability of coal enabled the industry to flourish at sites around the Forth, for example at Culross where by 1663 there were at least fifty saltpans in operation. However, the Scottish industry faced competition from the more superior Biscayan salt exported via La Rochelle or St Martin's. In Scotland, probably the single most important use of salt, for which there was a substantial local demand, was the curing of fish.

According to available Scottish sources, three consignments of salt were recorded as being shipped to Charleston; two of which were processed in the saltpans of the Fife coast. In 1743 the Magdalene, master William Carse, voyaged from Leith to Charleston with a part-cargo of Scottish salt. In the month of March, he loaded eight hundred bushels of Fife salt, and again in July, he took on a further eighteen bushels of "salt from Anstruther".[70] In April 1748, four and a half bushels of salt were exported from Dundee to Charleston.[71] Probably the most productive of the saltpans of the period lay on the coast between St Monance and Anstruther. These, established in 1771, were called the St Philips Saltworks, and owned by Sir John Anstruther who lived locally, and Robert Fall, a merchant in Dunbar. Fall also made use of the salt in the curing of herring exported to Charleston in the late colonial period.

It is reckoned that output of salt in Scotland during the first half of the eighteenth century amounted to between 250,000 and 300,000 bushels

69 NRS.CS96.64
[70] NRS.E504.22.1
[71] NRS.E504.11.1

per annum[72] and therefore the Charleston market was a very minor one for Scottish salt, no doubt also for the reason that Scottish salt was coarser than that obtainable elsewhere.

Linen

The linen industry was by far the single most important manufacturing industry and employer in contemporary Scotland, [73] and linen, in its various forms, represented the single most important export. Although the Customs records refer to *'linen cloth of British manufacture'* in reality much of the linen was almost certainly produced in Scotland. At that point in time the linen industry in England was relatively small with industrialists concentrating on other textiles, specifically woollens and cottons, and leaving the production of linen to the Scots and the Irish. A very limited quantity of the linen exported from Scotland to Charleston, perhaps around five per cent, seems to have come from Ireland and there was the occasional consignment from Danzig. Although a range of linens was exported the emphasis seemed to be on the cheaper and coarser varieties which were woven in east-central Scotland. In the 1740s the British government introduced bounty payments on such cloth exported to the colonies. These bounties were extremely effective in stimulating colonial demand. Consequently the industry experienced a boom during the second half of the eighteenth century when production more than doubled in quantity. While much of the linen exports were in bales there were also considerable quantities of handkerchiefs, table cloths, lawns, cambrics, ticking, thread, shirts, etc. The finer linen products tended to be woven in west

---

[72] Ian D. Whyte, *Scotland before the Industrial Revolution, An Economic & Social History, c1050-c1750*, London, England, 1995, p. 306

[73] see Alastair J. Durie, *The Scottish Linen Trade in the Eighteenth Century*, Edinburgh, Scotland, 1979, pp. 158-162

central Scotland, mainly around Glasgow. Printed linens, which were produced by craftsmen such as Alexander Buchanan or Daniel McInnes, both in Glasgow, were in regular demand throughout the colonies. In Charleston, Scottish linen was advertised in the South Carolina Gazette. John Crockett and George Seaman, two Scots merchants from Leith, advertised '*Negro cloth and Scotch linen*'[74] which suggest that the cheaper and rougher linen produced in eastern Scotland found a market for their produce among the slave owners. Robert Deans, from Scotland, offered '*lawns, checked handkerchiefs, striped and checkered lawns for aprons, checked linen, Scots and Holland Osnaburgs, striped and plain ticken and white threads*'.[75] Later, he advertised goods from Edinburgh such as '*striped hollands, checked handkerchiefs, women's thread gloves, lawn handkerchiefs, thread stockings, and Scotch linens.*'[76]

Table 1/2

Linen exports to South Carolina from Scotland, 1743-1772 (5-year totals)

1743-1747	43,283 yards	
1748-1752	104,830 yards	
1753-1757	371,347 yards	
1758-1762	283,356 yards	
1763-1767	224,074 yards	
1768-1772	424,286 yards	(Source: NRS E504)

According to the Scottish Port Books, in total, 1,835,593 yards of linen were exported from Scotland to South Carolina between the years 1743

[74] SC Gaz, No. *98*, dated 11 November 1734
[75] SC Gaz, No. 820, dated 29 August 1750
[76] SC Gaz, No. 869, dated 7 January 1751

and 1774. The ports of Greenock and Leith handled about a third of this quantity each, while the balance was shipped through the harbors of Bo'ness, Dundee, Dunbar, Glasgow, Kirkcaldy, Irvine and Ayr. The majority, over a million yards, was sent via the east coast, with about three-quarters of a million yards being sent from the west. Scottish linen exports to Charleston have been analysed by year and by port,. These figures do not include any consignments shipped to London and subsequently exported from there to Charleston. To place the exports to Charleston into proportion it should be noted that total exports of linen from Scottish ports 1743 to 1774 amounted to approximately fifty-five million yards,[77] which means that Charleston took only about four per cent of the total.

Sailcloth

This specialised type of canvas was intermittently exported to Charleston during this period and it has been generally possible to identify the sources of consignments. Sailcloth was quantified in 'ells' an old Scots measure which was roughly equivalent to a metre. Manufacturers were, as might be expected, located in the ports where there was a constant demand for their produce. Among those producing sailcloth for export to South Carolina were Robert Auchterlony in Dundee, Alexander Ogilvie in Leith, Thomas Brown and Charles and Robert Fall, all of Dunbar, Andrew Donald and Company, and later Donald, White, and Company in Greenock, and William Laird and Company in Port Glasgow. On one occasion, in August 1769, a complete set of sails was despatched on the Britannia of Greenock which also carried: one mizzen sail, one top sail, one main sail, one top galliot, and two additional sails.[78] Leaving from a Scottish

77 A. J. Durie, 'The Markets for Scottish Linen, 1730-1775', G. Donaldson, (ed), *Scottish Historical Review*, Volume 52, Edinburgh, 1973, pp. 32 [78] NRS.E504.15.17

SCOTTISH TRADE WITH
COLONIAL CHARLESTON, 1683-1783

port, was a shipment of German canvas which may also have been used for sail-making. This comprised eleven hundredweight of Hessian and 'Spruce' or Prussian canvas, brought from Bremen and Danzig, to be shipped onward to Charleston in August 1769.[79]

Between 1743 and 1774, according to the Scottish port-books, a total of forty-eight thousand, four-hundred and eighty ells of sail-cloth were exported from Scotland to Charleston. Approximately a quarter of this figure was shipped through the ports of Greenock and Port Glasgow, and the rest via Dundee and the Forth ports. The most important port engaged in this traffic was Dunbar, which between the years 1763 and 1773 shipped a total of twenty thousand, five hundred and eleven ells or roughly forty per cent of the Scottish total.

Cordage

All manner of ropes are required on-board ship, collectively known as cordage, were manufactured in many port towns and exported to the colonies. This item was an essential import of maritime centers such as Charleston. It has been recorded in the port books that in September 1772, the large Leith sail-cloth manufacturer, Alexander Ogilvy, shipped two hundred and seven hundredweight of cordage to Charleston. Cordage was retailed in Charleston by the Scottish merchants, Johnston and Simpson, who advertised *'sail-duck and cordage from Scotland'* in the *South Carolina Gazette*.[80] Between the years 1746 and 1772, approximately two-hundred and fifty hundredweight of cordage was shipped to South Carolina; with eighty seven-hundredweight, that is about forty per cent, being shipped through the port of Dunbar.

[79] NRS.E504.15.17
80 SC Gaz. 30 November 1767

36

SCOTTISH TRADE WITH
COLONIAL CHARLESTON, 1683-1783

Woollens

In the seventeenth century, raw wool and cheap woollens were important Scottish exports, and while much of this industry was concentrated in the southern half of the country, Aberdeen was an important manufacturing centre for woollen hosiery. In 1727 government began to encourage production of woollens in Scotland without much success and the domestic production of coarse woollen cloth continued much as before. The Scottish woollens industry was one of low cost, and low quality, with exceptions such as hosiery. There was, however, a market for cheap, low quality, rough woollen products in the colonies which the Scottish industry was in a position to supply. Generally English woollen products were of a higher quality and appealed to a different market both at home and abroad. It has been claimed that *'new products were developed to suit the growing Plantation trade'* and that *'low labor costs enabled the Scots industry to compete with the higher quality English products'*. The woollen products that were sent from Scotland to Charleston included tartan, blankets, caps, hose, stockings, hats, vests, gloves, bed covering, plaids, and clothing. These were manufactured mainly in the Central Lowlands, but also in Aberdeen and Shetland.[81]

Carpets

Small quantities of carpets manufactured in Scotland, around fifty, and approximately six thousand yards of carpeting were exported from Scotland to Charleston between 1753 and 1772. The great majority was shipped from the Forth ports of Leith, Bo'ness, and Dunbar, with one consignment through Port Glasgow, and another via Dundee. The

---

[81] C Gulvin, 'The Union and the Scottish Woollen Industry 1707-1760', *Scottish Historical Review*, Volume 50, Aberdeen, Scotland, 1971, p. 121

main manufacturing centres for carpet production of the period were Kilmarnock, Glasgow and Paisley.

Haberdashery

Consignments of haberdashery, small articles of dress and sewing accessories, were regularly shipped in the holds of vessels as part of Scotland's exports to Charleston. Sixty-nine loads of haberdashery have been identified between 1743 and 1774, of which forty-seven left from Greenock, fifteen from Port Glasgow, four from Leith and three from Bo'ness. These shipments collectively totalled approximately one thousand and ninety-two hundredweight. In addition to the above collective quantity, there were itemised haberdashery consignments of needles, ribbons, hairnets, thimbles, and thread exported to Charleston. The marked variation in the quantities shipped from the Clyde and the Forth ports may simply reflect a more stringent record keeping by the Customs Controllers in Leith.

Indian Textiles

Small, intermittent, consignments of calico, fustian, silk handkerchiefs, satin, and cotton handkerchiefs were exported, mainly from the port of Leith, to South Carolina in the colonial period. These products had been imported into London by the East India Company, and via the United Company of London, and the Leith merchants, were exported once again to the American colonies.

Glass

The manufacture of glass in Scotland began in 1610 when Sir George Hay, later the Earl of Kinnoull, was granted a patent. In 1661 two Acts were passed by the Scottish Parliament[82] which were designed to assist

82 Acts of the Parliament of Scotland (hereafter APS), Vol. VII pp. 255-261

SCOTTISH TRADE WITH
COLONIAL CHARLESTON, 1683-1783

the industrial development of Scotland though offering naturalisation to skilled foreign workers, by giving tax exemptions, and by authorising the formation of joint stock companies. These, together with the 1681 Act for Encouraging Trade and Manufactures,[83] fostered the establishment of several manufacturing concerns, such as glass-making, in the latter seventeenth century.

The earliest known glassworks in Scotland was established at Loch Maree and continued in operation until the 1620s. This site had been chosen due to a local supply of wood, the only suitable fuel at that time, however improvements in technology around 1615 meant that thereafter glassworks would be established on or near a site of a coalfield, and most of the 'glassaries' were to be found around the Forth, particularly at Leith, and also in Glasgow. The range of products included window glass, drinking glasses, beads, apothecary ware, mirrors, plate glass, and bottles. Scotland's centuries old wine trade with France and the Iberian Peninsula had brought great quantities of barrelled wine into Scotland, where it was bottled before being sold on, creating a demand for the production of bottles. The Glass Works of Leith, was established in the Citadel of Leith by Robert Pape in 1663. Another early glass-works was founded in 1678, again in Leith, and specialised in bottle-making, for which there was a substantial local demand. This firm, latterly known as the Leith Glass Company, operated until the premises were destroyed by fire in 1747. It was replaced by a new company, entitled the Edinburgh Glasshouse Company, which expanded operations in order to produce 'white-glass' bottles as well as the traditional 'green-glass' bottles. Probably the first

---

[83] APS, Vol.VIII p. 348

SCOTTISH TRADE WITH
COLONIAL CHARLESTON, 1683-1783

bottle making firm in Glasgow was a 'glassarie' built at the Broomielaw during the year 1700 by the Montgomerie family, which was also involved in the manufacture of soap and sugar.[84]   Another early Glasgow glassmaking firm was The Jamaica Street Bottle Works founded in 1730 by Richard and Alexander Oswald, George Murdoch, and others, which by 1752 was also producing crown or window glass. As can be seen, therefore, by the mid-eighteenth century Scotland had an established glass manufacturing industry producing a limited range of products, mainly bottles, and was ready to take up the challenge of expanding markets both at home and abroad.

An expanding domestic industry satisfied the increased domestic demand, and this expansion was further driven by the flourishing export of wine and ale bottled in Scotland and shipped to the colonies including South Carolina.   Glass bottles, of different descriptions, either empty or full, were regular cargo items on most vessels leaving the Forth and the Clyde ports, and this comprises a generally overlooked export to the colonies.   It is difficult to accurately assess the quantity of bottles on the evidence available as sometimes a number of bottles is noted, and in other documents, the weight.   There were, too, different sizes of bottles, for example 'chopin' bottles, or quart bottles.

Although glass bottles were the most common type of glassware exported to South Carolina, other kinds, such as flint glass and crown glass, could also be found listed among the cargoes.   Flint glasses and other types were manufactured in Newcastle, but were part of the export

[84] T M Devine and Gordon J Jackson, (eds), *Glasgow, Volume 1, Beginnings to 1830,* Manchester 1995, p. 81

SCOTTISH TRADE WITH
COLONIAL CHARLESTON, 1683-1783

consignments from the east coast ports of Leith and Dundee.[85] One example, also, has been found of the export via a Scottish port of continental glass bottles from the Dutch Staple port of Veere, shipped onwards via Greenock to Charleston in January 1754.[86] Veere also occasionally supplied more specialised wares brought from the continent, such as crystal mirrors.

Leather Goods

There were regular and substantial cargoes of leather goods, particularly shoes, boots, saddles, gloves and horse-whips shipped to Charleston without any indication of place of manufacture, and it is therefore very difficult to assess the specific quantity and value of these. The bulk of raw material, particularly tanned hides, was imported from Ireland, which was then converted in Scotland into a range of leather products, partly for export. Much of the capital invested in tanneries, boot, shoe and saddles manufactories in the west of Scotland at this period came from profits from the tobacco trade.[87]The two Scottish saddlers who are known to have practised their trade in Charleston were Hugh Graham and Hugh Pollock.[88] Possibly some of the saddles and associated wares exported to Charleston were destined for their stores.

---

[85] NRS.E504.11.8
[86] NRS.E504.15.6
87 L E Cochran, *Scottish Trade with Ireland in the Eighteenth Century*, Edinburgh, 1985, p66
88 TNA.AO19.99.336; AO13.133.437; APS.IX.321

SCOTTISH TRADE WITH
COLONIAL CHARLESTON, 1683-1783

Chaises

There was a small but unexpected trade in the luxury item of chaises
between Scotland and Charleston in the mid-eighteenth century. There
is no evidence to show the place of their manufacture in Scotland, but
since they were shipped from Leith and Dunbar, it is reasonable to
assume that they were constructed in the area of the ports. Several
consignments of cartwheels were also exported. The manufacture of
both these items required the availability of skilled craftsmen, coach-
builders, wheelwrights and lorimers, and Edinburgh being the area of
Scotland with the largest concentration of people, and wealth, it would
add to the belief that this would have been where the items were
produced.

The Edinburgh Parliament in the 1690s, allowed a William Scott
permission to establish a manufacturing business to produce coaches,
"chariots, sedans, coach harnish and glasses .." and undertook to bring
in appropriately skilled foreign artisans "until these of this nation be
capable and instructed in the said trade".[89] As far as can be established,
the only coach-maker in mid-eighteenth century Edinburgh was a Mr
Lancashire, possibly an English craftsman,[90] presumably the Thomas
Lancashire, coach-master, who married Christine Farrier in the
Canongate Kirk in 1749.[91] Wheelwrights were more common, but the
same source identifies only four working in Edinburgh at the same
period; James Ballantine in Cant's Close, Thomas Balderstone,

[89] APS.IX.321
90 James Gilhooley, *A Directory of Edinburgh in 1752,* Edinburgh, Scotland, 1988, p. 100
91 Francis J Grant, *Parish of Holyroodhouse or Canongate Marriage Register, 1564-1800,*
Edinburgh, Scotland, 1915, p 288

SCOTTISH TRADE WITH
COLONIAL CHARLESTON, 1683-1783

Andrew Millar in Fishmarket Close, and James Nisbet in Stonelaw's Close. Between 1750 and 1766, thirty chaises are recorded as having left Scotland for Charleston.

Metalware
The Scottish Customs books record regular consignments of copper, tin, pewter, and iron ware, such as tea kettles, saucepans, coffee pots, needles, buttons, buckles, firedogs, frying-pans, knives, axes, spades, shovels, pikes, hatchets, fire-grate tongs, thimbles, and cutlery, all 42 products in constant demand by the colonists and Indians in Charleston and its environs.

These articles were the output of small scale producers or craftsmen in the towns and villages of central Scotland. However the Industrial Revolution changed the structure of the industry from what was virtually a cottage industry to the factory system, and the Smithfield Company was established in 1734 on a site on the Kelvin River as a slitting mill to manufacture nails. Soon it was producing nails, adzes, axes, hoes, spades, shovels, chisels, hammers, bellows and anvils for the colonial market. In 1769 the Dalnottar Company was formed with the object of producing a similar range of iron goods. In both cases the capital was derived from profits generated in the tobacco trade.[92]

The Carron Company, established in 1759 near Falkirk, produced a wide range of products in demand by the colonists, ranging from simple tools, such as hoes, spades, shovels, and axes, to domestic items such as pots, pans, saucepans and skillets. Most of these were also suitable for marketing to the Indians. The company also produced stoves,

---

[92] T. M. Devine, *The Tobacco Lords,* Edinburgh, Scotland, 1975, p. 37

grates, pipes, chimneys, nails, and other cast iron goods all of which found a ready market in colonial America. The production of nails in contemporary Scotland had been concentrated in a few locations in the central belt, specifically in Bannockburn, Kirkcaldy, Glasgow, Rutherglen, Edinburgh, but increasingly it became centred on Carron. Traditionally the nailers had depended on supplies of iron from Sweden and Holland but by the 1760s a supply of rod-iron was at hand at the Carron Iron Works. The market for nails which was originally highly localised expanded to include England and the American colonies during the eighteenth century. The Scots nailers had one major advantage over their English rivals in that the centers of production in Scotland were generally closer to the coast which made transport costs lower and therefore their nails were more price competitive.   John Glassford, and other merchants engaged on overseas commerce, soon began to export the iron wares produced by the Carron Company.[93]

There were a number of consignments of cast iron goods being exported from south Forth ports which in all probability came from the nearby Carron Works. On 30 March 1765 Johnston and Simpson, merchants in Charleston, advertised in the South Carolina Gazette, a range of products which had just arrived from Scotland aboard the brigantine Jane, master John Smith.   Among the goods listed was 'a large assortment of cast metals from the new works at Carronshore'.[94]

There is some evidence of small quantities of continental ironware being shipped via Scotland to South Carolina: in 1772 a consignment

[93] Roy H Campbell, *The Carron Company*, Edinburgh, 1961, p. 105
94 SCGaz, 30 March 1765

of iron chests brought from Rotterdam; four tons of Russian and Swedish iron sent via Dunbar in 1764, and in 1771, iron-hoops and ten hundred weight of steel.

In addition, some of the hardware exported to Charleston through Scottish ports was manufactured in England.   The South Carolina Gazette announced the arrival of 'Sheffield wares' on the Industry, Captain Cowan, from Leith.[95]   In August 1752 the Industry returned with two and a half hundredweight of Birmingham and Sheffield hardware *'for want of sale'*.[96]

While the vast majority of metal goods being shipped from Scotland to Charleston were everyday items, there was evidence of a luxury
Item demanded by the affluent merchants and planters of Charleston, such as silver plated cutlery.   In 1753 Ebenezer Oliphant, an Edinburgh goldsmith, despatched a consignment of eighteen tablespoons, forty tea spoons, four pair tea tongs, two punch spoons, equal to sixty ounces troy weight British silver plate, from Leith bound for Charleston. Ebenezer Oliphant, was a member of the Oliphant of Gask family, noted for its Jacobite sympathies.   Son of James Oliphant of Gask, Ebenezer was admitted as a burgess and guilds-brother of Edinburgh on 26 October 1737 having served an apprenticeship under James Mitchelson an existing goldsmith burgess and guilds-brother of Edinburgh.[97]   It is just possible that the cutlery was destined for another

[95] SCGaz, No 869, 7 January 1751
[96] NRS E504.22.10
[97] Charles B Boog-Watson, *Register of Edinburgh Register of Apprentices, 1701-1755,* Edinburgh, Scotland, 1929, p. 67; Charles B. Boog-Watson, *The Roll of Edinburgh Burgesses and Guild-brethren, 1701-1760,* Edinburgh,1930, p. 156
98 NRS.RD3.235.265

member of the family, as Dr David Oliphant had sought refuge in America after the defeat of the Jacobites in 1746 and settled in Charleston as a physician.[98] The Oliphant family is another example of the elite chain migration that was a feature of emigration from Scotland to America. In the years immediately after the American Revolution another David Oliphant, son of James Oliphant a goldsmith and jeweller in Edinburgh, settled in Charleston as a painter, as did his sister Jemima.[99] Dr David Oliphant was among the Loyalist refugees that settled in Jamaica in the aftermath of the American War of Independence.[100]

The other commodity designed for an affluent market which was shipped from Scotland to South Carolinas was clocks. In total only five are known to have been exported to Charleston, and all in the period 1772-1773. These would have been expensive luxury items made by highly skilled craftsmen. In 1772 two clocks were sent, one an eight-day clock made by John Sasley in Edinburgh, and another constructed by James Duff in Edinburgh exported in same ship. The following year, 1773, a further consignment was sent to Charleston, and again through the port of Leith. This comprised of three eight-day carriage clocks made by Robert Clydesdale. It has been possible to identify the clockmakers.[101] Robert Clydesdale was a clock and watchmaker in Edinburgh from 1738 to 1786[102]; James Duff, also in Edinburgh from

98 NRS.RD3.235.265
99 NRS.CS17.1.6/196, NRS.CC8.8.135
100 TNA.AO13.88.96-104
101 Donald Whyte, *Scottish Clock and Watchmakers, 1453-1900*, Edinburgh, Scotland, 1996
102 NRS.CC8.8.126/1

1758 to 1774; and John Sasley, again in Edinburgh, from 1764 to 1803. James Duff, watchmaker, was admitted as a burgess of Edinburgh, by right of his father Alexander Duff an armorer burgess, on 6 December 1758. Robert Clydesdale, watchmaker, was admitted a burgess of Edinburgh on 12 June 1754 having been apprenticed to Alexander Brand a watchmaker burgess and guilds-brother.[103] However, surprisingly John Sasley does not appear in the published roll of Edinburgh Burgesses and Guild-brothers.

Specialist Tools, Equipment and Weapons

There are a small number of these in the Customs records. These are generally unique entries which may represent goods being supplied in response to orders or they may be the tools of craftsmen bound for Charleston. In September 1766 among the cargo of the <u>Magdalene</u> which left Dunbar bound for Charleston were one turning lathe, one trunk of mathematical instruments, and one box of tools[104]. Seven years later, one box of jeweller's tools, three boxes of cutting knives, and two drill barrows, was shipped on the <u>Happy Janet</u> from the same port again bound for Charleston.[105] The records for Leith list a chest of carpenter's tools being despatched to Charleston in June 1749, also 'two presses for book binders' in August 1768, and in August 1774 one box of wrights' tools, valued at £1 was sent on the <u>George</u>.[106] The only such export in relative quantity occurred in October 1758 when six anvils and three 'screws' were shipped from Bo'ness to South Carolina. The biggest single item of this category was a printing press sent to

[103] See Charles B Boog-Watson, *Roll of Edinburgh Burgesses and Guild-brethren, 1701-1760*, Edinburgh, Scotland, 1930, pp 40, 59
[104] NRS.E504.10.5
105 NRS.E504.10.5
106 NRS.E504.22.19

SCOTTISH TRADE WITH
COLONIAL CHARLESTON, 1683-1783

Charleston from Leith in 1766. Three ploughs were on board the <u>Pearl of Glasgow</u> which sailed for Charleston in August 1767.[107] The smallest item was a barrel of mousetraps sent from Leith in August 1750. There were only two consignments of weapons noted, thirty-six muskets in 1754, and a single fowling piece in 1760, but there were several shipments of gunpowder sent to Charleston from Scottish ports. Interestingly on the 26 September 1754, a Scots merchant, named Balvaird, advertised "superfine Highland pistols" for sale in the South Carolina Gazette.[108] One consignment of toys which had been brought from the Scots Staple port of Veere in Zeeland, was exported from Leith on the <u>George of Leith</u> in October 1771.[109]

Other unexpected commodities were golf-clubs and golf-balls. One consignment of ninety-six golf clubs and four-hundred and thirty-two golf balls, exported via Leith on board the <u>Magdalene</u> bound for Charleston in April 1743.[110] Two later consignments of twelve golf-clubs came aboard the <u>Black Prince</u> in 1763, and another of twenty-four golf clubs on the <u>Magdalene</u> in 1766, both from Dunbar.[111] As far as can be established, there were no full-time golf club-makers or golf-ball makers active in contemporary Scotland. Clubs may have been made by bow-makers originally though by the mid-eighteenth century it may have become the task of the wrights. Golf-balls however were

107 NRS.E504.15.18
[107] SCGaz No 1058
[107] NRS.E504.22.18
[107] NRS.E504.2.1
111 NRS.E504.10.3

generally produced by the cordiners, "The Minute Book of the Craft of Shoemakers in the Canongate" refers on 7 January 1641 to an "Andro Dicksoun, prentess to Wm. Dicksoun, cordiner and gowff ball maker in Leith".[112]   As the Lothians, especially the vicinity of Edinburgh, was one of the main centres for golf in contemporary Scotland it is highly likely that the clubs and balls exported originated there also.

Tobacco

Tobacco was imported from Virginia, Maryland, and North Carolina, and processed, mainly in Glasgow, before being exported or sold on the domestic market as roll or cut tobacco.   Some of this was destined for the markets of Charleston.   Among the tobacconists in Glasgow involved in this trade with South Carolina were Archibald McKendrick, James Tennant, David Black, and George Kippen.[113]   As well as consignments of tobacco being sent to Charleston, there were occasional cargoes of tobacco pipes and snuff.   While Glasgow was the main source of such exports there were small quantities of snuff produced in Aberdeen and in the Netherlands shipped from Leith and Dundee to South Carolina.

Soap

Soap boiling was established in Leith around 1620 by Nicolas Udwart, a prominent entrepreneur of the period. By the mid-seventeenth century there were two soap-works there, one operated by the Riddell family, and the other by Robert Douglas. While soap-making became one of Leith's staple industries it was not a major employer. The raw

---

112 A W C Hallen, *The Scottish Antiquary,* Vol.X, Alloa, Scotland, p102
113 NRS.E504.15.- passim

material for this industry was whale oil and fish offal, which were available in Dundee as well as in Leith. In Dundee, the industry was sited to the east of the town and close to the harbor where soap was made by a William Mitchell in his premises at Peep O'Day. Hard soap produced by William Mitchell was regularly exported from Dundee to Charleston in the late 1760s and early 1770s, for example twenty-three hundredweight of hard soap shipped in March 1771.[114]

Tallow Candles

The candles were manufactured from animal fat, usually sheep, and the wick from hemp or linen. As these were relatively common materials, candles could be easily produced. Candles were manufactured in large quantities only in major urban centres such as Glasgow, Dundee, Edinburgh and Leith, and it was more a cottage industry than a factory product. Tallow candles featured regularly in the ships manifests, bound for the colonies, and among those tallow chandlers in Glasgow who exported to Charleston were James King in Newark, William and Margaret King in Port Glasgow, John Hope, Archibald and James Paterson Archibald Paterson; in Greenock, there was George Thomas; and in Leith, George Anderson.

Wigs

Three small consignments of wigs were shipped from Greenock and Port Glasgow in the mid-1750s, an example being eighteen on the Edinburgh from Greenock in November 1754.[115] In the following year, thirty pounds in weight of human hair was also exported through Port

---

[114] NRS.E504.11.8
[114] NRS.E504.15.7

SCOTTISH TRADE WITH
COLONIAL CHARLESTON, 1683-1783

Glasgow bound for Charleston,[116] and it is possible that they were destined for the premises of John Bothwell, a peruke or wig-maker from Aberdeen, who had settled in Charleston.[117]

Paper

During the early modern period, much, if not most, of the paper products used in Scotland was imported from England, France or the Netherlands. The first attempt at a domestic industry occurred in 1590, followed by about a dozen other attempts before the Act of Union in 1707. One such was 'The Society of the White-Writing and Printing Paper Manufactory of Scotland' which was founded in 1694. The founder of this manufacturing company was a Huguenot, Nicolas Du Pin, who brought the skills of papermaking together with skilled workers from France.[118] Almost all of paper mills were sited in or around the capital city. Edinburgh housed the parliament, the law courts, the university, printing and publishing, and was the major commercial centre of the country. This being the case, its demand for paper was greatest. By the mid-eighteenth century, although the Lothians remained the major source of paper products, production of paper had spread through much of the country, with mills in operation from Aberdeenshire to Ayrshire. One of the latest paper-mills, and one which is known to have supplied customers in Charleston, was Melville Mill, Lasswade, established around 1760 by John Hutton, an Edinburgh merchant'.[119] As far as can be determined the paper

[116] NRS.E504.28.7
[117] probate SC, 1777
118 NLS.ms.1913
119 A G Thomson, *The Paper Industry in Scotland, 1590-1861*, Edinburgh 1974, p.120

exported to Charleston was made in the mills at Dalkeith, Lasswade, Ormiston, and Penicuik. Varying types of papers produced by James Hutton papermaker in Dalkeith, John Hutton in Lasswade, also by Duncan and Company of Penicuik found their way to South Carolina. In total, approximately nine-hundred reams of papers, ten hundredweight of pasteboard, and four gross of pressing papers were shipped to Charleston, mainly through Leith but also Dunbar, Bo'ness and Ayr, between 1767 and 1774. Also exported was a consignment of seventeen thousand goose quills.

Books

Regular consignments of books, unspecified apart from Bibles and New Testaments, were sent by the hundredweight. Around forty-six hundredweight of books were shipped from the ports of Greenock, Dunbar, Bo'ness, but particularly Leith to Charleston between 1749 and 1773. There were a couple of instances, in Leith in 1754 and in 1771, of part consignments being returned through lack of demand. The sale of books in Charleston created jobs in printing, book-binding, and publishing in Edinburgh as well as causing a derived demand for the produce of the local paper-mills. In mid-century Edinburgh, there were fourteen master printers and a dozen master book-binders who in turn employed a number of journeymen and apprentices. In Charleston, the only evidence of this trade are the advertisements appearing in the South Carolina Gazette. Apart from the mention of bibles, only on one occasion is a particular title given; on 15 April 1732, the book, *Lindsay's History of Scotland* is advertised for sale.[120] One of the most likely destinations for some of the books exported from Scotland to Charleston would have been the Charleston Library Society in King Street. This society was founded in 1748 by seventeen young

[120] SCGaz, No 15, 15 April 1732

gentlemen of various trades and professions who wished to avail themselves of the latest publications from Great Britain. It is the third oldest library in the United States.

Earthenware

Although pottery had been produced on a small scale in Scotland since the medieval period, the adoption of the factory method of production only dates from the mid-eighteenth century. 1749 saw a short-lived attempt to manufacture Delftware in Glasgow, but the main area of the Scottish potteries, dating from 1750, was along the south shore of the Forth from Bo'ness to Prestonpans, and across the estuary in Kirkcaldy. The industry began in Prestonpans with William Cadell's factory, and was aided by the expertise of Dr John Roebuck and Samuel Garbet, the founders of the Carron Iron Works. The Prestonpans Pottery exported to Italy, Russia, North America and the West Indies. Soon there were three additional pottery manufacturers; West Pans Pottery founded in 1764, Hilcote's Pottery founded in 1760, and Bankfoot Pottery in Prestonpans, 1764. All of these would have been able to supply earthenware for export. A total of nine cargoes shipped to Charleston contained earthenware or Delft. Six shipments left Greenock, two from Glasgow, and one from Leith. However, due to the different methods used for quantifying, namely hogsheads, crates, pieces and weight, it is impossible to estimate the quantity exported to Charleston. The single consignment of earthenware shipped from Leith was described as "Two crates of English earthenware".

Furniture

There is clear evidence of furniture being shipped from Scotland to

SCOTTISH TRADE WITH
COLONIAL CHARLESTON, 1683-1783

Charleston in the colonial period, albeit on a small scale, for example a consignment of two chests of drawers and one table shipped from Dunbar in 1773.[121]

What is not clear is whether these pieces of furniture were sent for sale in Charleston or whether they were the property of passengers intending to settle in South Carolina. What is perhaps more important than the shipment of furniture is the transfer of skills, techniques and ideas that occurred at that time. Edinburgh had for centuries been the main centre for craftsmen in Scotland, but the development of the New Town of Edinburgh from the mid-eighteenth century gave a boost in demand for furniture and an increased need for skilled craftsmen such as cabinetmakers. On the other side of the Atlantic, urban growth, especially in cities like Boston, New York, Williamsburg, and Charleston, caused a similar phenomenon. The town houses built by affluent planters and merchants in Charleston had to be furnished and while furniture could be imported it was increasingly being produced locally using colonial cedar, mahogany and walnut. The craftsmen who produced furniture in colonial America were predominantly English or German but there was a significant number of Scots also employed in the trade. It has been claimed that between 1790 and 1820, of the sixteen cabinetmakers known to have worked in Charleston, two thirds were Scottish immigrants.[122] Charleston, being a wealthy city, provided a market for the items produced by the town's cabinetmakers throughout the colonial period and thereafter.

[121] NRS.E504.10.3

[121] R Hurst and J Prown, *Southern Furniture, 1680-1830*, Williamsburg, Virginia, 1997, passim

SCOTTISH TRADE WITH COLONIAL CHARLESTON, 1683-1783

Cabinetmakers are recorded in Charleston from the 1720s, six by 1730, fourteen by 1750, twenty-eight by 1760, and twenty-one by 1775. Thirty cabinetmakers, joiners, carvers, furniture painters, chair-makers, and coopers, all bearing Scottish surnames, have been identified as working in South Carolina, predominantly Charleston before the Declaration of Independence in 1776, and these are listed below. It cannot be claimed with any degree of certainty that they were all Scots, some may have come from Ulster, and others may have been born in America.

Table 1/3
Scots Cabinetmakers in Charleston, pre 1776

Burn, Andrew, an upholsterer and cabinetmaker, 1769-1774
Burnett, Henry, a carver, 1750-1760, died 1761
Carmichael, John, a joiner, 1718-1725, died 1736
Cochrane, Robert, a furniture painter, 1750-
Deans, Robert, a joiner, cabinetmaker, carpenter, 1750-1776
Drummond, James, a cabinetmaker, 1769-1773
Ferguson, William, a cabinetmaker in Beaufort, 1744-1770
Finlayson, Mungo, a cabinetmaker, 1768-1793
Fisher, John, a cabinetmaker and chairmaker, 1767-1776
Fyfe, John, a cabinetmaker, 1776
Kirkwood, James, a cabinetmaker and joiner, 1746-1766
McClellan, David, a carpenter before 1739
McClellan, James, a cabinetmaker, 1733
McGillvray, Farquhar, a cabinetmaker, 1754-1767
McLenning, Andrew, a carpenter, 1741
Moncreiff, Richard, a carpenter and joiner, 1737-1777
Rannie, Charles, a carpenter and cabinetmaker, pre 1734

SCOTTISH TRADE WITH
COLONIAL CHARLESTON, 1683-1783

Scott, William, a cabinetmaker, Edisto Island, 1716-1722
Scott, William, a carpenter and joiner, SC, 1729-1735
Stephen, James, a cooper, pre 1766
Stewart, George, cabinetmaker, SC, 1774-1785
Stuart, Thomas, joiner, Berkeley County, 1709
Urquhart, Lennard, a carpenter, SC, pre 1758
Walker, Robert, 1772
Wallace, James, a cabinetmaker, pre 1755
Watson, Alexander, a joiner, SC, pre 1761
Watson, Thomas, a cabinetmaker and joiner, 1720-1736
Welch, William, a cabinetmaker and joiner, 1753-1754
Wilkie, George, a cabinetmaker, St Andrew's parish, pre 1787
Wilkie, John, a cooper, 1769.

Robert Deans, who was born in Scotland, was a joiner, cabinetmaker and carpenter in Charleston from around 1750. His talents extended to surveying, building and inventing, and his single most important invention was a machine for pounding and beating rice and indigo which reduced the need for slave labor by two thirds.[123] John Fisher, another Scot, was a cabinetmaker and chair maker in Charleston from 1767 to 1776. His Loyalist sympathies caused him to relocate to Jamaica after the American War of Independence broke out.[124] There are occasional references in the Scottish port books to '*cabinet-makers wares*' being shipped to Charleston. While these could have been the personal property of emigrant craftsmen, it is more likely that they were sent for sale. In Williamsburg, the then capital of Virginia,

[123] TNA.AO13.127.107
124 TNA.AO12.51.256

56

cabinetmakers sold imported furniture and tools, as well as locally produced items. Anthony Hay, a Scots cabinetmaker living there from 1748 to 1767 sold imported tools in his Williamsburg 'wareroom'.[125] A similar situation may have existed in Charleston.

Provisions

Since the seventeenth century Ireland, rather than Scotland, had directly supplied the colonies in the West Indies and in North America with provisions, especially salted beef, pork and butter.[126] But there were restrictions imposed by England on free trade between Ireland and the American colonies, unlike Scotland which enjoyed free trade with England and its colonies as from 1707. The restrictions on Irish trade benefited Scottish merchants who brought home colonial wares, such as tobacco and sugar which were, in part, then promptly shipped over to Ireland. During the colonial period, Ireland was a major supplier of provisions to the colonies across the Atlantic. However, there was some Scottish involvement in the shipment of provisions; several consignments of Irish and other beef were sent to South Carolina via Greenock and Bo'ness, and intermittent small quantities of barley, oats, cheese, beans, potatoes, butter, pork, flour, jelly, vinegar, pickles, sweetmeats, 'thornberries', and honey, appear in the Customs lists. South Carolina was at least self-sufficient in agricultural produce such as grain, pork and in rice, all of which were exported. The West Indies and the other mainland colonies were markets for all of them, and Europe was a major market for rice. As can be seen, therefore, there was only a small export of provisions from Scotland during the period.

[125] Michael Olmert, *The Official Guide to Colonial Williamsburg,* Williamsburg, Virginia, 1997, pp. 105-107

[125] See T M Truxes, *Irish American Trade, 1660-1783,* Cambridge, England,2000

SCOTTISH TRADE WITH
COLONIAL CHARLESTON, 1683-1783

Fish

In the seventeenth century, the Dutch were the predominant fishing, and indeed seafaring, nation in Europe. Their fishing industry was the most efficient and technologically advanced of its kind. The Scottish government, impressed by the success of the Dutch fishing activities off Scotland, attempted to improve the native industry by various measures, such as establishing the Royal Fishing Company with a monopoly of catching, curing and selling fish. Greenock was developed as a base for the fishing industry of the west coast and acted as the main port of export during the eighteenth century. In 1750 the British government introduced bounties to encourage the use of improved fishing vessels which resulted in an expansion of the Scottish fishing fleet. The expansion of the industry included the curing of herring, the main fish caught around Scotland. As well as a growth in the catch of fish and the numbers directly employed in the industry, there was an expansion in ancillary trades, especially shipbuilding and barrel-making. There was a growing market for herring both at home and abroad for Scottish fish including South Carolina. The fishing communities were located all around the coast, and it was there that the shipbuilding, curing and packing occurred. Consignments of fish, packed in barrels, were then shipped to the main ports on the Forth and Clyde from where they were exported to Charleston and elsewhere in the Americas. Fish merchants based in Lerwick, Loch Fyne, Loch Broom, and Thurso, are known to have been among those supplying fish, particularly herring but also ling and tuskfish, to the markets in Charleston. The fish merchants included Francis Grant in Shetland, and Alexander Miller in Thurso. Charles and Robert Fall, merchants in Dunbar who traded with Charleston, also cured the fish they exported. Most of the fish shipped to Charleston is believed to have been used to feed the slaves there.

SCOTTISH TRADE WITH
COLONIAL CHARLESTON, 1683-1783

Salmon, which for generations had been shipped to continental markets as far away as Venice, was not in great demand in South Carolina. There were occasional consignments of salmon sent, and one was despatched by a Perth merchant in 1764.[127]

Beer

Localisation of the brewing industry was largely determined by the supply of raw materials; grain, fresh water, fuel, particularly coal, as well as a market. Many of the burghs had their own small breweries which supplied their local needs. By the mid-seventeenth century Edinburgh had grown to become the center of brewing in Scotland, with the largest brewery located in Leith. This brewery had been established around 1670 by Sir James Stansfield, an English entrepreneur who had settled in Scotland. Stansfield was also associated with the erection of a glass and bottle works at Leith built to service his brewery. Here too Huguenot workers brought the skills to the benefit the Scottish economy,[128] one such being John De-Hew, a glassworker in Leith around 1689.

Between 1742 and 1774, seventy-eight consignments of beer and spirits left Scotland bound for Charleston. The vast majority, about seventy-five per cent, was shipped through Forth ports, especially Leith which handled about forty-two per cent of the overall total, with the balance being shared between Dundee and the Clyde ports. The terms 'beer' includes in its meaning, ale and porter. 'Beer' was recorded using a 60 variety of measures; hogsheads, barrels, firkins, gallons, bottles and chopin bottles, it is difficult to be accurate regarding the total quantities exported to Charleston, but a figure approaching nine-hundred barrels,

[127] NRS E504.11.9
[128] RPCS.XIV.382;

each containing thirty-six gallons, is a reasonable assessment. In 1747, three hundred gallons of 'spirits' were shipped from Leith.

Two brewers are particularly prominent in the Customs records for providing much of the cargoes of 'strong ale', beer and porter brewed in Scotland and exported to South Carolina. One was John Milne in Dundee, and the other was Hugh Bell in Edinburgh. John Milne, then a shipmaster and son of David Milne a maltman and a burgess of Dundee, was admitted as a burgess of Dundee in 1747.[129] By 1760 he was a Dundee wine-merchant[130] and by 1767 he had diversified into becoming a brewer in the Pleasants, Dundee.[131] Hugh Bell, merchant, was admitted as a burgess and guilds-brother of Edinburgh on 8 September 1756 by right of his father John Bell a brewer burgess and guilds-brother. Bell's Brewery was situated in Cleghorn's Close, off the Grassmarket, in Edinburgh, and from around 1762 Hugh Bell's Edinburgh Strong Ale was being exported to Charleston.[132] In Charleston advertisements for Scottish ale appeared in the South Carolina Gazette. On 30 November 1767, Johnston and Simpson, a firm of Scots merchants there, advertised 'Bell's Ale, and Cunningham's Ale' for sale.

Wine
This has been a regular import into Scotland since the medieval period, especially through the port of Leith. By the eighteenth century substantial quantities of French, Spanish, and Portuguese wine were

129; Dundee City Archives, The Lockit Book of the Burgesses of Dundee, ms
130 NRS.CE70.1.3
131 NRS.E504.11.6
132 NRS.E504.6.7

arriving in Scotland, also ships returning from America or the West Indies often brought back cargoes of Madeira wine which they obtained on the homeward voyage. While much of this wine was for home consumption some was for export to the colonies. The Customs records of Port Glasgow, Leith, Kirkcaldy, Bo'ness, Greenock, Dunbar, and Dundee all show regular shipments of wine to Charleston. The records use different measures, such as gallons, tuns, and bottles which make estimating the total of wine re-exports from Scotland to Charleston between 1742 and 1776 difficult. However, a figure in the region of twenty-nine thousand, five hundred gallons is reasonably accurate. Wine exports to Charleston from Scottish ports between 1743 and 1774 totalled approximately twenty-nine thousand, five hundred gallons of which around eight thousand gallons were sent from the west coast ports of Port Glasgow and Greenock and the rest from Dundee and the Forth ports, particularly Leith, which despatched about forty-five per cent of the Scottish total. Scots and other merchants in Charleston would advertise wine and other produce from Scotland in the South Carolina Gazette. In issue eighty, dated 21 July 1733, Alexander Nisbet, offered 'choice claret imported on the Betty from Glasgow'.

Refined Sugar

The sugar refining industry had been established in Scotland during the 1660s when John Brown, who had a patent to establish a sugar works in Scotland, was granted a licence by Charles II of England to send four ships annually from Scotland to the English West Indies for sugar which would be refined in Scotland. [133] Skilled sugar refiners were recruited in the Netherlands and Germany to provide the technological expertise necessary for the successful operation of the project, and

[133] NLS, MS7003, fo.3/7003, fo.29/31

SCOTTISH TRADE WITH
COLONIAL CHARLESTON, 1683-1783

continental names, such as Mark Kuhl and Casper Clausen, could still be found among the sugar refiners a century later. Caribbean sugar was processed in Greenock and Glasgow from the late seventeenth century onwards, and after refining, the sugar was mostly destined for the domestic markets of Scotland and Ireland, although some was exported to colonial markets including Charleston. The South Sugar House in Glasgow, dates from the 1740s, was founded by Alexander Houston, William McDowall, and the Oswald brothers, all wealthy West Indian merchants. By the mid-eighteenth century, sugar refining houses could be found in Greenock, Glasgow, Dundee and Edinburgh, with a flourishing export trade operating from their respective ports. Another sugar refinery in Glasgow was the King Street Sugarhouse. By 1772, Alexander Houston, was in partnership with Casper Clausen and James Dougal, sugar refiners in Glasgow. Robert Douglas, an entrepreneur who owned a soap making firm in Leith, established the first sugar refinery in Rotten Row, Leith in 1677. This refinery was still operating in the eighteenth century. The Edinburgh Sugar Company was established on 24 April 1752 and built a sugar house in the Canongait.[134] There was St Christopher's Sugar House in North Foulis Close off the High Street in Edinburgh, [135] and in 1757 another sugarhouse was built in Kirkgait, Leith, by Alexander Innes and partners. In Dundee sugar was being refined by James Fairweather, a merchant in Murraygait, who shipped the product to Charleston around 1772. Between 1742 and 1776, seventeen consignments of loaf refined sugar were despatched from Scotland to Charleston from four ports. In total three hundred and thirteen hundredweight was shipped to South Carolina, of which one hundred and sixty two hundredweight went via

[134] Journal of the Old Edinburgh Club, Volume XII, Edinburgh, 1923, p. 117
[135] James Gilhooley, *A Directory of Edinburgh in 1752,* Edinburgh, 1988, 11

Greenock, one hundred and nine hundredweight via Dundee, twenty-three hundredweight via Leith, and nineteen hundredweight via Port Glasgow. A typical consignment would have been the ten hundredweight, three quarters, and ten pounds of sugar refined at the King Street Sugar House in Glasgow and shipped on board the Crawford from Greenock in June 1752 bound for Charleston.[136] Confectionery, a closely related product, was also shipped, and two hundredweight was exported through the ports of Dundee and Leith in roughly equal proportions.

Livestock

This trade was almost non-existent, although trade in horses between Scotland and the English colonies was permitted under the Navigation Acts. In the post-Union era there was only one instance of livestock being shipped from Scotland to Charleston, a single horse in 1773.

III - Comparisons between Scotland and Charleston and the Chesapeake

Colonial markets, such as that of Charleston, were of supreme importance to the development, expansion and diversification of the Scottish economy during the eighteenth century. Access to such markets provided new opportunities to Scots merchants as sources of raw materials and as outlets for goods from Scotland. In order to generate growth in the economy, capital and skilled labor as well as entrepreneurs had to be brought in from abroad, especially from England, in a number of cases. While there were areas where exports from Scotland supplemented those from England entering the colonial markets, there were other areas where Scottish exports were significant,

[136] NRS E504.15.6

SCOTTISH TRADE WITH
COLONIAL CHARLESTON, 1683-1783

such as linen. By the outbreak of the American War of Independence in 1776 trade between Scotland and Charleston was well established and the two areas were increasingly interdependent. These bonds were so deeply entrenched that within a brief period of the cessation of hostilities in 1783 trade was soon reaching its pre-war level.

Evidence exists in the Scottish port-books of the stimulus given to Scottish industry through trade with Charleston, South Carolina.[137] Charleston was the single most important port in Colonial America south of the Chesapeake, and as well as acting as the main port of South Carolina it controlled part of the trade of the neighbouring colonies of Georgia and of North Carolina. The port of Charleston had trading links along the American coast, to the West Indies, Africa, the Mediterranean and the British Isles and Scottish exports could be of the Atlantic seaboard from the Chesapeake in the north to the Caribbean in the south, and possibly west as far as the Mississippi River, and back across the Atlantic to Africa. While the demands from the markets of Charleston did have an impact on Scottish industrial production, only a small proportion of that found its way across the Atlantic to Charleston.

The goods loaded aboard vessels in Scottish ports are listed in some detail in the port books from 1742 onwards. In a number of cases there is sufficient information to identify the place of manufacture and sometimes the company or individual concerned. An analysis of the exports from Scotland to South Carolina in 1684 based on the Scottish port-books[138] and a more detailed one for the period 1742 to 1774 based

---

[137] NRS.E504 Series
138 NRS.E72 Series

SCOTTISH TRADE WITH
COLONIAL CHARLESTON, 1683-1783

on a similar source,[139] provide a virtually complete breakdown of the commodities and their quantities sent from Scotland to Charleston in the colonial period.

The overall evidence points to the fact that in the late seventeenth century Scotland was able only to provide a limited range of basic goods, but as the eighteenth century progressed the range, quantity, and possibly the quality of goods made in Scotland and available for export was significantly greater. This, in part, reflects the growth and sophistication of the market based in Charleston, and also demonstrates how the Scottish economy had expanded. At the same time Scotland's growth in trade with other European countries meant that it developed as an entrepot, shipping colonial wares to the continent, and European goods, especially wine, to America.

Hitherto it had been believed that the west coast ports of Port Glasgow and Greenock had a near monopoly of Scotland's transatlantic trade of the American colonial period and that the Glasgow controlled tobacco trade alone had generated the profits which financed much of the growth of industry in contemporary Scotland. This study has revealed, however, evidence which partly challenges the historical orthodoxy. In a following chapter it will be established that trading voyages to Charleston and the Lower South originated in roughly equal proportions between east and west coast Scottish ports. It will be seen that in the colonial period a total of ninety-three voyages were made from east coast ports, of which seventy-five originated in the Firth of Forth, and ninety-five voyages began on the west coast, of which seventy-nine sailed from the River Clyde. The only published study of Scottish-American trade for the period stresses the predominance of

---

[139] NRS.E504 series

SCOTTISH TRADE WITH
COLONIAL CHARLESTON, 1683-1783

Glasgow in the tobacco trade, and more general studies assume or imply
that transatlantic trade between Scotland and the Americas in the
seventeenth and eighteenth centuries was almost wholly Clyde ports
based.   While admittedly the west coast ports certainly had the
geographical and strategic advantages for transatlantic trading, it is
nevertheless clear that east coast merchants also seized the
opportunities with both hands. This obviously impacted beneficially
on the economy of the whole country.   A brake, however, was applied
to the success of the east coast shipping activities during the period of
the Seven Years War, 1756-1763, when direct shipping from eastern
Scotland to America was almost decimated due to the presence of
French warships and privateers in the North Sea and the English
Channel, a problem that Clyde based shipmasters engaged in the
transatlantic trade were generally able to avoid.[140] Most vessels leaving
the Clyde bound for Charleston headed first for Madeira, the Azores, or
some other islands before sailing via the West Indies to Charleston,
while the ships from the Forth had to run the gauntlet in the English
Channel.

It is quite clear that, at least as far as Charleston was concerned, the
traditional view of Glasgow and Greenock being the dominant Scottish
ports trading with America is inaccurate. In order to be absolutely clear
on the overall situation, what is needed is a study of Scots trade with
the other major maritime centres of the Thirteen Colonies, of
Philadelphia, New York, and Boston. This author has elsewhere in the
series *Ships from Scotland to America, 1628-1828*,[141] based on primary
source material on both sides of the Atlantic, identified the voyages of

---

[140] see Eric J. Graham, *A Maritime History of Scotland, 1650-1790*, East
Linton, Scotland, 2002, pp.205-207
[141] David Dobson, *Ships from Scotland to America, 1628-1828*, Volumes I,
II, III, and IV, Baltimore, Maryland, 1998, 2002, 2004, 2011.

SCOTTISH TRADE WITH
COLONIAL CHARLESTON, 1683-1783

the period.   Volume II of the series is largely based on the Scottish port-books dating from 1742 and is therefore the most reliable source in print.   It is clear from random samples taken from Volume II, that Greenock was by far the single most important port trading with the Thirteen Colonies if number of voyages is the measure.   Scottish east coast ports seem, however, to have maintained a substantial part of the trade with American ports south of Cape Fear and with the West Indies, and can be explained by an examination of sailing routes.   The Clyde was admittedly well placed for trade with the colonies on or north of the Chesapeake, but Charleston and the Caribbean could be as effectively reached from Leith as from Greenock.

The most important port on the east coast which traded with Charleston was Leith, and on the west coast the major port was Greenock. Between 1742 and 1774 the Leith port books record thirty-eight voyages bound for Charleston while the equivalent for Greenock totalled seventy-eight voyages, a ratio of about one to two.   Despite this imbalance, Leith seems to have done particularly well.   The cargoes shipped from Leith and Greenock bound for Charleston have been extracted from the port books and analysed.[142]   These exports have been broken down into the following: textiles, metal-ware, leather, provisions, and miscellaneous.   There are twenty-two different commodities listed under 'textiles', of which linen is the single largest and probably most valuable item.   Of these twenty-two, fifteen different types of textiles, including linen, were shipped from Leith, and this exceeded the quantity of textiles sent from Greenock to Charleston. Of the eight categories of metal-ware, Greenock exported more then Leith in four cases, while a substantially greater quantity of leather was sent from Greenock than from Leith.   Under the fourteen categorised

[142] See Appendices

as 'Provisions', exports from Greenock generally greatly exceeded those from Leith, if wine, beer, and spirits are excluded. Those listed under 'Miscellaneous' were usually exported from Leith, and included products as varied as coal and cartwheels, and as a general rule the volume shipped out of Leith bound for Charleston exceeded that of Greenock. It should be noted that this comparison deals with volume of exports, rather than their value, and it cannot, therefore, be established where the greater profit was achieved. The comparison is interesting, however, in that it shows that despite roughly twice as many vessels leaving Greenock, a greater quantity of goods was shipped from Leith to Charleston.

While providing great detail on contemporary exports, the Port Books are limited by the absence of a uniform standard of weights, and it must be imagined that in many cases this makes a comparison extremely difficult. For example, the Customs at Leith measured woollens in yards while in Greenock they were measured in pounds. Liquid measures used for wine, ale, beer and porter, were variously measured in gallons, bottles, mutchkins, tuns, barrels, and firkins. The considerable imbalance in the quantity of haberdashery shipped through Greenock, four hundred and sixty-one hundred weight, compared to Leith, nine and a half hundredweight, may be a result of a variation in definition of the commodity. This is supported by the fact that textile products appearing on the Leith list are absent from those of Greenock.

South Carolina was clearly an important, though not necessarily a major market for Scottish exports, but one which in conjunction with the English, Irish and other colonial markets enabled the economic base of Scotland to widen and develop during the eighteenth century. Imports

68

SCOTTISH TRADE WITH
COLONIAL CHARLESTON, 1683-1783

from the colony were not always used domestically, and Scottish vessels off-loaded commodities such as rice in Spain and Portugal, exchanging this and other colonial products for wine and fruit, before returning to their port of origin.

SCOTTISH TRADE WITH
COLONIAL CHARLESTON, 1683-1783

CHAPTER TWO

EXPORTS FROM CHARLESTON

From the beginning it was obvious that the South Carolinians would have to develop a substantial and stable export trade in order to finance the level of imports necessary to enable the economy to grow, and also to provide the colonists with a reasonable standard of living. This chapter will examine the raw materials grown in the Carolinas together with and semi-processed goods which were exported Charleston to Scotland.

Many immigrants who had arrived from Barbados to settle in Carolina did so in the expectation of being able to develop trade links with the colonies of the West Indies creating a viable export trade which they hoped would provide a financial surplus which would enable them to buy the necessary manufactured goods required by the colony from Great Britain. While a thriving, regular trade was established and maintained between these colonies, the profits proved to fall short of the increasing demand for imported manufactured goods.[143] The Charleston trade with the Caribbean islands largely consisted of imports of sugar, molasses, rum, fruit, coffee and cocoa, while exporting naval stores, lumber, barrel staves, roof shingles, beef, leather, and in particular, rice; its Caribbean markets being located in Jamaica, Antigua, St Kitts, the Bahamas, and their largest, Barbados.

---

[143] See Karen O Kupperman, *Major Problems in American Colonial History, second edition,* Boston, Massachusetts, 2000, pp. 250-253

SCOTTISH TRADE WITH
COLONIAL CHARLESTON, 1683-1783

As early as the year 1669, the Proprietors of Carolina employed one Joseph West to test the viable growth of a number of potential staple crops which had been brought to South Carolina from Barbados, and these included cotton, indigo, ginger, canes, vines and olives. None were successfully grown,[144] and despite all efforts by 1687 the colonists had failed to find *"any Commodityes fit for the market of Europe but a few skins ...and a little Cedar... "*[145] Some idea of the extent of the trade of South Carolina before the commencement of the Charleston Naval Officer's accounts in 1710 was provided by Thomas Nairn, a Scot who had emigrated to South Carolina in 1698. By 1710 he was settled in Granville County, and had been appointed the colony's first official Indian Agent in 1707,[146] dying at the hands of Indians in 1715.[147] In a letter dated 1710, designed to reassure prospective settlers about the environment and trade of South Carolina, Nairn provided a description of the colony's contemporary trading pattern. He stated that twenty-two merchant ships annually traded between Great Britain and South Carolina and there were also sixty ships trading between Charleston and the West Indies, New England and the Middle Colonies, Madeira and Guinea. The goods brought in from Great Britain included various types of textiles, iron-ware, earthenware, haberdashery, guns and beer. Exported from the colony at an earlier period had been indigo but that

[144] Converse D Clowse, *Economic Beginnings in Colonial South Carolina, 1670-1730*, Columbia, South Carolina, 1971, pp. 58-59; John J McCusker and Russell R Menard, *The Economy of British America, 1607-1789*, Chapel Hill, North Carolina, 1985, p. 175
[145] McCusker & Menard, *The Economy of British America*, p. 171
[146] V W Crane, 'The Southern Frontier in Queen Anne's War', *The American Historical Review*, Volume XXIV, Washington, DC, part 3, p. 379
[147] David Dobson, *Scots in the Carolinas, 1680-1830*, Volume 1, Baltimore, Maryland, 1986, p. 252; David Dobson, *Scots in the Carolinas, 1680-1830*, Volume 2, Baltimore, Maryland 2004, p. 126

had ceased, and in Nairn's time exports included furs, tar, resin, raw silk, rice and most lucrative all, deerskins. There was a considerable trade imbalance between the exports of Great Britain and South Carolina and this was compensated for by goods brought in from the West Indies, which included consignments of coconuts, sugar and tortoise-shell. Charleston's exports of timber products and rice to Jamaica, St Thomas, Curacao, Barbados and the Leeward Islands were exchanged for imports of sugar, molasses, rum, cotton, chocolate, and Negro slaves. The captured Africans brought into Charleston from Guinea and elsewhere in the West Africa, arrived on vessels which had been dispatched from London with cargoes of trade goods which were off-loaded in Africa. The northern colonies of New England, New York, and Pennsylvania, sent foodstuffs to Charleston in exchange for its general hides, deerskins, gloves, rice and Indian slaves. Madeira and the Atlantic Islands sent wine and took in return provisions, staves and barrel-heads. Salt was obtained by South Carolina from the Bahamas.[148] As goods were recorded as being imports from 'Great Britain', it is possible than some of these goods originated in Scotland, especially in the light of the fact that almost all the goods listed were being produced there at the time.

Trade of the South Carolinian colony during the seventeenth and early eighteenth centuries was heavily dependent on the export of deerskins, timber products and meat. Later rice and indigo were to become major exports. A surplus of rice was available from the 1720s, and indigo from 1750. The markets for both expanded rapidly, creating wealth that allowed the colony to greatly increase its imports, especially from

[148] Thomas Nairne, 'A Letter from South Carolina', London, 1710, Jack P. Greene, *Selling a New World,* Columbia, South Carolina, 1989, p.42

SCOTTISH TRADE WITH
COLONIAL CHARLESTON, 1683-1783

the British Isles.   By the outbreak of the Revolution, South Carolina was probably the wealthiest of the mainland colonies largely to its ability to grow rice and indigo.   The volume of these exports played its part in Charleston becoming an important entrepot, through which the produce of Great Britain, its colonies, and elsewhere were processed and distributed.   For this reason, Jamaican rum would arrive in Scotland via Charleston, while linen, exported from Scotland to Charleston might well end up in the plantations of Georgia.

The Rice Trade

It is still unclear just when rice was first introduced into the Carolinas. It had been intended to be grown in Virginia, but the difficulty of producing it, combined with the success of tobacco growing caused it to be abandoned.   The market for tobacco was a growing one, and allowed Virginia to expand its European market. Like the early settlers in Virginia, those hoping to become established planters in the Carolinas later that century had to find a cash crop which could be exported to finance the cost of imported goods.   In the seventeenth century and during the early eighteenth century, the planters and merchants of Carolina had concentrated their efforts in supplying deerskins and the essential naval stores of pitch, tar and turpentine, for export, and South Carolinian export of naval stores was only made economically possible due to the British government's subsidy in the form of bounties.   When this was withdrawn in the 1720s, demand and output fell which put a severe strain on the colony's balance of payments.   Although they had already experimented with rice as a possible crop as early as 1671, the particular strain they had used was found to be unsuitable for the climate of Carolina.   Later, sometime around 1690, another variety of rice brought from Madagascar proved

74

SCOTTISH TRADE WITH
COLONIAL CHARLESTON, 1683-1783

to be highly suitable for local conditions. It is said that it was brought by an early colonist named Dr Henry Woodward. The Carolinian House of Assembly, however, gave this distinction to a shipmaster named John Thurber, and by way of thanks in 1715 awarded him an honorarium of one hundred pounds. During the 1690s, rice was to become a major cash crop of the colony. The key factor to its successful production was not only its suitable strain, the soil and the heat, but also the terrain. The coastal area around Charleston, known as the Low Country, was flat and watery due to heavy rainfall patterns, and most of the land surrounding the town was swampy. These were, of course, ideal growing conditions for a rice crop. Early crops had been planted on the dry, upland soil, with rainwater being used for irrigation, but it was soon discovered that the inland swamps produced a much better crop and so production was re-located to the lowland areas. These, in turn, by mid-century, were supplanted by the marshy areas along the sea coast, which proved to be even more productive. The swamps were drained, divided into squares, and separated by ditches surrounded by banks to avoid flooding. The swamps in the neighborhood of Charleston were the first to be developed for rice growing, but by 1750, more was produced around Georgetown, along the coast to the north. The conversion of swamps into rice-fields was laborious, trees had to be cleared, ditches and canals had to be dug, banks erected, and floodgates constructed. The major markets for rice were continental Europe, the nearby West Indies and the northern colonies of America and production rose with demand. Increasing consumer demands led to the requirement for more labor for both its cultivation and the industrial infrastructure. Since this labor force could not be found locally, nor be satisfied by the incoming immigrant indentured servants from Europe, planters and merchants began their dependence on black slave labor brought in from the African continent.

SCOTTISH TRADE WITH
COLONIAL CHARLESTON, 1683-1783

It has been suggested that the expansion of rice plantations was due in no small part to the knowledge of Africans who had experience of its cultivation in rice-producing parts of Africa.[149] These people were now actively sought, and slave owners were willing to pay premium rates to the slave traders for native Africans who had experience of rice farming. Traders in slaves began to advertise the geographical origins of particular imported slaves as being from areas they knew to be rice producing. These localities included Angola, Gambia, the Windward Coast, and the Gold Coast. An advertisement of the sale of a vocationally desirable Africans was published on 11 July 1785 in the Charleston Evening Gazette, which announced the arrival of a Danish ship bearing *'a choice cargo of Windward and Gold Coast Negroes, who have been accustomed to the planting of rice'*.

While rice neatly filled the gap of the withdrawn subsidy on naval stores as an export, and there was an ever increasing demand for the product in Europe and the Americas, there arose an issue with regard to the regulations of the English Navigation Acts. While inter-colonial trade was permitted and encouraged, colonial exports destined for markets other than England were required to call into English ports as their first port of call. After the Union of Parliaments in 1707, Scottish ports were included in this regulation. The rule was designed to bring financial and trade benefits to the British economy but a side effect was to increase costs. This was especially true in the case of rice exports, because its main European markets lay in Spain and Portugal. Carolinian rice shipped via England had to compete with rice imported from other European colonies in the Americas. In order to overcome this problem, in 1729 the British government introduced the 'Mediterranean Pass' which authorised shipmasters to sail for ports

---

[149] Peter Wood, *Black Majority,* New York, 1974, pp. 75-130

76

SCOTTISH TRADE WITH
COLONIAL CHARLESTON, 1683-1783

south of Cape Finisterre without calling first at a British port. Mediterranean Passes were issued by the local Collector of Customs before a transatlantic voyage and collected from the shipmaster on the vessel's return. Local Customs Collectors around Scotland recorded the issue of these passes in their letter books and advised the Board of Customs in Edinburgh. An example dated 15 September 1756 from the Customs Collector in Dundee records '*enclosed is a certificate for obtaining a Mediterranean pass for the ship the <u>Mercury of Dundee</u>, James Strachan master, for Charles Town, South Carolina*'.[150] By this means deliveries of cargoes of rice which had become the major export of South Carolina, was enabled to access directly the Iberian and Italian ports where fruit, wine, vinegar or salt would be loaded before and onward journey to Scotland or England.

The increasing demand in Europe for Carolinian rice was caused by a the general increase in population together with economic growth and at the time there was also a growing social change from agrarian-based economies to more emphasis on industry. No longer being self-sufficient, European countries were beginning to supplement their food supply from external sources. Fluctuating domestic output owing to poor harvests, or the impact of wars, contributed to an increasing reliance on America as a major source of foodstuffs. Before the outbreak of the American War of Independence about two-thirds of the rice exported from South Carolina and Georgia was destined for the markets of northern Europe, in particular Germany and the Netherlands. Spain and Portugal took about one-sixth of the total exports and the West Indies roughly the same amount. The situation was otherwise in Britain, where relatively little rice was consumed, and the population continued to rely on cereals, such as wheat or barley for their staples.

[150] Dundee City Archives: CE70.1.3

SCOTTISH TRADE WITH
COLONIAL CHARLESTON, 1683-1783

Latterly the main market for Carolinian rice was in northern Europe, partly as Spain and Portugal turned to cheaper rice from Turkey and Brazil, and the French, for political reasons, banned imports of rice from North America.

The amounts of rice shipped by Scottish merchants at various dates from Charleston to ports south of Cape Finisterre, particularly in Spain and Portugal, but also to Italy and possibly North Africa, can be seen below. The figures have been taken from the Scottish port books of various Customs Collectors and provide an almost complete record of exports and imports dating from 1742. All data referring to rice imports from South Carolina have been extracted from these records.

Table 2/1
Rice exports from South Carolina on Scots ships, 1742-1775

Year	Quantity	Destination
1742	x	
1743	3242 cwt	[all to Lisbon]
1744	3255 cwt	[of which 1565 cwt to Lisbon]
1745	2819 cwt	
1746	12,905 cwt	
1747	4,177 cwt	
1748	1933 cwt	
1749	1,265 cwt	
1750	x	
1751	1,435 cwt	
1752	3,081 cwt	[all to Lisbon]
1753	2,140 cwt	[1,729 cwt to Lisbon]
1754	10,653 cwt	[1499 cwt to Lisbon/Oporto]

SCOTTISH TRADE WITH
COLONIAL CHARLESTON, 1683-1783

1755	4,204 cwt	
1756	6,836 cwt	[3,035 cwt to Lisbon]
1757	37,877 cwt	[8,310 cwt to Lisbon]
1758	23,236 cwt	[1,556 cwt to Lisbon]
1759	21,695 cwt	[3,767 cwt to Lisbon]
1760	19,836 cwt	[1,027 cwt to Figuera]
1761	29,090 cwt	[10,231 cwt to Lisbon]
1762	11,348 cwt	
1763	12,868 cwt	[10,476 cwt to Lisbon]
1764	13,203 cwt	[2,693 cwt to Lisbon]
1765	9,554 cwt	[3,163 cwt to Lisbon]
1766	15,031 cwt	[5723cwtLisbon/ Barcelona]
1767	12,464 cwt	[12,302 cwt to Lisbon]
1768	15,251 cwt	[14,151 cwt Lisbon/Leghorn]
1769	21,986 cwt	[15,508 cwt Lisbon /Figuera]
1770	38,668 cwt	[35,278cwtLisbon / Valencia]
1771	16,294 cwt	[11,073 cwt to Lisbon, Seville and Figuera]
1772	9,226 cwt	[2,619 cwt to Lisbon]
1773	11,168 cwt	[2,748 cwt to Lisbon]
1774	12,828 cwt	[Lisbon, Oporto & Barcelona]
1775	9,314 cwt	[Lisbon, Barcelona & Cette]

Source: Scottish Port Books[151]

In Charleston, the roughly equivalent sources are the Shipping Records kept by the resident Port Officer.[152]   These records date from 1712 but are incomplete. It has been possible, however, to analyse the shipments for a forty year period from 1727 to 1767.   During that period one

[151] NRS.E504 series
[152] TNA. CO5.508-510
79

SCOTTISH TRADE WITH
COLONIAL CHARLESTON, 1683-1783

hundred vessels, either Scottish, English or colonial, left Charleston bound for Scotland, with cargoes which included rice.   Forty-six of them were bound directly for Scots ports, twenty-six to Iberian ports, twenty for English ports, and eight for colonial ports in the West Indies or North America.   Roughly a third of the ships destined for Scotland sailed for Orkney, thirteen for Glasgow, three for Dundee, and the rest for Forth ports.   Half of the twenty ships bound for England sailed for Cowes on the Isle of Wight and the others for ports lying between London and Bristol.   Nineteen of the twenty-six vessels which left for Iberian ports were docked at Lisbon, and the other ports mentioned were Cadiz, Leghorn, Barcelona and Oporto.   While the records are clearly incomplete, it is possible to see that the Seven Years War, 1756-1763, had a considerable impact on the sailing routes used by the merchant vessels operating out of Charleston, in an attempt to avoid the French navy and privateers.   Before and after the war, ships bound for Great Britain opted for ports along the English Channel, but during the war ships were directed north to Scotland, especially to Stromness in the Orkneys.

Stromness seems to have acted as an entrepot, distributing Carolinian rice and other colonial produce to the markets of northern Europe, especially those of Rotterdam and Hamburg.   In 1756, John Murray, a Scottish resident of Charleston, proposed that during the current war against the French, merchants of Charleston should consider sending their vessels via the Orkney Islands to avoid the possibility of being attacked and captured by the French navy or privateers.   This suggestion was rejected by the merchants on the grounds that they were adequately insured with companies in London.   In 1757, twenty-one ships, laden with colonial produce, including six hundred thousand pounds of indigo, left Charleston bound for England and the markets of northern Europe, and all but two were captured at sea by the enemy.

SCOTTISH TRADE WITH
COLONIAL CHARLESTON, 1683-1783

Although there was insurance to cover these vessels, it was no longer available for shipments thereafter. Planters and merchants belatedly took Murray's advice and from that time, during the period of warfare, sent their cargoes via Orkney.[153] The route from America via the Northern Isles to London was not, however, without its perils. A few years earlier, on 14 June 1748, the Aberdeen Journal contained an extract of a letter from Crail dated 3 June 1748 which reported that on 10 May the Friendship of London, master William Cleland, and another vessel, having taken the north passage to London from South Carolina, were unsuccessfully attacked by a French privateer off Rona. [154]

At specified ports along the south coast of England there were agents, known as factors, employed by Scottish merchants to act on their behalf on cargoes being shipped from the American colonies. These men directed the onward passage of consignments of rice, occasionally to Leith, but mostly commonly, directly to the markets of Rotterdam, Amsterdam, Bremen or Hamburg. One factor, James Mackenzie, was based in the port of Cowes on the English Channel. In January, 1773 he received instructions from his superior, James Inglis, an Edinburgh merchant, concerning a cargo of rice aboard the Bachelor of Leith due from Charleston. This is the same merchant and ship which achieved infamy through an abortive attempt to transport a group of emigrants from northern Scotland to North Carolina later that year.[155]

[153] NRS. Murray of Murraythwaite Muniments, GD219.290
[154] *Aberdeen Journal*, No 14
[155] NRS.CS96.2250/222; NRS.CS238.J5.69; probably the best account of this is in Bernard Bailyn's 'North Carolina: The Wreck of the Bachelor', *Voyagers to the West. A Passage in the Peopling of America on the Eve of the Revolution,* New York, New York, 1986, pp. 499-544.

SCOTTISH TRADE WITH
COLONIAL CHARLESTON, 1683-1783

This pattern of distribution demonstrates that very little of the rice arriving at Scottish ports was for domestic consumption. The majority of rice cargoes were quickly re-exported across the North Sea to continental markets. Evidence for this can be found in many of the contemporary port books. According to the Leith Port Book [156] in July 1744 the Charming Rachel, master John Perkins, brought a cargo of rice from South Carolina to Leith, and this was then dispatched from there to Rotterdam by Robert Clerk, a factor acting on behalf of James Crokatt, a Charleston merchant. Similarly, in April 1744, the Magdalene, master William Carse, was bound from Leith to Rotterdam, with rice sent by Hugh Clerk of Leith. The same ship had brought five-hundred and twenty four barrels of rice to Leith from Charleston, South Carolina the previous month. On 11 December 1755, Andrew Cowan, master of the Industry of Leith, who had arrived from Leith with a wide ranging assortment of Scottish wares, advertised these, at the same time announcing that he required rice for shipment to Lisbon, Hamburg and Bremen.[157]

Newspapers of the time also record the import and export of rice. The Edinburgh newspaper, the *Caledonian Mercury*, noted that the Carolina Packet of London, Captain Stewart, and the Indian Queen of Hull, Captain Reid, arrived in Leith from South Carolina with rice on 24 September 1745.[158] It also mentions that the Sarah of New York, Captain Knox, docked in Leith on 25 August 1746 after sailing from South Carolina with a cargo of rice, which was shipped onwards to Amsterdam on 11 September 1746.[159] Another issue announced the arrival of the Christian of Glasgow, Captain Butcher, and the Mally of

[156] NRS.E504.28.1/152
[157] *South Carolina Gazette*, No 1120
[158] *The Caledonian Mercury*, No 3894
[159] Ibid No 4037

SCOTTISH TRADE WITH
COLONIAL CHARLESTON, 1683-1783

Glasgow, Captain Petticrew, on the 16 August 1746 with rice from Carolina which was unloaded at Bo'ness.[160] On 4 September 1746, the Magdalene of Leith, Captain Mackenzie, was reported sailing from Leith to Bremen with rice.[161] While much of the shipping trade was kept in the hands of British shippers and seamen, occasionally continental ships would collect the rice from British ports for shipment to foreign markets. On 5 November 1747 the Christianna of Bremen, Captain Keiper, sailed from the harbour of Leith with a cargo of rice bound for Bremen in Germany. [162] This was probably the same rice which had arrived in Leith aboard the Magdalene of Leith, Captain Mackenzie, from South Carolina on 10 September 1747.[163]

This practice of trans-shipment of rice has been noted elsewhere also. In the Dunbar Customs House Letters of 1765,[164] the Jean of Elie, master John Smith, arrived in Dunbar from Charleston, South Carolina on 24 July with a cargo for Charles and Robert Falls, comprising one hundred and eight tons rice, one hundred and eleven barrels pitch, two hundred and sixty nine barrels tar, one thousand six hundred and seventy one pounds indigo, six hundred and seventy gallons rum, on hundred and nine pieces mahogany, sixty pounds of cotton wool, and having unloaded everything apart from the rice the ship sailed on 1 August 1765, bound for Bremen, Germany, with one hundred and eight tons of Carolina rice. Of the rice that did stay in Scotland, not all was for domestic consumption:

---

[160] Ibid No 4044
[161] Ibid No 4034
[162] Ibid No 4042
[163] Ibid No 4224
[164] T C Smout, The Dunbar Customs House Letters of 1765, *Transactions of the East Lothian Antiquarian Field Naturalist Society,* Volume XL, pp. 17-36

SCOTTISH TRADE WITH
COLONIAL CHARLESTON, 1683-1783

> "to be sold by public roup on Thursday 6th of November next betwixt the hours of three and four afternoon at James Cheap's, wine cooper, in his loft, head of Quality Street, Leith, A PARCEL OF RICE, fit for making STARCH or DISTILLING which by trial makes a fine spirit. The rice may be seen any day before the roup."[165]

An insight into a trading voyage to Charleston for rice in 1756 is provided by a case brought before the High Court of the Admiralty of Scotland. The voyage of the <u>Elizabeth and Peggy of Leith</u>, master Walter Scott, ended up as a case held in the Admiralty Court on 11 November 1757, involving Alexander McDougall versus John McKenna, Leith. The evidence produced in court included an inventory of the wide range of merchandise including tartan, shoes, hats, Shetland stockings, linen, glass, drugs, copperware, candles, and also eleven indentured servants, to be exchanged in South Carolina for rice.[166]

Entrepreneurs by definition take risks and those merchants involved in the rice trade were no exception. Considerable capital was required to finance the import and export trade, and before the days of the limited company, extended or joint partnerships were formed. Ships could be owned by as many as twenty-four individuals. The perils of sea trading were many, and included piracy and privateers, enemy action, storms and other natural disasters, as well as the risks to unseaworthy ships. For additional security, where possible, cargoes were distributed over a number of vessels. Merchants sending a ship to the colonies for goods such as rice appear to have been required to advance money to the local

[165] *Caledonian Mercury*, No 4063
[166] NRS.AC7.49.1293-1534

SCOTTISH TRADE WITH
COLONIAL CHARLESTON, 1683-1783

Customs Collector prior to a voyage, as the following extract from the Dundee Customs Collectors letter book shows:

> 'Dundee, Collector to Board, 22 May 1761, " Sometime ago John Fyffe, Alex Strachan and Company came here and consigned the half subsidy of the cargo of rice shipped at Carolina in January last on board the <u>Mercury</u> of Dundee, Robert Stirling master, for Lisbon, and then protested that as they had no advice of the ships arrival anywhere in Europe to the southwards of Cape Finisterre that possibly she might have been taken by the enemy or perished at sea and in that event they might recover or have their money repaid but the other day advice being received of the ship's arrival at Lisbon Mr Fyffe came and offered to make a formal entry of said cargo.....".'[167]

The date when rice became commonly available in Scotland is hard to establish, but there is documentary evidence that it was consumed here from at least the early eighteenth century. According to the letter-book of the Inverness merchant, John Steuart, he was importing small quantities directly from Italy in the 1720s. In 1726 Bailie John Steuart wrote a memorandum to Alexander Steuart, commissioning him to purchase specified commodities at particular prices when he was in Livorno (Leghorn, Italy), and these included one hundred pounds of rice of Lombardy at £1.50. Later, in April 1735 the Inverness merchant, wrote to John Reid, master of the <u>Adventure of Cromarty</u>, on whose ship he had loaded salmon for the London market, *'When, please God, you come to any port in the Mediterranean, pray but me a barrel of rice, about two-hundred weight...'* [168]

[167] NRS.CE70.1.3
[168] William Mackay (ed.), *The Letter Book of Baillie John Steuart of Inverness, 1715-1752,* Edinburgh, Scotland, 1915, pp. 265,.388

SCOTTISH TRADE WITH
COLONIAL CHARLESTON, 1683-1783

Published domestic financial records also show that rice had become part of the normal diet of at least the households of lairds in different parts of Scotland by the early eighteenth century. Lady Grissel Baillie bought four pounds of rice costing £1.4/- on 10 June 1707, and on 1 March, 1710 bought two stone of rice at 8/- per stone, 16/-.[169] The publication, *Life and Labour on an Aberdeenshire Estate, 1735-1750* is based on the estate papers of Sir Archibald Grant of Monymusk in Aberdeenshire. His household accounts, within the book, reveal that rice was purchased in small quantities from merchants in Aberdeen, Old Meldrum, and Banff in 1735, amounting to twenty-five pounds in a five-month period.[170]

Even during the height of the American Revolution cargoes of rice were still being shipped across the Atlantic, and one cargo was inadvertently was landed in Scotland. The ship George, from South Carolina, in the service of the US Congress, was laden with rice and indigo and bound for Bordeaux when she was brought into Port Glasgow by her mate and part of the crew.[171]

The Indigo Trade

During the seventeenth and eighteenth centuries, probably the single most important industry in England and Scotland was the manufacture of textiles. Most of the dyes for this industry could be found in Europe, but one of the most commonly used dye, giving a blue color, was derived from indigo, and this could only be grown in tropical climates. The supplies which English manufacturers relied upon came initially

[169] Robert Scott-Moncreiff, *Lady Grissell Baillie's Household Book, 1692-1733*, Edinburgh, Scotland, 1911, pp. 70-82
[170] Henry Hamilton, *Life and Labour on an Aberdeenshire Estate, 1735-1750*, Aberdeen, Scotland, 1946, p. 42
[171] NRS. Minutes of the Scots Board of Customs, 1723-1828

SCOTTISH TRADE WITH
COLONIAL CHARLESTON, 1683-1783

from American colonies largely under Spanish rule, which meant that the Spanish could control both the price, and quantity available on the market. Jamaica, originally a Spanish colony, was a major producer of indigo which supplied the English market. In times of political turmoil, this reliance affected the industry adversely. When the island was captured by Cromwell during 1655, one of the benefits accruing to the English economy was that textile manufacturers could be sure of a continuous supply of this essential raw material.

Planters in Jamaica, as elsewhere in the English colonies, became subject to the English Navigation Acts of the 1660s. These Acts brought in laws which demanded all colonial produce to first enter an English port even if the eventual destination for the ship's cargo was elsewhere. While the planters had a guaranteed market in England, and English textile manufacturers now had a guaranteed supply, these Acts increased the cost of the product. In addition, an import duty was applied to the product of indigo by the English Parliament in 1670, and these new laws increased the cost of the product to textile manufacturers. One outcome of this increased cost to planters was that in the English West Indies they began to concentrate their efforts more on the production of sugar which was becoming more profitable, and in turn reduced the land given over to the growing of indigo. The replacement crop of sugar cane was to become a far more profitable crop than indigo had been.

Profits in the West Indies were not available to all as the European population grew, and this combined with the unhealthy climate caused a second leg of migration, particularly from Barbados, to the mainland colony of South Carolina during the late seventeenth century. These

SCOTTISH TRADE WITH
COLONIAL CHARLESTON, 1683-1783

new settlers brought with them slaves with the intention of establishing another slave based economy of the type they had left in the Caribbean. One of the cash crops they tried to grow was indigo, but the indigo seeds brought with them from the West Indies did not grow well in South Carolina, and these planters abandoned attempts to produce this crop for the time being.

Although British industry could rely on limited supplies of indigo from Jamaica, the rapid expansion of the textile industry during the eighteenth century and the consequent demand for indigo exceeded the abilities of the Jamaican planters to supply the market. Britain was back in the position of being reliant for additional supplies on the plantations of the Spanish and French West Indies, but this meant she might endure severe shortages of indigo should there be an outbreak of war. The position could have been relieved if British colonial planters changed from sugar cane crops to indigo, but by this time the increasing demand for sugar made this crop far more profitable.

In 1739, the daughter of a plantation owner on Wappoo Creek, west of Charleston, South Carolina, named Elizabeth Lucas, later Pinckney, experimented with growing, on her father's land, a different type of indigo seed which had been brought from the Bahamas. By 1744 she had succeeded in producing a good dye in marketable quantities. As far as British textile manufacturers were concerned, this timing was fortuitous, in that it was the period of the War of Jenkins' Ear, a conflict between the imperial powers of Britain and Spain, in which the French sided with the Spanish, and affecting the Caribbean area. Owing to this dispute, the British textile industry experienced a suspension of supplies of indigo from these foreign colonies, and was clearly badly in need of locating other sources of indigo. This same war had caused the suspension of trade between British colonies, including South Carolinian, and their Spanish markets. This in turn led to a glut in rice supply and prices fell. In these circumstances, planters of South Carolina grasped with enthusiasm the new strain of indigo which Miss Lucas had shown to be viable, and began to grow crops for the hungry British market, and by the war's end in 1748, the growing of this crop had become well established. Among those who encouraged planters to switch production from rice to indigo was the Scots-born South Carolinian merchant based in London, James Crockett who distributed pamphlets and articles on indigo cultivation in the late 1740s.[172]

Extra encouragement in the production of indigo came in the form of a bounty to growers from the colonial government, to be superseded in 1749 by one paid by the British Government. The British Government's bounty was paid to British importers, and effectively subsidised the price of South Carolinian indigo, making it cheaper than the indigo from the Spanish and French Caribbean when it once again became available. Without this subsidy, Carolinian indigo producers could not have competed for the British market with those of the French or Spanish. The same situation arose during the Seven Years War, between 1756 and 1763, when French suppliers were prohibited from trading with Britain, giving opportunities for more indigo to be sourced from South Carolinian producers.

It was during this period that indigo exports reached their highest level to date; 876,000 pounds, weight. After 1763, in addition to subsidising their colonies, the British government imposed taxes on imported

[172] Joyce E Chaplin, *An Anxious Pursuit. Agricultural Innovation and Modernity in the Lower South, 1730-1815,* Chapel Hill, North Carolina, 1993, p. 193

indigo from foreign sources, thereby adding to the advantages already enjoyed by South Carolinian indigo planters. South Carolinian indigo was, however, considered to be inferior in quality to that produced elsewhere. This meant that prices achieved for South Carolinian indigo in the London indigo market were lower than those achieved for supplies from other sources. Any assistance the British government could provide was essential to ensure a market.[173] At the close of the colonial period, in the year 1775, over a million pounds in weight of indigo was shipped to Great Britain from South Carolina, representing around one-third of the colony's total exports. It is therefore evident that the British textile industry and the South Carolinian indigo planters had become highly interdependent and the American War of Independence had significant consequences for this arrangement. One of these was the loss to the colony of Imperial Preference in the British domestic market for indigo. After this date, the British turned their attention to establishing production of indigo to land over which they still had dominion. The colonies in the east, India and the East Indies were to supply their indigo needs in the future, and it is interesting to note that among a small group of Scots who settled as indigo planters in Bengal in the 1780s was a Hugh Baillie, possibly a member of the Baillie family who were planters in Georgia before the American Revolution.[174]

Scots in the Indigo Trade of South Carolina

Scots could be found at every stage in the chain of production of indigo in South Carolina, especially in the roles of planters and merchants. As has been seen above, indigo only became economically viable due to the experiments of Elizabeth Pinckney during the 1740s. While indigo

[173] Chaplin, *An Anxious Pursuit*, p. 202
[174] India Office, O series, 5

SCOTTISH TRADE WITH
COLONIAL CHARLESTON, 1683-1783

planting had ceased in South Carolina around the late seventeenth century, there was an attempt by a Scots immigrant in Georgia to plant indigo as well as cotton in the late 1730s. Patrick Houstoun, who arrived from Scotland in 1734, is recorded as having the intention to plant cotton and indigo in 1737, but his labor was unsuccessful.[175] In South Carolina, many planters, including some Scots, began to diversify their agricultural crops to include indigo from around the time of the 1750. The Scotsman, Francis Kinloch of Santee, was described in his obituary which appeared in the South Carolina Gazette as 'one of the most successful indigo planters in South Carolina'.[176]

Scots merchants and factors in Charleston, such as John Simpson and Company,[177] would buy indigo from planters and supply it to the masters of Scottish vessels arriving in the harbor. On 24 February 1757 Alexander Rintoul advertised[178] that he had goods for sale which could be bought for ready money, rice or indigo at market prices, delivered in Charleston. Similarly, on 19 September 1758 James Strachan who had brought a range of products from Leith aboard his ship the Mercury offered them in exchange for ready money or indigo.[179]

The Scottish Domestic Market

In the beginning, any colonially produced indigo used in Scotland would have originated in the Caribbean, from one or other of the English, French or Spanish colonies. A possible supplier of indigo for Scots during the late seventeenth century was a John Swinton, later

---

[175] NRS. Clerk of Penicuik Muniments, GD18/5360
[176] *South Carolina Gazette* (hereafter SCGaz), 1 June 1767
[177] NRS.CS96.2250.791
[178] SCGaz, No 1184
[179] SCGaz, No 1057

known as Sir John Swinton of that Ilk, Berwickshire. Swinton was a Quaker and doubtless part of their mercantile network which spread around the British Atlantic World. When he was a merchant in London during the 1670s he was known to have dabbled in consignments of indigo.[180] The odd reference has been found in Scotland to the use of indigo, for example John Tyler, a merchant in Dumbarton, is known to have supplied a quantity of indigo to Lord Neil Campbell, Governor of Dumbarton Castle, before 1691.[181] In a case brought before the High Court of the Admiralty of Scotland in 1677 there is evidence that a few years earlier Charles Charters, a merchant in Edinburgh, had unsuccessfully attempted to import ginger, indigo and musk skins from New England.[182]

In early eighteenth century Scotland, there are also a limited number of references to indigo. Among these, Charles Stewart, a merchant in Perth, sold the Earl of Breadalbane quantities of both rice and indigo around 1704.[183] Indigo was also available at the market in Kenmore, Perthshire, in 1704.[184] Lady Grisell Baillie, in Mellarstaine, Roxburghshire, bought four and a half ounces of indigo at seven shillings per ounce on 1 January 1709.[185] William Ferguson, a merchant in Perth, also traded in indigo in 1714.[186] Archibald Bothwell in Edinburgh was retailing indigo in 1716, when he supplied Menzies of Weem.[187] John Gardiner, a merchant in Perth, was recorded selling

---

[180] NRS.CS96/3264
[181] NRS, Breadalbane Muniments, GD112.63.7
[182] NRS.AC7.4
[183] NRS, Breadalbane Muniments, GD112.35.21
[184] NRS, Breadalbane Muniments, GD112.15.108
[185] Scott-Moncreiff, *Household Book*, p. 73
[186] NRS, Breadalbane Muniments, GD112.15.146
[187] NRS, Miscellaneous, GD1/368/30

hides, iron, indigo, and oil, between 1731 and 1737.[188]   The domestic
records of Sir Archibald Grant of Monymusk disclose that in 1735
small quantities of indigo, about three pounds, weight, were purchased
from a Mr Lesslie, a merchant in Aberdeen.[189]   There is evidence in the
Letterbook of Baillie John Stewart of Inverness that he obtained his
supplies of indigo between 1718 and 1721 from Rotterdam. *'I wrot Mr
Andrew of Rotterdam anent the tuo firkins indigoe of fifty lb wght. Sent
per John Mackay, to exchange the same, and send the like quantity of
good float indigoe'*, Inverness, 15 February 1718.[190]   This predates the
availability of indigo from South Carolina and was presumably a
produce of the West Indies.

Despite the supreme importance of the textile industry, and in particular
the manufacture of linen, to the Scottish economy, the level of indigo
imports coming directly from South Carolina was surprisingly low.
Both the Scottish Customs Records[191] and the Charleston Naval
Officer's Shipping Records[192] on inspection reveal that the direct indigo
trade between Charleston and Scotland was absolutely minimal.   The
reasons for so little indigo being shipped directly to Scotland, despite
its important textile industry, is explained in a recent essay by R. C.
Nash, who claims that *'virtually all indigo exports were shipped to a
single market, London'*.   This, he suggests, was due to the high value
to bulk ratio, and the fact that London during the eighteenth century
was fast becoming the main European market for dyestuffs.[193]   The

[188] NRS.CS96/469
[189] Henry Hamilton, *Life and Labour on an Aberdeenshire Estate, 1735-1750,* Aberdeen, Scotland, 1946, pp. 9-10
[190] Mackay, *Letter Book of Baillie John Stewart,* p. 70
[191] NRS.E504 series
[192] TNA.CO5.508-511

SCOTTISH TRADE WITH
COLONIAL CHARLESTON, 1683-1783

period of this limited trade was also mainly confined to 1756-1763, the time of the Seven Years War between Great Britain and France. The implication of this is that the ships were sailing to Scotland to avoid the French. Seventeen ships arrived in the ports of Montrose, Dundee, Leith, Bo'ness, Greenock and Port Glasgow, with cargoes that totalled approximately eighteen thousand, five hundred pounds of indigo – a minute fraction of the total indigo exported from Charleston to Great Britain during the period. A single Scots ship, the <u>Ferdinand,</u> transported seven thousand, eight hundred and thirty-two pounds of indigo to Liverpool in a single voyage in 1761. Most of the indigo used by the Scottish textile industry presumably, therefore, arrived indirectly from the colonies via the London dyestuffs market.

Possibly the most prominent merchant in Scotland specialising in the supply of indigo to the textile industry was Duncan Campbell. Duncan Campbell was a son of Duncan Campbell MA (1633-1707), minister of Rosneath in Dunbartonshire, and his wife Elizabeth Schaw. Duncan, junior, had trained as a merchant in Glasgow before crossing the Atlantic to work in New York and later in Kingston, Jamaica, during the 1720s. He may have first come across indigo in Jamaica which was then the main British colony producing the crop. For a period around 1740 he worked as a grocer in London before moving north to Edinburgh with his wife, the daughter of an Edinburgh merchant. In Edinburgh he soon established himself as a merchant and as a manufacturer of indigo with a workshop in the Grassmarket, where he was known as 'Duncan Campbell at the Blue Manufacturing in the

193 C Nash, 'The Organization of Trade and Finance in the Atlantic Economy, Britain and South Carolina, 1670-1775', Jack P Green, Rosemary Brana-Shute and Randy J. Sparks (eds), *Money, Trade, and Power. The Evolution of Colonial South Carolina's Plantation Society,* Columbia, South Carolina, 2001, p. 78

SCOTTISH TRADE WITH
COLONIAL CHARLESTON, 1683-1783

Grassmarket'. Campbell seems to have had the monopoly of the supply of indigo in Edinburgh but for an undisclosed reason had trouble with the Excisemen who in 1752 occupied his property for a month and removed certain unspecified articles from there. Among his business records, which have survived, is his 'blew book' which contains recipes for making various kinds of dyes based on indigo, for example '*for flat blue fifty-six pounds whites at 16/8, eight pounds rock at £1.14/-, three and a quarter pounds ashes at four pence, making 4/-, total sixty-nine and a half pounds at £2.15 shillings and 6 and a half pence*'. His financial records reveal that he was supplying merchants in Aberdeen, Kincardineshire, Angus, Fife, Renfrewshire, Ayrshire, Glasgow, Roxburghshire, and Berwickshire, and he also had links with Robert Cumming, a Scots Episcopalian minister and tutor in South Carolina, who sent him small quantities of indigo around 1750.[194]

The Cowans, a family of merchants based in Bo'ness, were Scots who are known to have sent their vessels, the Industry of Leith and the Friendship of Bo'ness, to Charleston with great regularity between 1748 and 1768. To begin with the family's ships were under their own command, for example Andrew Cowan was the skipper on Charleston bound voyages on eleven occasions between 1748 and 1756,[195] but latterly the Cowans seem to have been generally content to manage the ships rather than to sail them. There is no evidence that they established a store in America, unlike other seafaring merchant families, such as the contemporary Gammell family of Greenock. The only mention of the Cowans in Charleston, apart from the shipping returns of the local Naval Officer and the South Carolina Gazette, is in the records of the St Andrew's Society where Andrew Cowan is noted

[194] NRS.RH15.69; RD2.28.11
[195] See Appendix 13; NRS.AC8/723

95

as being a member between 1751 and 1753.[196]   Cowan voyages were not limited to South Carolina, for example Patrick Cowan, sailed the 96 Christian, from nearby Airth to Virginia in 1772.[197]   At home in Bo'ness, the family busily distributed indigo and other colonial commodities they had brought into Scotland.   Records of the Court of Session in 1770 outlines details of a case brought it by a Margaret Carlyle, a shopkeeper in Glasgow.   Carlyle claimed that John and Robert Cowan, merchants in Bo'ness, had undertaken to supply her with indigo but that the consignment had been lost somewhere between Bo'ness and Glasgow.[198]   The Cowan link with Charleston can be seen to have continued after the Revolution, with Margaret, daughter of James Cowan and wife of George Ogilvy recorded in Charleston around 1790.[199]   The family was also represented in the local civil service with Thomas Cowan (1757-1828) a Customs Controller there.   Alexander, his son, died at St John, New Brunswick, in 1810, aged seventeen, probably due to following the family's seafaring tradition.[200]

During the American War of Independence textile manufacturers were generally cut off from what had become their most important source of indigo, that being South Carolina, and were forced to look for alternative suppliers.   After 1783 these were increasingly in Asia. William Wilson and Son, tartan weavers in Bannockburn, who were major users of dyes such as indigo, obtained the product from Peter Bald and other merchants in Glasgow whose suppliers were in the Spanish West Indies and later the East Indies.   Peter Bald also imported

---

[196] See Appendix 12
[197] NRS.AC7/55
[198] NRS. Henderson Collection, GD76/342
[199] NRS.CS17.1.9/13
[200] Bo'ness Gravestone

dyewoods, shumac, and indigo from the Caribbean.[201]

The Timber Trade

For many years, Scotland had been importing timber from Scandinavia, but when an increased variety of timber became available from the American colonies a transatlantic trade was established for both hardwoods and softwood. As with other imports, it was strategically advantageous to secure a source of supply within the Empire rather than be at the mercy of changing political circumstances when essential supplies could suddenly be cut off because of international conflicts. Inter-empire trade links also had the advantage of strengthening the transatlantic economic bonds between Great Britain and the American colonies.

Timber was required for a wide range of uses in Great Britain, such as construction, shipbuilding, and furniture making, and was available for export from a number of colonies, including South Carolina. Charleston merchants shipped a wide range of timber to Scotland, some of it local and some brought in from the Caribbean, particularly Jamaica and the Mosquito Coast. Mahogany and pine were always part of the wood consignments for Scotland, and as well as occasional cargoes of cypress, cedar, brazil-wood, walnut, lignum, and logwood. The records show also one single delivery in 1754 of one thousand pounds of bark, presumably for use in Scottish tanneries. The most significant type of timber exported from Charleston for the Scottish market was,

---

[201] H C Rawson, J Burnett and A Quye, 'The Importance of Textile Dyes to Scotland: the case of William Wilson and Son, tartan weavers of Bannockburn, 1780-1820', *Review of Scottish Culture,* No. 13, Edinburgh, Scotland, 2000; NLS, ms6682

SCOTTISH TRADE WITH
COLONIAL CHARLESTON, 1683-1783

by far, mahogany. Such was the demand, that in time, ever greater quantities also began to be shipped directly from Jamaica and the Bay of Honduras.

Mahogany was imported from Charleston almost annually from 1744 to 1771.[202] Unfortunately the method of measurement had not been standardised at the time, and while for the most part it is quantified in tons, occasionally customs staff referred to 'pieces' and at other times it was measured in feet. For this reason, it is difficult to provide an accurate estimate of the quantity imported, but as far as can be reckoned; the year that the greatest quantity of mahogany was imported to Scotland was 1753, when 87.5 tons and 10,000 feet were landed. This large demand for timber came from a number of sources. Significant amounts of mahogany were used by furniture makers and boat builders. A derived demand for timber was a direct result of the contemporary construction country houses for the gentry also rich merchants, and after 1767[203] the New Town of Edinburgh with all the timber requirement that implies, together with a demand for modern mahogany furniture to equip these homes.[204]

Cargoes of wooden oars and spikes made in South Carolina were occasionally exported from Charleston as were the semi-processed barrel staves. These were made from local hardwood and exported to Scotland for use by coopers who completed the process of barrel

---

[202] NRS.E504 series
[203] An Act of Edinburgh Town Council dated 29 July 1767 approved James Craig's plan for the New Town and construction started almost immediately
[204] See Ian Gow, 'The Eighteenth Century Interior in Scotland', Wendy Caplan ,(ed), *Scotland Creates, 5000 Years of Art and Design,* London, England, 1990, pp. 90-106

SCOTTISH TRADE WITH
COLONIAL CHARLESTON, 1683-1783

making in Scotland. This is another product which again is hard to quantify because of the variations in measurements; both 'hogsheads' and 'hundredweight' being used. It would appear, however, that the import of staves was at its height in 1761, when fourteen thousand hogsheads plus 3,475 staves were landed. The barrels produced from this import were used to pack goods such as herring and strong ale, some of which were in turn exported to South Carolina.

In the Customs records, appended alongside the details of the cargoes of ships, is found the notation 'PB' or 'BB'. This gives indication of a timber import from South Carolina which might easily be overlooked; the manufacture of ships for the British merchant fleet in the colonies. 'PB' indicates 'Plantation Built' to distinguish them from those built in Scotland or England which appear as 'BB' or 'British Built'. Some of these 'PB' ships may have been constructed in South Carolina because its shipyards, together with others in the American Colonies, built many of the vessels that formed the British merchant navy. It is, however, generally not possible to identify in which colony the 'Plantation built' ships originated until the introduction of more formalised ship registration documents later in the eighteenth century.

Scots were prominent among the shipbuilders of colonial Charleston, and one of the main centres of shipbuilding in colonial South Carolina was at Hobcaw Creek on the Wando River. This site lay across the Cooper River from Charleston, and had been established in 1702. In 1753 the shipyard was purchased by two Scottish shipwrights, James Stewart and John Rose. The Stewart and Rose shipyard covered over one hundred acres and could have three vessels being constructed at the same time. In 1769 the shipyard was once again sold, and again to Scots; two recent immigrants, William Begbie and Daniel Manson. By

1773 they had built a dozen ships at Hobcaw, the largest being of 300 tons. Having supported the Loyalist cause, however, they found it expedient to sell their shipyard in 1778.[205] Another contemporary shipbuilder in Charleston was a Robert Cochrane who owned a shipyard at Shipyard Creek, just north of the city, running it from 1763 to 1788, and during the American Revolution supported the rebel cause.[206] Among the other Scottish shipbuilders of Charleston were Robert Claghorn,[207] and John Imrie.[208]

Table 2/2

Stave Imports, 1748 to 1766

Year	Hogsheads	Cwt	Units
1748	1,000	-	-
1751	1,000	-	-
1758	7,500	30	-
1759	4,000	-	-
1760	1,500	20	-
1761	14,000	-	3,475
1762	3,000	-	-
1764	2,000	-	-
1766	1,000	-	-
Totals	**35,000**	**50**	**3,475**

(Source: NRS.E504 series)

[205] TNA.A0.12.51.184: A0.12.50.213
[206] P C Coker III, *Charleston's Maritime Heritage, 1670-1865,* Charleston, South Carolina, 1987
[207] Probate 1751 SC
[208] TNA.AO12.3.252

SCOTTISH TRADE WITH
COLONIAL CHARLESTON, 1683-1783

Table 2/3
Mahogany Imports, 1744 to 1771

Year	Tons	Feet	Pieces
1744	-	600	-
1747	-	80	-
1749	-	456	-
1750	-	1,150	-
1751	28	-	-
1752	2	-	-
1753	88	10,000	-
1754	18	-	-
1755	5	-	-
1756	22	-	-
1757	2	-	-
1758	3	282	-
1759	10.5	734	-
1760	-	403	-
1761	7	-	-
1762	24	200	-
1763	9	-	-
1764	8	-	-
1765	-	1,400	-
1766	-	340	-
1767	3	-	64
1768	-	460	-
1769	-	600	-
1770	-	1,000	210
101			
1771	-	-	65

Totals	229.5	17,705	339

(Source. NRS.E504 series)

The Deerskin Trade

For a significant period of time the fur trade was one of the most profitable businesses of colonial America. Demand both from within the colonies and Europe continued to outstrip an increasing supply. This trade can be subdivided into the northern branch which was mainly comprised of beaver and fox and the southern fur trade, based largely on deerskin. The northern fur trade was concentrated in Canada, New England and New York and was controlled by the merchants of Montreal, Albany and Philadelphia. In the south, the fur trade was mainly in the hands of merchants resident in Charleston whose supplies came, for the most part, from the Carolinas, Georgia, and the Indian lands beyond.

During the late seventeenth and early eighteenth centuries the export of deerskins was of paramount importance to the economy of the colony of South Carolina.[209] From the earliest days, until the 1720s, fur was probably the single most important primary product being shipped from the port of Charleston to English and later British markets. Deerskins fell into secondary importance as an export only when rice began to be

[209] See Eirlys M. Barker, 'Indian Traders, Charles Town and London's Vital Link to the Interior of North America, 1717-1755', J. P. Greene, R. Brana-Shute, and R. J. Sparks, *Money, Trade, and Power. The Evolution of Colonial South Carolina's Plantation Society,* Columbia, South Carolina, 2001, pp. 141-165

SCOTTISH TRADE WITH
COLONIAL CHARLESTON, 1683-1783

produced, and in the 1740s, indigo reduced its status still further, pushing it into third place in the export league.

The guarantee of supply was never, however, without its problems owing mainly to the fact that deerskins were largely acquired in the backcountry of South Carolina and beyond.   In addition to this, for most of the colonial period, the backwoods locations from which the deerskins were obtained were often disputed territory, fought over by the British and the other colonial powers of France and Spain.   This rivalry between Europeans drew in the local Indians, particularly the tribes of Creeks and Cherokees and a major disruption to supply occurred during the period of the French and Indian Wars in mid-century, causing a depression in the market.   These fluctuations in supply of a prime export commodity obviously had major economic consequences for the colony's balance of trade.   The trade in furs, known as 'The Indian Trade' was controlled by merchants based in Charleston.   Indian trails led deep into the interior, and along these were conveyed trade goods for barter by colonists in exchange for the Indians' deer and other skins.   Skins were taken back along the trails to Charleston for sale and exported to Great Britain. Packhorses, used to convey commodities, were supplemented by shallow boats, pettiaguas and canoes and these plied the rivers of South Carolinas.   Scots could be found at each and every level of the fur trade. In addition to those in transit with packhorses or boats, there were some who lived with the Indians in their villages.   Jacobite prisoners who were sent to guard the South Carolinian frontier in 1716 soon became involved in the deerskin trade, and some, such as Ludovick Grant, integrated with the tribes.[210]   In Charleston, Scots merchants and

210 E Merton Coulter, and Albert B. Saye, *A List of the Early Settlers of Georgia,* Baltimore,1983, p. 76; Charleston Probate Book, 1754-1758, p. 301

103

factors purchased the deerskins for shipment to Great Britain, and others manned wharfs and warehouses and loaded the furs onto the ships.   W.O. Moore lists one hundred and seventy six merchants involved in the export trade.   In total he calculates that six hundred and sixty four persons and firms were participants in the export of deerskins, and possibly, as many one-third, based on their surnames, were of Scottish origin.[211]

In colonial South Carolina, it can be seen that the barter system was not limited to trade with Indians; it was also a feature of the deerskin trade between the colonists, as evidenced by advertisements in the local newspaper, the South Carolina Gazette.   In the issue dated 16 November 1753, Andrew Cowan advertised *'an assortment of Scots manufactures'*, stating that, *'merchantable rice, pitch, tar, turpentine, mahogany, deerskin, beaver, or indigo, will be taken in payment at market prices provided it be mentioned at making the bargain'*.[212]   In the same newspaper on 11 July 1761, Alexander Fyffe from Dundee announced that he was opening a store in Savannah for the Indian trade, and that deerskins or cash would be accepted in payment of debt.[213]

However, from the evidence of the Scottish port books, the deerskin imports into Scotland from Charleston were insignificant; a total of only ten consignments arriving in the Clyde and Dundee between 1758 and 1767, amounting to a total of fifty-six thousand, seven hundred and ninety-two pounds of deerskins.   In addition to this there were two

---

[211] W O Moore, 'The Largest Exporters of Deerskins from Charles Town, 1736-1775', *South Carolina Historical Magazine*, Volume74, Charleston, South Carolina, 1973, pp. 144-150
[212] SC Gaz No 1013
[213] SCGaz No 1407

SCOTTISH TRADE WITH
COLONIAL CHARLESTON, 1683-1783

consignments of beaver skins; one comprising seventy-three skins arriving in Greenock aboard the <u>Rebecca</u> in 1756, and another of fifty-three skins and fifty cowhides, arriving in Leith during 1769. Since it is the case that all the recorded arrivals of skins into Scotland took place during a period of hostilities with France, one might conclude that this import may have been a temporary arrangement during the period of conflict.

Naval Stores

One of the smaller exports from the colony of South Carolina was collectively known as 'naval stores'. This term covered items such as tar, pitch and turpentine, which were predominantly used in shipbuilding and the ship-repair industries of the period. No doubt some of these items were also used in the construction industry and turpentine in the manufacture of paint.

According to a case study carried out by R C Nash,[214] the export of naval stores substantially declined during the eighteenth century. Between 1718 and 1722 the average annual export value was £16,000. This compares with rice valued at £19,000, and deerskins valued at £17,000. Fifty years later, between 1768 and 1772, the comparative average annual values had become £5,000 for naval stores; £284,000 for rice; and £15,000 for deerskins. In the export of naval stores, Charleston was always secondary to Georgetown, South Carolina, which lay northwards along the coast and was closer to the pine forests of the colony which were the centres of their production.

[1] R C Nash, 'Urbanisation in Colonial Charleston, South Carolina', *Journal of Urban History* ,London, England, 1992, volume 19, p. 7

SCOTTISH TRADE WITH
COLONIAL CHARLESTON, 1683-1783

Some naval stores were landed in the ports of Leith and the Clyde from South Carolina for use in shipbuilding or for ship repair. As has already been established, about half the Scots vessels employed in transatlantic shipping were 'Plantation built'. Scottish shipyards of the seventeenth and eighteenth centuries were relatively small scale operations. Shipbuilding which had been started in Leith during the medieval period probably represented the main centre of the industry in the eighteenth century. During the 1720s, although ships as large as one hundred tons were occasionally built, on average most were between twenty and forty tons.[215] Vessels of three hundred tons had been built in the late seventeenth century, but mostly the demand was for small coasting vessels. On the west coast, one of the oldest shipbuilding companies was Scott's, founded in Greenock in 1711, and on the Moray Firth, Alexander Stephen's was founded in Lossiemouth in 1750.

The trend, however, was to order ships to be built in America, it being more economic to construct them close to the supply of timber, and it was no doubt for this reason that Scottish interests commissioned American built ships or bought them second-hand. In 1754, trade goods were sent to Boston by a Methil merchant, Walter Orroch, the price of which was to be used to finance construction of a ship to be sent back to Scotland.[216] James Watt, a merchant in Greenock was another who bought a ship built in America. He purchased a sloop built in Massachusetts in 1738 which he named the Roanoke.[217] Part

---

[215] Sue Mowat, *The Port of Leith, Its History and People,* Edinburgh, Scotland, 1994, p. 231
216.NRS.AC7.46.101
217.NRS.AC9.1626

owner of the Theodosia of Aberdeen which had been built in Boston in 1733 was John Burnett, a merchant in Aberdeen.[218]

This healthy construction business was enabled by the investment of both capital and skills originating in Scotland. Scottish shipbuilders had become established in South Carolina, as elsewhere in the American colonies. In 1752, John Rutherford, a Scot, recruited three carpenters from Dundee and Leith to work in his shipyard in Wilmington, North Carolina,[219] and in 1775 a group of eight carpenters from Ayrshire sailed to Quebec to work in the shipyards there.[220] This transfer of skills and technology to the American colonies where the main raw materials were located, worked to the disadvantage of the small-scale Scottish industry. The outbreak of the American Revolution put a temporary stop to this transatlantic drain on skilled labor in Scottish shipyards, and stimulated the domestic industry. As a result of this, and the disruption of supply of ships from the American colonies, Britain became more self-sufficient in shipbuilding.

The Scottish Port Books suggest that between the dates 1742-1776, naval stores were landed at three ports in Scotland. Leith was the main port of import and the main centre of contemporary shipbuilding. Small amounts, however, were also landed at Dunbar and Greenock. Tar amounting to five hundred and seventy lasts and one last were landed at Leith and Greenock respectively, pitch totaling one hundred and thirty one lasts, seventy lasts, and five lasts at Leith, Dunbar, and Greenock, and Leith received one thousand seven hundred and sixty hundredweight of turpentine and Greenock fifty seven hundredweight. As has been shown, the relatively small amounts of naval stores

[218] NRS.AC9.1472
[219] NRS.RD4.178.365
[220] TNA.T47.12

107

imported by Scotland during the colonial period can be explained by the existence of the highly efficient and economically superior contemporary American shipbuilding industry.

Other Imports from South Carolina

There were additional commodities, albeit in small quantities, shipped from Charleston bound for the Scottish market. The majority of these were landed at the ports of Leith, Greenock, and Glasgow, with the occasional, often more specific, consignments at Dunbar. Over three thousand eight hundred gallons of rum, the produce of the British West Indies, arrived at Scottish ports via Charleston. Rum was landed at four ports, Greenock, Glasgow, Leith and Dunbar in ascending order of volume, with Dunbar receiving about ninety percent of all the rum brought to Scotland via South Carolina. Dunbar was also notable as being the only port where orange juice and lime juice was landed. The Dunbar port books show this import totalled nearly five hundred gallons for the period between the years 1767 and 1773. Small quantities of hemp were landed at Leith and Dunbar, presumably for the rope-making companies there. Around ninety hundredweight of Muscavado sugar was unloaded, especially in Glasgow, probably for the sugar works in Glasgow and Greenock. Two consignments of cotton-wool arrived, one in Glasgow and the other in Leith, possibly for the textile industry, and amongst these other commodities imported from Charleston were two-thousand cane reeds, ten thousand five hundred vocat reeds, six hundredweight of sasafras, and one hundred pounds of wax, all of which were delivered to the ports of Leith, Glasgow, and Greenock. While some of these products may have been re-exported, the majority would have been used as the raw material of local industrialists, enabling the economy to diversify and further develop its economic base.

SCOTTISH TRADE WITH
COLONIAL CHARLESTON, 1683-1783

The impact of the American War of Independence had both short and long-term consequences. During the period of hostilities from 1776 to 1783, the city of Charleston was sometimes under British occupation and at other times under American occupation. The war did not completely cut off trade between Scotland and Charleston although emigration was halted. The Scottish port books record vessels intermittently bound for South Carolina, with cargoes largely containing items which were to support the war effort. Cargoes were also dispatched from Charleston, bound for Great Britain during the British occupation of the city, and others could be seen from contemporary newspaper articles to be bound for shipment directly to continental markets during the time of the American occupation. The absence of port books for Charleston for the period of the Revolution makes it impossible to ascertain with any accuracy the types of cargo dispatched and received. Sometimes American vessels sailing from Charleston to European ports were intercepted by the Royal Navy or by privateers and the ship brought to a British port where both ship and cargo were confiscated by the authorities and subsequently sold. Most such prize vessels were taken to English ports where they fell under the jurisdiction of the High Court of the Admiralty of England. Far fewer prize ships were brought into Scottish ports, in total only fourteen such were adjudged by the High Court of the Admiralty of Scotland. Of these, only one ship had sailed from Charleston, the Minerva of Charleston in 1778. The Minerva, master William Sextroh, had been bound from Charleston for Gothenborg, Sweden, with a cargo of tobacco, rice, indigo, and logwood, but was captured at sea and brought to Greenock by the crew of the privateer Sally of Greenock in May 1778.[221]

221 NRS.AC7.58

109

SCOTTISH TRADE WITH
COLONIAL CHARLESTON, 1683-1783

While trade between Scotland and Charleston was drastically cut during the war years, commerce did not completely stop. After 1783 the legal position changed as the new United States of America was not subject to the Navigation Acts which had determined that almost all trade between the American colonies and Europe went via British ports and on British ships. On the other hand, Americans no longer had any preferences in the form of lower tariffs or subsidies which they had previously enjoyed from Great Britain, and were viewed as any other foreign supplier. An example of this was that their former free access to the British West Indian market for their fish exports was withdrawn. South Carolina was now able to supply European markets directly, but were still dependant on imported manufactured goods from Great Britain, this being the only source of many of the items they required. This had the effect of maintaining traditional markets which might otherwise have dissolved. Raw materials, therefore, continued to be shipped from the port of Charleston, with vessels returning with the commodities they needed from Great Britain.[222] The indigo market was an exception. During the period of the war, Great Britain increased its orders for this commodity with the more dependable colonies located in the West Indies, and later sourcing also from India. The effect of this change was that residents of South Carolina began to increase their production of rice as their major cash crop, with the invention of the first water-powered mill in 1787, followed in 1792 by the tide-operated rice mill further increasing the profits of their rice crops.

222 See Anthony McFarlane, *The British in the Americas, 1480-1815,* London, England, 1994, pp. 285-286

SCOTTISH TRADE WITH
COLONIAL CHARLESTON, 1683-1783

Table 2/4

American Exports to Scotland, 1770-1787 (Abstract)[223]

Year	SC £	%	Total VA £	TotalGB£
1770	10,363	2.0	315,236	482,206
1771	8,874	1.5	423,105	606,464
1772	4,262	3.0	385,556	541,896
1773	3,563	3.7	374,243	517.954
.....				
1784	1,795	4.0	32,720	48,140
1785	8,559	7.0	88,097	117,705
1786	7,811	8.0	75,548	99,476
1787	17,186	15.0	76,142	113,191

The above table enables some measure of the change that had occurred as a result of the American Revolution. In absolute terms, Scottish imports from South Carolina initially showed a marked decline, but thereafter imports increased substantially, although never exceeding the pre-war levels. As an overall share of total imports from America,

[223] Jacob M Price, 'New Time Series for Scotland's and Britain's Trade with the Thirteen Colonies and States, 1740-1791', *William and Mary Quarterly*, Volume XXXII, Williamsburg, Virginia, 1975, p. 319

SCOTTISH TRADE WITH
COLONIAL CHARLESTON, 1683-1783

those from South Carolina rose dramatically in the post-war period. Between 1770 and 1773, South Carolina provided between 0.7% and 3% of the total Scottish imports from America, but in the period 1784 to 1787 imports rose, both absolutely and relatively from 4.0% in 1784 to 15% in 1787. From 1740 to 1791 most of the imports, by value, came from Virginia. For example, between 1770 and 1773, about 70% of American imports came from Virginia while in the post war years, 1784 to 1787, although the total values had fallen the ratio of goods coming from Virginia remained steady, ranging between 67% and 77% of the total. As can be seen, therefore, Scotland's trade with South Carolina expanded substantially in the post-war years.

SCOTTISH TRADE WITH COLONIAL CHARLESTON, 1683-1783

CHAPTER THREE

MARITIME ASPECTS OF THE SCOTTISH-CHARLESTON TRADE

Transatlantic trade of the eighteenth century clearly depended on shipping and this chapter will examine the issues surrounding the practicalities of operating trade between the shores of Scotland and South Carolina. To this end, the numbers of ships involved in the trade, the types of vessels and their place of construction will be identified, alongside an examination of the direct and indirect impact on the Scottish economy of the Carolina trade. It will show the increasing demand for labor in the areas of both shipbuilding and the manning of vessels, together with giving insight into, and naming, the Scottish merchants who owned and operated these vessels, and how these were financed. Since trade was often not directly across the Atlantic, the trade routes which these vessels used between Scotland and Charleston will also be identified. The orthodox view of vessels bound for America, originating almost exclusively from Clyde ports, will be questioned. This research, albeit exclusively concerning Charleston, will show that the number of voyages from Scottish east coast ports, primarily, but not exclusively the Forth ports, were almost equal to the numbers leaving from the Clyde and raises the question as to whether this was the case with other American colonies.

Information on ships and voyages comes largely from the records of the Customs and Excise Department. The Scottish port-books of the seventeenth century are incomplete, and those of the eighteenth century are only continuous from 1742 onwards.

113

SCOTTISH TRADE WITH
COLONIAL CHARLESTON, 1683-1783

Scottish newspapers of the eighteenth century as well as the South
Carolina Gazette also contain information on shipping and international
trade, but here too there are gaps in the records. There is no continuous
run of Scottish newspapers for the eighteenth century. The Aberdeen
Journal is continuous from the date of 1748, but contains only a limited
amount of shipping news. The South Carolina Gazette, founded in
Charleston in 1732 provides a great deal of useful detail on trade and
shipping, but again is not comprehensive. Shipping records maintained
in America by the ports' Naval Officers are now housed in London and
Charleston date from 1712.[224] These, together with a few documentary
sources, do provide a reasonably comprehensive insight into the degree
to which Scotland participated in Charleston and South Carolina's
international trade during the colonial period.

Scottish trade with America and the West Indies during the seventeenth
century was small scale when compared with that of England's. As
indicated earlier, one reason for this was the English Navigation Acts,
passed by the Westminster Parliament in the 1660s, which effectively
outlawed direct trade between any port, other than an English one, and
the English colonial ports across the Atlantic. Not only that, but that
any trading could only be carried out by ships owned by Englishmen,
under an English captain, and largely crewed by Englishmen. This
legislation was designed, largely to combat the rising power of the
Dutch mercantile marine, but had the double effect of curtailing the
trading activities extant of the Scots with the English colonies on the
Atlantic coasts.

224. NRS.GD29.106/1439/1962; Register of the Privy Council of Scotland, Vol III, p. 46; Acts of
the Privy Council Colonial, 1669, No 848

SCOTTISH TRADE WITH
COLONIAL CHARLESTON, 1683-1783

These regulations, however, were widely ignored, and a number of Scots merchants, both in America and at home, continued to trade as before, but clandestinely through smuggling. Despite embargoes on commodities, Scotland continued to be permitted to send cargoes of indentured servants and horses without restriction because of the need for skilled labor to further develop colonial settlement. This exception, together with the fact that the Navigation Laws were not designed primarily with the intention of stopping Scottish trade, allowed a certain degree of comfort to those circumventing English law. It is unlikely that the English Parliament had any realistic expectation that vessels carrying men and horses from Scotland would not also carry some contraband or that they would voluntarily return with empty holds. Although officials in the colonies were eager to reap the financial rewards of apprehending and prosecuting ships captains contravening the regulations because of their portion of the ship's value when sold by the Order of the Admiralty Court, the evidence shows that colonists were less keen to co-operate in the prosecution. One might assume that this was because they wished to continue the trade, or that they had links with the owners. That this is evidenced to be the case on the Chesapeake makes it likely that the situation was no different, except in terms of scale of profit, in Charleston.

Later parliamentary acts allowed a waiving in certain circumstances of the terms of the Navigation Acts, and a notable example of restrictions being lifted was when a settlement of Scots was proposed for the area about New York around 1669. This settlement, however, did not happen due to the shipwreck of the vessel, The Hope of Leith,[225] which was carrying new colonists of 'merchants, planters and fishermen' but included in the 400 people were those from Edinburgh's jails.

[225] D. Dobson, *Transatlantic Voyages 1600-1699*, Baltimore, Maryland, 2004

SCOTTISH TRADE WITH
COLONIAL CHARLESTON, 1683-1783

Despite incomplete records, it is possible to identify one hundred and thirty-four voyages departing from Scotland for the Americas, and forty-eight arriving in Scotland from there before 1707.[226]

Surviving records record thirty-seven transatlantic voyages occurred from Scotland to the West Indies, thirty-four voyages to Virginia, and the rest to the other English colonies lying between Surinam and Newfoundland. Scottish trade with Carolina was limited to eight voyages during the 1680s. These recorded figures cannot, however, be taken as the total number of voyages, and there is little doubt that the level of trade between Scotland and America was significantly higher. A large number of the outgoing vessels are not recorded as having returned, but these were not lost at sea as they can be shown to have undertaken later voyages.

These sources indicate that between the years 1684 and 1784, one hundred and eighty-three individual vessels were used by merchants trading between Scotland and Charleston, South Carolina. The majority of these, one hundred and fifty one, were owned or registered in Scotland; twenty two were registered in the American colonies; nine in England, and one in Ireland. An analysis of these vessels can break them down into their types, often pinks, brigs, brigantines and snows. Pinks were narrow-decked, round-sterned Dutch bulk carriers with a flat floor interior; brigs, or brigantines as they were also known, were two-masted, square-rigged, wide-decked seagoing vessels of various sizes; snows, were a variation of the brig, where the rear mast had a

226 Eric J Graham, *A Maritime History of Scotland 1650-1790*, East Linton, Scotland, 2002, pp. xi-xii

separate upright from which to set the mizzen sail.[227]   In addition, there were others simply described as 'a ship.'   Below is a breakdown of these ships by nationality.

Table 3/1

Types of vessels on the Scotland-Charleston trade route 1684-1784

Type	Scots	English/Irish	Colonial	Total
Pink	2	0	0	2
Brig	6	0	3	9
Brigantine	24	2	4	30
Snow	37	2	10	48
Ship	82	7	5	94
	151	10	22	183

The indications are that the overwhelming majority of vessels (eighty-two per cent) used on the Scotland-South Carolina trade routes were owned in Scotland, and a minority by English, (five per cent), Irish or Colonial (twelve per cent) residents.

227 David MacPherson, *Annals of Commerce, Manufactures, Fisheries and Navigation,* Edinburgh, Scotland, 1805

SCOTTISH TRADE WITH COLONIAL CHARLESTON, 1683-1783

The actual tonnage of the combined 'fleet' can be estimated to some extent. Tonnage figures exist for one hundred and eighteen vessels, which amount to twelve thousand and twenty tons cumulatively, however there are a further sixty-five vessels with an unknown capacity. At a rough guess the total tonnage may have amounted to eighteen thousand tons. Individually, tonnage varied from forty to two hundred and forty, with one hundred tons being the most common.

Twenty-three vessels were each said to have a capacity of one hundred tons, seventeen had a capacity of eighty tons, and the rest were in single figures. The significance of tonnage is that it allows a picture of capacity for cargo and by extenuation, the amount of trade carried out. With available figures, a comparison could be made with English trading patterns.

The contemporary writer, David MacPherson, makes the claim that half the Scottish tonnage prior to 1783 was American-built.[228] The data for the Scots-Carolina fleet suggest that, out of a sample of forty-six Scottish vessels recorded in Charleston by the Naval Officer between 1717 and 1767,[229] nineteen had been built in Britain, two in Ireland, twelve in New England, one in Pennsylvania, six in Virginia, and another six in 'the Plantations'. This means that from a total of forty-six vessels twenty-five were American-built, which is proportionately roughly in line with MacPherson's figures, however it contrasts with Dell's figures for the Clyde Tobacco Fleet for the period 1700-1769,

228 TNA.CO5.508-511
[229] R. F. Dell, 'The Operational Record of the Clyde Tobacco Fleet, 1747-1775', T. M. Devine and T. C. Smout, (eds), Scottish Economic and Social History, Volume 2, Glasgow, Scotland, 1982, p. 14

SCOTTISH TRADE WITH
COLONIAL CHARLESTON, 1683-1783

roughly in line with MacPherson's figures, however it contrasts with Dell's figures for the Clyde Tobacco Fleet for the period 1700-1769, which claim which claim that 35 ships were British Built and 195 were Plantation Built.[230]   There is no evidence, among the Scots-Carolina fleet, of any 'prize ships', enemy vessels taken during wartime and sold to local skippers or merchants.   This is slightly surprising considering the major conflict that occurred with France, the Seven Years War, during which time many ships were captured and sold on by both sides. Possibly the 'prize ships' had been taken to ports in England and sold there.

Nineteen vessels were described as 'British built' but there is no indication where construction took place. After the passing of the 1786 Act for the Further Increase and Encouragement of Shipping and Navigation" this information becomes available, when all vessels had to be registered in their home port, and a certificate issued giving the names of the owners, name of vessel, name of master, where and when built and by whom, and a description of the ship.   However, for our period no such record exists and the place of construction is generally unknown.   But as the Leith yards were among the foremost in shipbuilding in contemporary Great Britain, it is likely that at least some of the ships were constructed there by men such as Robert Dryburgh, Patrick Robertson, John Sime, or Thomas Willison. [231]   It is also reasonable to assume that the expansion of the Scottish mercantile marine during the eighteenth century must have had an impact on shipbuilding and the economy of ports such as Leith.   The construction of ships would have created employment opportunities not only in their

230 Sue Mowat, *The Port of Leith,* Edinburgh, 1994, p. 226
231 Dobson, *Ships, Vol.II,* Baltimore, 2002 p. 171

building, but in the repair and maintenance of these wooden ships, particularly through the regular replacement of timbers, sails and rigging.   All this would have contributed to the growth of ancillary industries such as rope-making and sail-making in ports such as Greenock and Leith. These new vessels would of course have required crew members and this would lead to the recruitment of seamen. Smaller vessels, such as the sloop, would have required around five men, while larger ships like the brigantine needed between fifteen and twenty sailors on board.   This number would have been supplemented in times of warfare if owners decided to arm their ships with cannon.

In total two hundred and forty seven voyages from Scotland to South Carolina between 1684 and 1784 can be identified.   These have been analysed on a decennial basis as follows:

Table 3/2

Years	Number of Voyages[232]
1684-90	8
1720-29	5
1730-39	15
1740-49	18
1750-59	63
1760-69	93
1770-79	32
1780-89	13

Of these there is sufficient information on one hundred and eighty - eight vessels (76%) to identify their port of origin in Scotland. Roughly

SCOTTISH TRADE WITH
COLONIAL CHARLESTON, 1683-1783

half sailed from the east coast and half from the west coast as is shown
below in Table 3.3.

Table 3/3

Ships from Scotland to Charleston 1684-1784[233]

East Coast		West Coast	
Leith	38	Greenock	78
Burntisland	2	Gourock	1
Kirkcaldy	4	Irvine	8
Bo'ness	20	Ayr	5
Cockenzie	1	Galloway	2
Dunbar	10	Kirkcudbright	1
Dundee	11		
Montrose	1		
Peterhead	1		
Inverness	1		
Orkney	4		
Total	93	Total	95
(Forth	75)	(Clyde	79)

Some of the ships followed routes south from the Clyde or Forth and
then crossed directly to Charleston, while others sailed first to the
Azores, Madeira, the Isle of Maia (one of the Cape Verde Islands), and
the West Indies before heading north to Charleston.   One of the best

232 See also NRS.E504.15.392
233 NRS.E504.15.39; *Caledonian Mercury*, 9 August 1784

SCOTTISH TRADE WITH
COLONIAL CHARLESTON, 1683-1783

accounts of a contemporary voyage from Scotland to the Carolinas is to be found in the famous 'Journal of a Lady of Quality',[234] the diary of Janet Schaw who sailed from Burntisland on the <u>Jamaica Packet of Burntisland</u> in 1775 by way of Antigua and St Kitts to Charleston and then to Wilmington, North Carolina.

Ships returning to Scotland from Charleston generally followed one of the following three routes: they could sail directly across the Atlantic to Scotland, or call in first at an English port, or by way of southern Europe. Based on a random sample of seventy four departures of 'Scottish' ships from Charleston, roughly half were bound directly for a Scots port, just fewer than a quarter headed for England, and the rest went to Iberia or Italy. In total, forty ships sailed directly to Scotland, sixteen to England, and eighteen to Mediterranean ports.

Under the Navigation Acts shipmasters were required to sail directly from a colonial port back to a British port. Shipmasters and owners lobbied against this practice because of its financial implications, making the goods they carried from the colonies uncompetitive in price and delivery dates, as well as the detriment to the freshness of produce being carried. Because of this, the 'Mediterranean pass' system was introduced enabling ships to go directly to the markets of southern Europe before returning to Great Britain. During periods of hostility between Great Britain and France, shipmasters wishing to avoid the warships and privateers in the English Channel sometimes chose to go via the Orkney Islands. Sailing time from Scotland to Charleston seems to have averaged at about three months, and the turnaround time

234 E W Andrews (ed), *Journal of a Lady of Quality: Being the Narrative of a Journey from Scotland to the West Indies, North Carolina, and Portugal, in the years 1774 to 1776,* Newhaven, Connecticut, 1922

took an additional three to four weeks.   However, there was wide variation.   On the basis of a sample of thirty-eight vessels in Charleston during the period 1732 to 1767, turn-around time varied from as little as ten days to as much as one hundred and fifty- two days. This lengthy turn-around time contrasts with that of the tobacco ships on the Chesapeake, when, with the use of port storage unavailable in Charleston, and early ships could be unloaded and loaded in a matter of a few days.   Of the attached random sample, half the ships took up to seven week to clear, three-quarters took up to eleven weeks, and the balance took up to twenty two weeks. It is possible to compare these figures with those for Scottish ships on the contemporary Clyde-Chesapeake route as calculated for the years 1750 to 1776. According to Richard F. Dell's sample of the turn round time of Scottish ships in the Chesapeake, fell from 53 days in 1750 to 33 days in 1775.[235]

Table 3/4

Scots ships from Charleston, 1684-1784, sample

To Scotland	40	Glasgow	11
		Orkney	12
		Irvine	1
		Dundee	2
		Leith	7
		Bo'ness	5
		Dunbar	1
		Anstruther	1

[235] Dell, 'The Operational Record ' p. 12

SCOTTISH TRADE WITH
COLONIAL CHARLESTON, 1683-1783

To England	16	Cowes	8
		Dover	3
		Bristol	2
		Portsmouth	1
		Liverpool	1
		London	1
To Mediterranean	18	Lisbon	13
		Leghorn	1
		Cadiz	1
		Oporto	3

Table 3/5

Scots vessels turn-around time at Charleston 1732-1767 based on a sample of 38 vessels.[236]

Johanna	1727	86 days
Robert and Jane	1727	77 days
Euphemia	1732	29 days
Helen	1734	29 days
Speedwell	1734	152 days
Neptune	1735	25 days
Anslie	1735	36 days
Rebecca and Mary	1736	107 days
Chance	1758	27 days
Peggy and Nelly	1758	27 days
Industry	1759	28 days

236 David Dobson, *Ships from Scotland to America, 1628-1828, Volume II,* Baltimore, Maryland, 2003, p. 154

SCOTTISH TRADE WITH
COLONIAL CHARLESTON, 1683-1783

Jenny	1759	125 days
Chance	1760	32 days
Nancy	1760	10 days
Industry	1761	88 days
Robert	1761	53 days
Montgomery	1761	35 days
Friendship	1761	67 days
Chance	1762	56 days
Dennistoun	1762	39 days
Chance	1763	16 days
Jamieson	1763	44 days
Loudoun	1763	26 days
Betsy	1763	19 days
Industry	1764	28 days
Mary	1764	20 days
Elizabeth	1766	59 days
Magdalene	1766	110 days
Two Brothers	1766	32 days
Jane	1766	98 days
Neptune	1766	66 days
Orangefield	1766	44 days
Betty	1766	43 days
Elizabeth	1766	59 days
Jenny	1766	65 days
Kinnoull	1767	52 days
Richmond	1767	39 days
Peggy	1767	72 days

SCOTTISH TRADE WITH
COLONIAL CHARLESTON, 1683-1783

The cargoes delivered in Scotland were not all for home consumption as some were re-exported to the markets of northern Europe, such as Amsterdam and Hamburg. Similarly, the ships bound for England generally called into Channel ports before heading for major European markets such as Rotterdam, Hamburg and Scandinavia. Ships that headed for Spain and Portugal generally disposed of their colonial produce there and loaded fruit and wine for delivery to Scottish ports.

Until 1786 and the introduction of compulsory ship registration there is no single source revealing ownership of ships, and therefore no official record of ship-owners involved in the Scotland-Charleston trade before this date. Some information can be found scattered in documents such as charter parties, or from cases brought before the High Court of the Admiralty of Scotland, but the identity of the majority of ship-owners may never be known. However, for the colonial period, a register was kept by colonial administrators called the Naval Officers' Shipping Lists and records were kept by the incumbent official for port of Charleston during this period. This is therefore a reasonably comprehensive register of ship-owners using this port from which it has been possible to assemble the list below.

Table 3/6

Scottish Shipowners using the Port of Charleston

Alexander of Glasgow: Adam Lorimer and Company
Amity of Glasgow: Alexander Morrison, James Taylor, Robert Craig
Anna Maria of Montrose: James Hercules, John Scott skipper, Alexander Turnbull

SCOTTISH TRADE WITH
COLONIAL CHARLESTON, 1683-1783

Anslie of Leith: George Anslie, and John Hay skipper
Aurora of Greenock: Simson, Baird, and Company, Patrick Crawford, James Gammell
Avon of Leith: Alexander Urquhart skipper, Isaac Forrest
Barbary of Leith: James Murray and Margaret Henderson
Bell of Glasgow: T. Peters, the Dunlops, J Jamieson, Walter Brock
Betsy of Greenock: William McCunn and John Brown
Betty of Leith: Angus McLarty skipper, Alexander Morrison
Brothers of Greenock: John and Joseph Scott
Catherine of Glasgow: John Glasford and Company
Chance of Kirkwall: George Smith skipper, James Crawford, John White
Christian of Leith: William and Robert Alexander
Diligence of Greenock: Alexander Wilson, George Brown, Robert Scott, John Munro, and Ebenezer Munro,
 Edinburgh of Greenock: John Lyon skipper, Alexander Ritchie skipper, Alexander and William Porterfield
Elizabeth of Bo'ness: Hercules Angus skipper, John Pearson, Robert Clark
Elizabeth of Glasgow: Alexander Keir skipper, J & J Alexander
Euphemia of Glasgow: John Lyon and Hugh Milliken
Expedition of Glasgow: Daniel Campbell, Colin Campbell, George Campbell, Charles Crawford
Fame of Dundee: John Rankin, ... Stormonth
 Friendship of Bo'ness: A., J. skipper, and R. Cowan
Helen of Leith: James Carmichael and James Seaman skipper
Industry of Leith: Andrew Cowan skipper, Robert and Hugh Clerk
Industry of Bo'ness: Andrew Cowan and C. Cowan
Industry of Berwick: Henry Liddell, George Chalmers, Patrick Miller

SCOTTISH TRADE WITH
COLONIAL CHARLESTON, 1683-1783

Jamieson of Leith: John Aitken skipper, Walter Forrest, Robert Robertson,

Jane of Anstruther: John Smith skipper, James Wood

Jenny of Greenock: John Glasford

Jenny of Greenock: Robert Erving, skipper, and William Erving

John of Bo'ness: Archibald McMillan skipper, John Glasford, James Gordon and Neil Jamieson

John & Robert of Gourock: John and Joseph Scott

Juno of Berwick: Ralph Foster

Keith: William Millar

King of Prussia of Greenock: Joseph Angus

Kinnoull of Leith: James Crawford, Patrick Miller, William Hogg, Robert Young, Alexander Alexander skipper, and Alexander Scott

Kitty of Irvine: Hugh Patterson, Robert Arthur, R and J Montgomerie

Little Donald of Leith: John Morrison skipper and John Rose

Lord Montgomery of Glasgow: Thomas Clark

Loudoun of Glasgow: James King, James Dennistoun, Nicholas Harries, Stevenson and Laird

Magdalene of Dunbar: C and R Fall

Martha and Sally of Montrose: Daniel Napier and Daniel Buchanan

Menie of Glasgow: Joseph Simson and George Buchanan

Mercury of Bo'ness: J and A Baillie

Minerva of Dundee: Alexander Strachan, Robert Stirling skipper, H. Smith, J. Fyffe

Molly of Dunbar: C and R. Fall, Robert McLeish

Montgomery of Greenock: Denniston, Stevenson, Laird, J.Witherspoon

Munro of Glasgow: James Glasford skipper

Nancy of Burntisland: Alexander Ritchie skipper, James Oswald, D. Cockburn

Nancy of Irvine: Crawford, Brown and Stevenson

SCOTTISH TRADE WITH
COLONIAL CHARLESTON, 1683-1783

Nannie of Glasgow: Andrew Crawford
Nelly of Greenock: John Cross, John Baird, Robert Bogle, Robert Glasford in St Kitts, John Munro
Neptune of Dumfries: James Corrie and Andrew Crosbie
Neptune of Glasgow: G and R Oswald
Peggy of Glasgow: John Douglas, Andrew Buchanan, Robert Hastie
Peggy and Nelly of Greenock: Robert Arthur, Hugh Morris and John Catlin
Prince Ferdinand of Greenock: Joseph Angus
Rebecca and Mary of Montrose: C. Godfrey, Alexander Turnbull
Richmond of Bo'ness: James Hamilton skipper
Robert of Irvine: D. Drew, D. Bryce, R. Boyd, A.Farrie
Robert of Greenock: J and H Ritchie
St George of Montrose: George Morrison, Patrick Stratton, George Ouchterlonie
Sally of Irvine: William Shaw skipper, James Boyd, James Kennedy
Speedwell of Glasgow: Richard Oswald, John Baird
Thistle of Greenock: G and J Buchanan
Tiverton Merchant of Montrose: Patrick Ogilvie skipper, George Campbell, John Watson
Two Brothers of Kirkcaldy: D and T Ballantyne

Out of sixty-seven vessels in the above list, twenty-four, approximately thirty- six per cent of the sample, were part owned by the skipper, the rest being owned by merchants who were generally local to the port of registration. Three vessels were partly owned by Scottish merchants resident in the American colonies. These were Neil Jamieson, one of the most prominent of the Tobacco Lords, then in Virginia, who owned part of the John of Bo'ness; Robert Glassford, a member of another successful Glasgow tobacco merchant dynasty, then in St Kitts, who

129

owned part of the Nelly of Greenock; and J and A Baillie, also in St Kitts, who owned part of the Mercury of Bo'ness. The only example of an English-based merchant owning part of a Scottish vessel was A Farrie in Liverpool who had invested capital in the Robert of Irvine.

The control of the shipping used in the Scotland-Charleston trade was therefore overwhelmingly in the hands of Scots who were based in Scotland. Scotland was self-sufficient as far as shipping was concerned, which meant that shipping services were invisible earners contributing to the economy. This had a beneficial effect on the balance of payments of the country. While the number of Scottish vessels trading with Charleston may not have been significant in relation to overall Scottish trade, in Carolinian terms they represented only around five per cent of the overall traffic entering or leaving the harbor of Charleston. Charleston's main trading links were with England or the other American colonies, including the West Indies. What is notable about these figures, is the fact that the Scots merchants were vertically integrated to the extent that they both owned the vessels and the merchant houses.

It may be the case that the Scots trade was too small to interest the larger London based merchant, and this enabled Scots merchant to remain independent of larger trading concerns.

'Tonnage' was formulated in the closing years of the seventeenth century under an English Act of Parliament of 1694. Tonnage was measurement formula which decreed the cubic capacity of a ship. It equalled the length of the keel within the board, by the midships beam from plank to plank, multiplied by the depth of the hold from the plank below the keel to the under part of the upper deck plank, divided by ninety- four. This formula was modified in the eighteenth century and continued to be used throughout the British Isles and colonies.

130

SCOTTISH TRADE WITH
COLONIAL CHARLESTON, 1683-1783

As a vessel's tonnage determined various costs such as insurance and harbor dues, shipmasters are known to have varied their calculations of tonnage to minimise harbor charges. One of the functions of the Customs Service was to randomly check the actual tonnage against the declared, but it should be kept in mind that the declared tonnages may not always be wholly accurate.

During the period of the American Revolution, emigration was suspended and restrictions were placed on free-trade between Great Britain and the Americas. This did not mean, however, that all trading activities stopped as evidenced from various port books and court records. The Susannah left Port Glasgow bound for Charleston in 1780, and again in 1781, also in the post war years of 1784, 1785, and 1786.[237] British shipping bound for America had to run the gauntlet of American and allied privateers and naval vessels, and some of vessels, as might be expected, failed to arrive at their destinations. For example, the Janet left the Clyde in 1781 bound for Charleston but was captured by a privateer and taken to Boston.[238] At the same time American merchants attempted to develop a transatlantic trade direct to the continental markets, where they would sell colonial produce for commodities formerly obtained from Great Britain. At times Charleston was in rebel hands, allowing it to participate in this trade, despite a British embargo and the existence of British privateers. Some vessels were intercepted at sea and taken to a British port. One such ship was the Minerva of Charleston, master William Sextroh, which left Charleston in April 1778 with a cargo of tobacco, rice, indigo, and

237 *Scots Magazine*, (hereafter SM), Volume 42, Edinburgh, Scotland, 1781, p. 222
238 NRS.AC7.58

logwood, bound for Gothenborg in Sweden. On 7 May the ship was captured by George Innes, a Greenock shipmaster, and brought into Greenock, where the ship and its cargo were declared 'prizes' and sold by order the Hugh Court of the Admiralty of Scotland. A letter found aboard the Minerva, which had been written by a merchant in Charleston to a correspondent in Gothenborg stated *'such has been the scarcity of dry goods in these United States and particularly in this that they will now bring from ten to fifteen hundred on the European cost'*.[239]

The likelihood of making good profits during war-time encouraged some merchants to trade in neutral colonial ports, such as those in the Danish and Dutch West Indies. A case in point was Ninian Menzies, a Scottish merchant and factor based in Richmond, Virginia, engaged in the tobacco trade between Glasgow and the Chesapeake, and operating under the name of Todd, Menzies and Company. He was also a partner in John Hay and Company with stores in Virginia and North Carolina. At the outbreak of the American Revolution he refused to take the rebel oath and in 1776 moved via New York back to Glasgow. From there he took up residence as a merchant in St Eustatia, a Dutch colony in the Leeward Islands, dying there in 1781.[240] In the two years 1773-1774, seventy-five and seventy-seven ships left Scotland bound for North America. During the period of the war, the number of voyages undertaken dropped, and in the last year of the war, 1783, these amounted to twenty-four voyages. In the post war period commercial opportunities ensured a relatively quick re-establishment of trade between Great Britain and the nascent United States, but it took

239 NRS.AC7.58
240 NRS.CC8.8.131/1; NA.AO12.109.192; SM.43.223

SCOTTISH TRADE WITH
COLONIAL CHARLESTON, 1683-1783

several years to reach the pre-war levels.[241]   Four ships left Scotland
bound for Charleston in 1783 and only three in 1784, all sailing from
the Clyde.

The emigrant trade seems to have recovered almost immediately.   On
5 June 1784 the Caledonian Mercury advertised that the <u>Wilmington</u>
was at Greenock bound for Charleston and that '*passengers – wanted,
house and ship carpenters, blockmakers, blacksmiths, coopers,
bricklayers, and tailors*'[242] and three months later, the <u>America</u> also left
Greenock bound for Charleston with passengers.[243]   With the end of
the war came a renewed period of trade and shipping between Scotland,
especially the Clyde, and South Carolina.

241 Dobson, Ships, Vol.II, Baltimore, 2002, p.171
242 see also NRS.E504.15.39
243 NRS.E504.15.39; *Caledonian Mercury,* 9 August 1784.

SCOTTISH TRADE WITH
COLONIAL CHARLESTON, 1683-1783

CHAPTER FOUR

THE EMIGRANT TRADE

During the sixteenth century Spain claimed jurisdiction over virtually all of the Americas, a claim which the northern European powers of England, France and the Netherlands increasingly disregarded. In 1565, French Huguenots had established a settlement named Fort Carolina on the St John River, in what is now South Carolina, but this settlement did not last for more than a few years before it was destroyed by Spanish forces. It was not until the seventeenth century that the northern Europeans began to establish and maintain colonies in the Americas, and this was made possible by the balance of naval power having shifted from Spain, to England and the Netherlands. Spain, as might be expected, did not take kindly to these encroachments, and from time to time tried to dislodge budding settlements on land to which they laid claim with the use of force. The early seventeenth century Spanish settlements stretched from the Gulf of Mexico along the Atlantic coasts as far as the area now known as the Carolinas.

The area claimed by the Spanish in the north was disputed territory from as early as 1585. The evidence for this is that an attempt at settlement took place by the English at Roanoke; an island in Albemarle Sound lying just to the south of Chesapeake Bay, now in North Carolina. That the period of English settlement there was very brief has been explained by the assumption that the local Indians were hostile. When a supply

SCOTTISH TRADE WITH
COLONIAL CHARLESTON, 1683-1783

ship arrived one year after the first settlers had landed, it found no remaining colonists, and no bodies.[244]

The location was, in any case, not ideal. Shifting sandbanks made it difficult to land provisions and emigrants, also the soil conditions were poor, so it was probably for these reasons that there were no further attempts to settle this area in the sixteenth century. Twenty-two years later, in 1607, the first successful English colony in America was established at Jamestown on the James River off Chesapeake Bay, and this was to be the beginning of permanent English presence in America. [245] From this period on, the area of the Chesapeake and later, New England, became the centre of most English colonisation, and it was not until Spanish power declined even more that the English turned their attention to the lands lying further south.

Interest in the Caribbean islands began with privateering activity against the Spanish. The English, Dutch and French were flexing their muscles, and their vessels plundered the Spanish treasure fleets carrying gold and silver from South America. Forays by these privateers to the local islands revealed that agricultural conditions would be conducive to a number of crops, and the opportunities for profit were quickly recognised. Settlements were soon established, and the planting and production of tobacco and sugar started. Barbados, which had been

243 John C. Appleby, 'War, Politics, and Colonisation, 1558-1625, Nicholas Canny, (ed), *The Origins of Empire. British Overseas Enterprise to the Close of the Seventeenth Century,* Oxford, England, 2001, p. 65
244 Ibid, p. 72
245 Hilary M. Beckles, 'The Hub of Empire: the Caribbean and Britain in the Seventeenth Century, Nicholas Canny, (ed), *The Origins of Empire British Overseas Enterprise to the Close of the Seventeenth Century,* Oxford, England, 2001, p. 221; Robert M. Weir, 'Shaftesbury's Darling : British Settlement in the Carolinas at the Close of the Seventeenth Century, ibid, p. 398

SCOTTISH TRADE WITH
COLONIAL CHARLESTON, 1683-1783

settled in 1627, was the first English colony, and its economic success led to an increase in the settling of other islands. The next to be developed were the Windward and Leeward islands, taken one after another during the 1630s. A pause occurred during the English Civil War, and then Jamaica was taken from the Spanish by an expedition sent by Oliver Cromwell in 1655. The capture of this large island from the Spanish demonstrated more than any other event, that the power of Spain was seriously on the wane, and the time had come for further colonial expansion by England. Some, who were established in the Caribbean islands, now turned their sights to mainland America.[246]

The colony of Carolina dates from 1629,[247] when Charles I granted all the land lying between 31 degrees north and 36 degrees north to Sir Robert Heath who had proposed to settle Huguenot refugees from La Rochelle there. Development was retarded for a while due to the English Civil War, and it was not until the period of the Restoration that an attempt to colonise the area occurred. In 1663, Charles II granted the area of Carolina to a group of eight English 'proprietors'. This group of men were eager to explore and exploit the benefits which colonial expansion often offered. Under this second charter, the Proprietors were named as Sir John Colleton, John and William Berkeley, Sir George Carteret, and the Duke of Albemarle, and later William, Lord Craven, Edward Hyde, and Lord Claredon.[248] Two of these men were experienced colonists. Sir John Colleton was a Royalist who had fled from England and become a planter in Barbados,

---

246 Warren Ripley, *Charles Towne, Birth of a City,* Charleston, South Carolina, p.4
247 Angus Calder, *Revolutionary Empire, The Rise of the English-Speaking Empires from the Fifteenth Century to the 1780s,* London, England, 1981, pp. 296-297
248 Ripley, *Charles Towne,* p.4; Calder, *Revolutionary Empire,* p. 297; Weir, *Shaftesbury's Darling,* p.380

SCOTTISH TRADE WITH
COLONIAL CHARLESTON, 1683-1783

and William Berkley had been the Governor of Virginia. To speed up settlement the Proprietors invited settlers in the colonies of Barbados, Bermuda, Virginia, and New England with the necessary skills, to avail themselves of an opportunity to develop the land of Carolina. The least successful of those who re-located to the Carolinas were the settlers originating from New England. They had moved to the region around Cape Fear, but found conditions were not to their liking, and as a result, most returned to New England. Between 1663 and 1665, groups of Barbadians, under the leadership of William Hilton and Robert Sandford, also attempted to colonise the Cape Fear region, but they too became discouraged and returned to Barbados. However, a series of natural disasters in Barbados, including a plague of locusts in 1663, a major hurricane in 1667 and a drought in 1668, ruined some planters and because of this, some planters decided to again try their luck in the Carolinas. In 1669 Barbadians established a settlement on Goose Creek, a tributary of the Cooper River.[249] The Proprietors, had in the meantime, also been recruiting for potential Carolinian colonists in England, and in 1669, three shiploads of hopeful emigrants left its shores bound for Carolina. In 1680 Charles Town, known as Charleston after the American Revolution, was re-sited to the junction of the Ashley and the Cooper Rivers, from where it was to become the centre of administration and chief port of the colony.[250] Contemporary maps illustrating early Carolina and the locations mentioned above are included. [251]

249 Ripley, *Charles Towne*, pp. 9-12
250 See maps
251 Guild Hall, London Record Office. MRE/93

SCOTTISH TRADE WITH
COLONIAL CHARLESTON, 1683-1783

Many of the early immigrants to Carolina arrived as indentured servants, which meant that in exchange for the cost of their passage they undertook to work for a period of years without pay. During this period of time they were fed, clothed and housed by their employers. To then encourage them to remain in the colony once their period of indentureship had ended, the authorities generally allocated them a tract of land, and sometimes tools and seeds to enable them to farm. Merchants and shipmasters advertised and recruited for those wishing to become indentured servants, especially those men or women with specific skills. Many of the unskilled indentured servants were found in London, which then, as now, attracted young people seeking their fortunes. Surplus agricultural laborers, demobilised soldiers from both the British Isles and parts of the continent and common vagrants were all grist for the colonial mill. Not all transatlantic passengers were willing, however, and kidnapping of the able bodied was not unusual by unscrupulous merchants and skippers. This practice was so widespread that it led to the authorities in port towns insisting on indenture-ship agreements being registered in the town records. Although not complete, many of these registers survive for the ports of London, Liverpool and especially of Bristol where many thousands of emigrants are listed. These records reveal personal details of emigrants, including their place of origin, their occupation and their destination; for instance, one dated April 1684, concerns a John Law from Scotland, aged 32, who indented with John Smith, a merchant in London to serve for four years in Carolina.[252]

To some extent the flow of emigrants reflected social and economic conditions at home and in difficult times emigration increased. Those wishing to emigrate to the Carolinas from English ports in the

252 TNA.E190.62.5

SCOTTISH TRADE WITH
COLONIAL CHARLESTON, 1683-1783

seventeenth century did so through London, Bristol and Plymouth. The individual Port Books identify the merchant vessels bound for Carolina, most of which probably carried passengers as well as cargo. One of the earliest on record is the doggar, _Edisto_, master John Cumming, which sailed from London to Carolina in 1675, and again in 1679.[253] Because the demand from the colonies for servants often outstripped the supply, a solution was found by emptying the town jails and transporting the felons. During the colonial period approximately 50,000 criminals and political undesirables were taken from the jails of England and sold off to planters in the colonies.[254] The authorities in Scotland and Ireland adopted this English practice and shipped a considerable, though much lower number. The first prisoner known to have been transported to the Carolinas was a Paul Hobson, who was released from the Tower of London on 28 April 1665 to be sent to Carolina. In June 1684 felons in London's Bridewell were given the choice of indentureship in Carolina. Although indenture-ship was how most English emigration to the Carolinas was affected, some people went as 'redemptioners'. This, slightly later development, meant that shipmaster paid the cost of the emigrant's passage, and was reimbursed by the passengers' friends or relatives on reaching the American port. If this payment was not made, the shipmaster was allowed to sell the individual as an indentured servant to cover the cost of the passage.

253 See Peter Wilson Coldham, _Emigrants in Chains,A Social History of Forced Emigration to the Americas of Felons, Destitute Children, Political and Religious Non-Conformists, Vagabonds, Beggars and other Undesirables, 1607-1776,_ Baltimore, Maryland, 1992; Peter Wilson Coldham, _British Emigrants in Bondage, 1614-1788,_ Baltimore, Md, 2005
254 W L Grant, _Acts of the Privy Council, Colonial,_ London, Volume I, Hereford, England, 1908, pp. 865-866; W. Noel Sainsbury, _Calendar of State Papers, America and the West Indies, 1677-1680,_ London, England, 1896, p. 428

SCOTTISH TRADE WITH
COLONIAL CHARLESTON, 1683-1783

During this period Huguenots were also, once again, showing an interest in emigrating to America, and to Carolina in particular. On 1 May 1679, Rene Petit, King Charles II's agent in Rouen, recruited eighty Huguenot families skilled in the manufacture of silk, oil and wine for settlement along the Santee River.[255] In late December 1679 an advance party of ninety Huguenots left England, bound for Charleston, on board the <u>Richmond</u>.[256]

The War of the Spanish Succession, 1702-1713, had implications for emigration, and the settlement of South Carolina. From 1685 Creek Indians had allowed white traders in Carolina to journey along the 'Creek path' to the Upper Creek centre of Coweta, giving merchants based in Charleston a monopoly of trade with these Indians. Deerskins, horses and Amerindian slaves were traded for muskets and other manufactured goods imported from England. The Creeks were the pre-eminent tribe in what is now Alabama. To the west lay the areas inhabited by the Choctaw and the Chickasaw tribes, and these traded with the French who had established a colony in Louisiana, and whose main population centres were Biloxi and Mobile.

Political alliances were fixed by the end of the seventeenth century. The English supported the Creeks, the French were allied to the Choctaw, and the Spanish were in league with the Apalachee in Florida.

Fearing a joint Franco-Spanish invasion, the English colonists and their Indian allies took pre-emptive action against the Spanish in Florida. This successful attack had the benefit of increasing trading

255. W L Grant, Acts of the Privy Council Colonial, Vol.i. Hereford, England, 1908, pp865-866
256 see St Julien Childs 'The Petit Guerard Colony' SCHGM, Charleston, 1942, Vol.XLIII,

opportunities, in that they took over the Indian trade of the seized Spanish territory, thereby strengthening the position of the British and at the same time advantaging the Creeks Indians. Within a few years, the Creeks allied with the Chickasaw and encouraged by the Carolinians attacked the French and Spanish settlements as far west as the Mississippi.[257]

The Treaty of Utrecht, which in March 1713 ended the War of the Spanish Succession, also caused a cessation of hostility in the American south-east. The British, with their Creek allies, had succeeded in expanding their hegemony throughout the area, securing the Indian trade essential to the economy of contemporary colonial Charleston. This comfortable position was, short-lived, however, as in 1715 the Yamasee Indians based along the Savannah River, who had formerly been regarded as allies, attacked the frontier settlements of Carolina. It is possible that this war was ignited by the activities of some Indian traders operating within Indian territory, who often took advantage of their goodwill. So serious was the Yamasee War that it threatened the very existence of South Carolina. Almost ten per cent of the white population was killed during this war with the Indians, trade was disrupted, frontier settlements were abandoned, and Indian raids occurred within twelve miles of the town of Charleston. The Creek, Shawnee, Guale and the Cherokee aided the Yamasee but this support gradually fell away and eventually hostilities ceased in 1727. The Proprietary government, having shown itself unable to protect the

257 NRS.AC10.317/318, a case re a coach maker from Wurtemberg who wished to abandon the voyage on the death of his wife and three children

SCOTTISH TRADE WITH
COLONIAL CHARLESTON, 1683-1783

Colony, lost its jurisdiction to the Crown, and the result of these Indian wars was that economic development of South Carolina slowed down, and emigration to the colony was halted.

For almost a generation after these events there was posed very little threat from the Spanish, French or Indian tribes, and the threat to the colonists' security was one of self-making. At this period the white population was increase at a slow rate, which the numbers of blacks were being increased constantly because of the slave trade. By 1729, when the overall population of the colony was estimated to be around thirty thousand people, only approximately thirty per cent were white, and this imbalance, added to their cruel treatment of the imported Africans, caused the whites to have concern for their personal security. In an attempt to increase the number of whites to a comfortable ratio with the blacks, the government took began to increase its attempts to encourage white immigration. For a two year period from 1716, former Yamasee Indian land was offered to potential immigrants from Ireland and this measure was successful in attracting an increasing number of Protestant Irish. Later, large land grants were allocated to individuals who undertook to bring over Protestants from the British Isles and continental Europe. Immigration of Catholics was discouraged because it was thought they might side with their Spanish or French co-religionists during periods of conflict. As a result of this incentive, during the 1730s around one thousand Swiss arrived and settled in South Carolina, with smaller contingents from France and Germany. Ireland was also considered 'foreign' because at the time it was a kingdom distinct from Great Britain.

Religious persecution was a reason that many emigrated from continental Europe. The Huguenots fled France after the Revocation

SCOTTISH TRADE WITH
COLONIAL CHARLESTON, 1683-1783

of the Edict of Nantes in 1685. The law which previously protected
this Protestant community were withdrawn with the rescinding of this
law, making their position within French society extremely precarious.
Half a million Huguenots left their native soil to settle in the Protestant
states of north-west Europe, and the more adventurous travelled via
England and Ireland to destinations in colonial America, with a few
hundred reaching Charleston. As elsewhere, the arrival of this highly
skilled, educated group of people greatly benefited the country in which
they took up residence.

More numerous were emigrants from German speaking areas,
especially the Palatines from the modern-day Rhineland whose
homeland been devastated during the War of the Spanish Succession in
the opening years of the eighteenth century. These came in waves
during the eighteenth century, travelling from Rotterdam or London to
Philadelphia. At least one vessel, the Hannah of Rotterdam, master
William Wilson, bound for Philadelphia in 1746 with Palatines, called
in at Leith.[258] During the 1720s many Germans took the Great Wagon
Road south, establishing communities in the backwoods of Carolina
and Georgia.

The Swiss who settled in South Carolina[259] were recruited by a Jean
Pierre Purry. Initially, in 1718, he had tried to recruit the Dutch, but
when they showed little interest, he moved his focus to Switzerland,

258W Stitt Robinson, *The Southern Colonial Frontier, 1607-1763,* Albuquerque, New Mexico,
1979, pp. 167-168
259 David Dobson, *Scottish Emigration to Colonial America, 1607-1785,* Athens, Georgia,
1994, pp. 118-121

SCOTTISH TRADE WITH
COLONIAL CHARLESTON, 1683-1783

and before he died in 1736, he had successfully recruited 600 Protestants for the colony of South Carolina, settling them on the east bank of the Savannah River, now known as Purrysburg.[260]

The pages of the South Carolina Gazette bear out the fact of Scots merchants of Charleston being active in both the transportation and the settlement of new immigrants. In January 1745, the Scot, Mackenzie, and his partner Roche advertised the arrival of:

> 'the ship <u>St Andrew</u>, Robert Brown master, from Rotterdam, with three hundred Palatines, among whom are several tradesmen and farmers, also a great number of young men and maids, the greatest part are indebted for their passage and are willing to serve any person inclinable to purchase their time.'

In late 1751, Austin (a Scot from Perth), and Laurens advertised:

> 'about two hundred German passengers. Amongst them are several handicraft tradesmen and husbandmen and likely young boys and girls. They are to be indented for a term of years to any person who will pay their passages.'[261]

In 1752 Benjamin D'Harriette and John McCall announced:

> 'A vessel is just arrived from Rotterdam with German servants in good health. Amongst them are tradesmen of all sorts, which will be indented on reasonable terms.'[262]

An entry in the South Carolina Council Journal of 31 January 1765 shows William Woodrop and Andrew Cathcart, merchants in

---

260 *South Carolina Gazette* (hereafter *SCGaz*), 23 October 1751
261 *SCGaz*.3.10.1752
262 *South Carolina Journal*, Volume 32, pp. 412-427

SCOTTISH TRADE WITH
COLONIAL CHARLESTON, 1683-1783

Charleston, to be agents for a London organisation for the Relief of Poor German Protestants. A number of these had recently arrived in South Carolina on the Dragon, Captain Hammett, and on the Union, Captain Smith, for which these agents received £5 sterling for each immigrant, and a bounty of £4 or £2 for passage.[263] Germans who landed in Charleston were generally en-route for Georgia or the frontiers of South Carolina to join their countrymen. It can be seen, therefore, that Scots merchants of Charleston were participants in the emigrant trade irrespective of the origins of the passengers. They were active in transportation, whether it be from the British Isles, continental Europe, or indeed Africa. When passages could not be financed by the individual, passages were paid for in different ways.[264] Germans normally arrived as redemptioners; their passages being paid for when they arrived by members of their family or community. In the case of those arriving from the British Isles, these were generally sold on arrival as indentured servants to the highest bidder. Under this system, families could be, and often were, separated. From the available evidence, it would seem that during the period of the late eighteenth century, Scots were more likely to be able to finance their passage to America and avoid indentureship than other immigrants from the British Isles. An analysis of emigrants from Great Britain to the American colonies, based on the Register of Emigrants 1773-1774,

263 Alan Taylor, *American Colonies, the Settlement of North America to 1800,* London, England, 2002, p. 319
264 Bernard Bailyn, *Voyagers to the West. A Passage in the Peopling of America on the Eve of the Revolution,* New York, 1986, pp. 170-171

SCOTTISH TRADE WITH
COLONIAL CHARLESTON, 1683-1783

indicates that 83% of emigrants from England left as indentured servants, whereas only 17% left Scotland on that basis.[265]

From 1699 there had been push factors at work in Ireland encouraging emigration to America. The Woollen Act of 1699, passed by the Irish Parliament in 1699 under pressure from England, had the effect of regulating the sale of Irish woollen cloth and wool, making it available only to the markets in England and Wales. The immediate result of this Act was the loss to the Irish of profitable European markets which they had built up over decades, which badly affected their economy. The Test Act of 1704 took the right to vote and the right to hold any but the most insignificant public office from all non-Anglicans. This was followed by the banning of Presbyterian ministers from officiating at marriages, funerals, and conducting church services. Finally, in 1717, the thirty-one year leases on many farms expired, renewable only on far harder terms. For many Ulster Scots, this was the last straw and a wave of large scale emigration to America began in 1718.[266] These pioneers first sailed for New England, but the welcome there was surprisingly muted. The attraction of New England for the Ulster Irish lay in the fact that the existing colonists were fellow Calvinists, but the reality was that these Congregationalist Protestants and the recently arrived Presbyterian Protestants found much in which to differ. The result of this was that later immigrants from Ulster instead chose Philadelphia, where the Quakers were more welcoming, and land more abundant. Flax seeds, formerly obtained from the Baltic, began to be supplied from Philadelphia and from 1731 direct shipping links between the two

265 See R J Dickson's, *Ulster Emigration to Colonial America, 1718-1775,* Belfast, Ireland, 1976, passim
266 see appendices

147

SCOTTISH TRADE WITH
COLONIAL CHARLESTON, 1683-1783

places commenced, and with it emigration between Ireland and
Philadelphia.   Many immigrants to Philadelphia from Ireland, like
others, took the Great Wagon Road south to Carolina and Georgia.
From 1732 onwards many Ulster Scots families began to arrive in South
Carolina, settling in Williamsburg and Kingston in the north-east of the
colony.   Some of these appear to have been encouraged to do so by
James Pringle and Robert Orr, Scottish merchants in Charleston.[267]
The new immigrants from Ireland brought with them the skills required
in the manufacture of linen, butter, cheese, tallow, flour and bacon.[268]
New arrivals included Presbyterian ministers such as the Reverend
Robert Heron who arrived from Ireland and served the community from
1740 to 1743 and the Reverend John Rae, from Dundee, who was a
minister in the Presbyterian Church in Williamsburg until his death in
1761.[269]   In November 1733 a James Gordon unsuccessfully petitioned
the South Carolina Assembly for aid to settle one hundred families in
Queensboro in the north-east but was refused.   He later transported
settlers to the colony at his own expense, and some of these would
appear to have been Scottish;[270] Colonial records refer to a '*Mr Gordon
and forty Highlanders in one of the northern townships.*'[271]   By 1751,

267 See Robert L Meriwether, *The Expansion of South Carolina, 1729-
1765,* Kingsport, Tennessee, 1940, pp. 79-88; Robinson, *The Southern Colonial Frontier*, pp.
163-165
268 Frederick L Weis, *The Colonial Clergy of Virginia and the Carolinas,* Baltimore, Maryland,
1976; passim; Public Records of South Carolina, Volume XXI.103.
269 Meriwether, *Expansion of South Carolina,* p. 89
270 TNA.CO5.363; Calendar of State Papers, Colonial, America and the West Indies, 1734-
1735, Volume XLI, London, 1953, fo.402.i
271 South Carolina Council Journal, Vol 34, pp 1-9

SCOTTISH TRADE WITH
COLONIAL CHARLESTON, 1683-1783

a number of religious denominations were represented in the colony of South Carolina, including Anglicans, Presbyterians, Lutherans, Huguenot, and Irish Quakers.

But more Protestants were wanted.   In 1761 the South Carolina Assembly passed an Act to encourage Protestant settlers to immigrate to the colony from Europe.   With the exception of Ireland, subsidies were extended only to non-English speaking Protestants, resulting in fewer British immigrants.   An example of how the subsidy was allocated is mentioned in the South Carolina Council Journal[272] dated December 1767, when it reports the Clerk of Council boarding the brigantine Chichester, master, William Reid, with one hundred and forty-seven immigrants from Belfast.   The Clerk ordered that a bounty of £4 and £2 sterling respectively be paid to the shipping agents, Messrs Torrans and Pouag in payment of their passages, and an additional £1 sterling was paid to the immigrants to assist their settlement.

In South Carolina, this payment, or 'bounty' of £4 per adult was paid to the shipping agents by the colonial authorities for every poor Protestant brought from Europe.   This gave incentive to ship-owners to actively participate in encouraging emigration and advertising passages.   The Charleston firm belonging to John Torrans, John Greg, and John Pouag had an established network of agents in Belfast and Londonderry who recruited emigrants for South Carolina.   All the emigrant ships from Ulster to South Carolina during the bounty years of 1763-1768 were consigned to Torrans, Greg and Poaug, and this firm successfully petitioned the Governor for two townships of twenty thousand acres on which they undertook to settle immigrants.   These were Boonesborough on Long Canes Creek, and Londonborough on

272 *Belfast News Letter*, 14 April 1767

SCOTTISH TRADE WITH
COLONIAL CHARLESTON, 1683-1783

Hard Labor Creek, and peopled, almost exclusively, by immigrants from the province of Ulster. In Belfast, the firm of Greg and Cunningham was the main recruiting agency for Torrans, Greg and Pouag, and this firm sent its representatives to market towns in the surrounding counties promoting emigration to South Carolina. Local newspapers regularly advertised the availability of ships from northern Irish ports bound for the colonies. During the Spring of 1767, one newspaper advertisement was inserted by the firm Bynan and Gaussan, merchants in Newry, promoting their ship, the Britannia, a vessel of three hundred tons, bound for Charleston, requesting that passengers to be on board by 4 May when 'the ship, by the blessing of God, will then proceed on her intended voyage for the Land of Promise'.[273] The vessel arrived in Charleston in late August with one hundred and seventy-four emigrants aboard.[274]

For a time, the bounty system achieved its objective of increasing immigration into South Carolina from Europe. The greed of ship-owners, however, led to the overloading of their vessels to the peril of its passengers. The worst example of this was on a ship called the Nancy, Captain Samuel Hannah, from Belfast. This vessel had a registered tonnage of eighty tons, which indicated that it could carry a maximum number of 80 adult passengers. On one voyage in 1767, however, it took on board nearly 300 passengers, and arrived at Charleston on its arrival on 25 June 1767 many were ill or dying.[275] This particular event was a significant factor in the disbanding of the

273 *SCGaz*: 31.8.1767; TNA.CO5.511
274 TNA.CO5.511
275 NRS.GD205, box 40, fo.10

bounty-system in the following year. The Passenger Acts which introduced regulations on minimum safety standards and maximum number of passengers, introduced in the nineteenth century, were still some years distant.

The Scottish participation in the settlement of Carolina during the seventeenth century developed in a number of distinct ways. There had been a steady trickle of Scots to the Chesapeake from 1607 and their numbers were inflated by almost one thousand prisoners of war sent by Oliver Cromwell around the period 1650, together with a number of felons and Covenanters banished over subsequent decades. By 1671 there is evidence of some interest within Scotland regarding the possibility of settlement in the region when the Lord Advocate was instructed to prepare a charter under the Great Seal of Scotland in favour of certain Scots, granting them the territory lying between the St Mathias River on the coast of Carolina and the southernmost part of Cape Florida.[276] Considering the relative proximity of the Spanish at St Augustine, such a project was risky and it may have been for this reason it was not followed through.

Scots could be found among the early settlers on Albemarle Sound which today forms part of North Carolina but was originally an offshoot of Virginia. The most prominent of these Scots settlers was William Drummond.[277] Little is known of this man, other than that he acted as deputy for the Governor of the district, and was executed in 1677 for

276 The Colonial Records of North Carolina, Vol. I, xii; Vol. II, p. 123; Probate October 1677, Prerogative Court of Canterbury (hereafter PCC)
277 North Carolina State Archives. (hereafter NCSA), SS978.1/26; 1/196

SCOTTISH TRADE WITH
COLONIAL CHARLESTON, 1683-1783

his part in Bacon's Rebellion. The Albemarle Sound area is also likely to have had its population boosted by Virginia settlers crossing the bay, possibly for fresh land after the soil for growing tobacco became exhausted in Virginia. Alexander Murray is noted to have made this move by 1693, as had Mary Maxwell a year later.[278] The earliest Scot known to have been in the vicinity of what is now South Carolina was a Robert Christie, a merchant from Culross in Fife, afterwards in Florida. He wrote home in 1667 to his wife, Margaret Sands, advising her of his intention to move on further south into Mexico.[279]

There was no emigration directly from Scotland to Carolina in the period before 1680 although there did exist a handful of people bearing Scottish names among the immigrants from England and from Barbados. These immigrants arriving aboard the Carolina, Captain Sullivan, from England in 1670 included Thomas Gourdon, William Lumsden, James Montgomery, Richard Alexander, and John Carmichael.[280] Similarly among the immigrants to Carolina from Barbados were time-served indentured servants such as George Gordon on the Plantation in 1679, or Alice and Robert Grigg on the Mary in 1678.[281] Scottish emigration to what is now South Carolina can be dated from 1682. In that year the Carolina Company of Scotland was

278 P Hume Brown, (ed), *Register of the Privy Council of Scotland*, 3rd series, Volume 4, Edinburgh, Scotland, 1911, p. 297
279 Warren Ripley, *Charles Towne, Birth of a City*, Charleston, South Carolina, 1998, p. 19
280 John Camden Hotten, *Original Lists of Persons of Quality and Others who went from Great Britain to the American Plantations, 1600-1700*, Baltimore, Maryland, 1983, pp. 370-372
281 Gilbert Burnett, *History of My Own Time*, Edinburgh, 1833, p.526

SCOTTISH TRADE WITH
COLONIAL CHARLESTON, 1683-1783

established with the objective of forming a plantation and trading settlement in southern Carolina. This is thought to have been a consequence of the Scottish Privy Council's Act for the Encouragement of Trade in 1681.

Some Covenanters, subject to persecution by the Scottish Government, took this opportunity to make a fresh start. The following entry in Gilbert Burnett's journal records that their leaving for the New World was not unappreciated by the government of Scotland:

> 'The Duke of York encouraged the motion as he was glad to have so many untoward people sent so far away who, he reckoned, would be ready upon the first favorable conjecture to break out into new rebellion'.[282]

In 1682 the English Proprietors of Carolina agreed to Scots' requests to settle in Carolina and allocated land on an area known as Port Royal, which lay between Charleston and the Spanish territory of Florida,[283] and accordingly, the Undertakers of the Carolina Company contracted with Walter Gibson, a merchant burgess of Glasgow, to supply a vessel to carry out an exploratory survey in Carolina.[284] The six company

282 NRS. National Register of Archives, Scotland (hereafter NRAS).0631.A20/1
283 NRS.NRAS.0631.A20/4
[284] NRS.NRAS.0631.A20/4

153

representatives on board were required to sell the cargo, and check for
navigable rivers and suitable sites for a port.   As part of this they had
to examine the soil conditions, available springs, amount of timber and
the friendliness or otherwise of the natives to ascertain the feasibility of
permanent settlement of the Port Royal area.[285]   The reconnaissance
expedition left the Clyde on the vessel James of Irvine in September
1682,[286] arriving in Charleston in March 1683, and returning to
Scotland on 4 July 1683.[287]   The results of this reconnaissance
expedition being encouraging, the Carolina Company of Scotland then
began to plan their settlement.   They first advertised for indentured
servants who, for the cost of their passage, would contract to work for
a period, and then be encouraged to remain in the colony by the offer
of an allocation by right of fifty acres of land each.[288] At the same time
the company attempted to attract emigrants who would pay their own
passages.   Walter Gibson, a prominent merchant in Glasgow, was an
agent who placed advertisements for interested individuals or families
to grasp the opportunity of a new, and possibly more prosperous, life in
the colony.[289]   Adults paying for their passages were to be charged five

285 NRS.E72.19.6
286 NRS.AC7/7; E72.19.6; NRS.NRAS.0631.600
287 NRS.NRAS.0631.A20/18
288 *Bannatyne Miscellany, Volume 3,* Edinburgh, Scotland, 1855, p. 383
289 See A S Salley jr, *Warrants for Land in South Carolina, 1672-1711,* Baltimore, Maryland,
1998

SCOTTISH TRADE WITH
COLONIAL CHARLESTON, 1683-1783

pounds sterling each, children aged two to fourteen, fifty shillings each, and there was to be no charge for an infant. Those unable to pay the cost of passage but wishing to take up the opportunity of a new life signed contracts in Scotland whereby they agreed to be sold to a colonist for a period of years labor, and in return the colonist paid the cost of his passage and gave him bed and board. Land grants were an additional incentive to those organising this provision of manpower, as they were given land in proportion to the number of servants landed. Tradesmen would require to indent for three years. The unskilled, between the ages of eighteen and forty-five, would indent for four years, and any under the age of eighteen would require to indent for five years. All servants who completed their period of indentureship, and all paying passengers, were allocated land; fifty acres for the former and seventy acres for the latter. Some of these former indentured servants who availed themselves of Gibson's offer can be identified through the South Carolina Land Warrants; Thomas Moody and his wife Mary had sailed on his ship the Carolina Merchant in 1684, and were granted one hundred acres of land on 23 July 1694.[290]

The 170 tons, Carolina Merchant, master George Lyon, left the Clyde on 21 July 1684 with 148 passengers, together with cargo, bound for Port Royal, arrived first in Charleston on 2 October 1684.[291] George Lyon, skipper of the Carolina Merchant, sold off some of the servants bound for Port Royal, at Charleston, and as a result caused the merchant

290 Henry Paton (ed), *Register of the Privy Council of Scotland*, (hereafter RPCS), 3rd Series, Volume 8, Edinburgh, Scotland, 1915, p.710; Walter McLeod, (ed), *Journal of Hon. John Erskine of Carnock, 1683-1687*, Edinburgh, Scotland, 1893, p. 72;
291 TNA. CO5.287.126]

SCOTTISH TRADE WITH
COLONIAL CHARLESTON, 1683-1783

Walter Gibson, to suffer a financial loss in respect of his expected land grants.[292]   Walter Gibson sent his other ship, the Pelican of Glasgow, whose master was his brother James Gibson, from Port Glasgow in June 1684 with 180 passengers bound for South Carolina,[293] and court records show that this voyage involved a case of kidnapping. The most famous example of kidnapping from a Scottish port was that of Peter Williamson, taken as a child of around 10 years, with other youngsters, from the streets of Aberdeen in 1743 by the shipmaster Robert Ragg in collusion with the town's merchants.   He was sold as a servant in Philadelphia, had many adventures in America, and later returned to minor celebrity in Edinburgh.[294]   Another unwilling emigrant was Elizabeth Linning, held on the ship the Pelican, Captain James Gibson, while it was docked in the Clyde, when she had boarded to say farewell to relatives being transported to Carolina. Gibson had hoped to sell her there as an indentured servant and she was only saved from this fate by the Governor of the colony hearing of her plight and ordering her release.[295]

In August 1684 another Scottish ship, whose master was Robert Malloch, sailed for Carolina bound for the Port Royal colony. This vessel evidently arrived in South Carolina by November of that year, and Malloch was awarded 3,700 acres for the 74 servants that he landed there. The landed passengers were mainly Covenanter prisoners

292 NRS.E72.19.9
293 Coldham, *Emigrants in Chains,* pp. 90-96
294 James King Hewison, *The Covenanters Volume II,* Glasgow, Scotland, 1908, p. 424
295 Paton, RPCS, 9.95

SCOTTISH TRADE WITH
COLONIAL CHARLESTON, 1683-1783

liberated from the jails of Edinburgh and forcibly transported.[296] It had been the law that prisoners were not allowed to be taken from jails and forcibly transported to the colonies, but this law was revoked on 5 May 1684 when the King authorised the Privy Council to banish any rebel who refused the Test Oath, requiring an individual's concurrence with the state's religious policies. This obligation effectively identified Covenanters, who were then arrested and as prisoners, became eligible for shipment to the Plantations.[297] It was not long before shipmasters like Gibson and Malloch were petitioning the Privy Council for these valuable prisoners and transporting them to the colony of Carolina, and also those of New York and East New Jersey.[298]

The Carolina Company of Scotland with which these shipmasters were involved was short-lived and the last document available is dated 27 October 1682. It is known that some members of the Company became disinclined to supply capital and this may have contributed to its demise, evidenced by a letter dated 29 September 1682, when the managing director, Hugh Archibald, wrote to the shareholders on the matter.[299] Court actions also provide evidence of a company in difficulties from the start, with petitioners to the High Court of the Admiralty of Scotland bringing cases of non-payment for the initial voyage of exploration in 1682 before the court. In January 1686, Robert Verner claimed that he was owed £20.0s.2p sterling in wages, plus half a rex dollar per day for time spent ashore at Charleston, and twelve shillings Scots per day for board for the boy who was left with

296 Paton, RPCS.8.508
297 Paton, RPCS.8.525; 9.111
298 Linda G Fryer, 'Documents Relating to the Formation of the Carolina Company in Scotland, 1682', *South Carolina Historical Magazine, Vol. 99,* Charleston, South Carolina, 1998, p. 123
299 NRS.AC7.7

him in Charleston.[300]   Similarly, on 6 April 1686, Patrick Crawford, a mariner in Edinburgh, sued the partners of the Carolina Company for £546 Scots for wages and expenses incurred when he went to Carolina.   Crawford stated that he had supplied a report on the colony as requested, and had made a map of it which he had handed over on his return on 4 July 1683.[301]

The Carolina Company had planned the development of the colony at Port Royal, which included the settlement at Stuartstown, intended to be laid out as a port town and the seat of justice for the county of Port Royal.[302]   The town land and the streets of Stuartstown would occupy 600 English acres, divided into 220 lots each having a garden.   No map or plan of Stuartstown appears to have survived, but one exists for the contemporary Scottish settlement of Perth Amboy in East New Jersey which reveals a similar layout.   By March 1685, forty-one town lots had been occupied by Scots, and some English colonists had joined them, with others expected to arrive from Antigua with the experience and intention to grow sugar and indigo.   One ship with emigrants from Belfast, bound for Port Royal, was wrecked off the coast of Carolina. The South Carolina Land Grants record that on 12 July 1685 an allocation of 1150 acres was made to Mr William Dunlop for himself and the twenty-three immigrants he had brought with him to the province.   On 6 October 1685, Henry Erskine, Lord Cardross, was granted 850 acres for himself and the sixteen immigrants he had brought.[303]

300 NRS.AC7.7
302 See A S Salley jr, *Warrants for Land in South Carolina, 1672-1711,* Baltimore, Maryland, 1998
303 SCHGM.30.81

SCOTTISH TRADE WITH
COLONIAL CHARLESTON, 1683-1783

Further emigration from Scotland to the settlement at Stuartstown was curtailed when a Spanish raiding party from St Augustine destroyed the township on 17 August 1686, and those who survived moved to Charleston.[304] The Spanish raid was motivated by a number of factors. Firstly, they considered the Scots to be intruders on Spanish territory; secondly, the pirate, Grammont, had taken refuge at Stuartstown in July 1686 after his unsuccessful attack on St Augustine; and thirdly the Scots had been considering annexing the former Spanish settlement at Santa Catalina.[305] The Spaniards returned to St Augustine with loot and three prisoners, one of whom was named as John Livingston, a young man from Edinburgh.[306] Although some of the survivors from the raid on Stuartstown who fled to Charleston may have settled there, there are indications that others may have gone north. A contract was drawn up in Charleston in 1687 between Lord Cardross and John Henderson, master of the Stephen of London for a voyage from Charleston to Virginia.[307] In April 1687, William Dunlop, a leading Scot at Port Royal returned from Charleston to Stuartstown and Port Royal on a reconnaissance voyage but decided against settling there again, and within two years had moved to London.[308] As a licentiate of the Church of Scotland, William Dunlop could well have acted in the role of minister to the Scots during his stay in Carolina, a post later filled by the Reverend Archibald Stobo.

304 John E Worth, *The Struggle for the Georgia Coast,* Athens, Georgia, 1995, p. 169
305 Archivo General de Indias, Seville, de Montiano, Auto fo.8
306 NRS.GD103.2.222
307 J G Dunlop, *Letters and Journals, 1663-1889,* London, England, 1953, passim
308 H Scott, *Fasti Ecclesiae Scoticanae,* Volume 7, Edinburgh, Scotland, 1928, p. 665

SCOTTISH TRADE WITH
COLONIAL CHARLESTON, 1683-1783

The only other Scots known to have settled in the area of Charleston in the seventeenth century was a group of refugees from Darien on the Isthmus of Panama, arriving in Charleston in August 1700 on the <u>Rising Sun</u> and the <u>Duke of Hamilton</u>. They had intended Charleston to be simply a port of call en-route home to Scotland but when most of the passengers and crew were ashore a hurricane arose which destroyed the ships. Most of the passengers decided to remain, the most prominent of these unexpected settlers being the Reverend Archibald Stobo. Stobo had been sent to minister to the Scots at Darien, and instead ended up establishing seven Presbyterian churches in the colony of South Carolina.[309]

By the end of the seventeenth century, hundreds of Scots had settled in South Carolina but existing records identify only a small number of them. Records of land grants prior to 1707 contain the Scottish surnames Abercromby, Abernethy, Alexander, Allan, Alston, Anderson, Annan, Burnett, Boyd, Campbell, Carmichael, Clark, Cochran, Cunningham, Drummond, Dunlop, Fenwick, Ferguson, Forbes, Fraser, Fullarton, Fulton, Gleddie, Gordon, Gourdon, Gunn, Hall, Hamilton, Johnston, Leslie, Lilly, Logan, McGregor, McKay, McLaughlin, Macley, McPherson, Macklane, Malloch, Martin, Moncur, Moody, Nairn, Paterson, Robertson, Ross, Scott, Simpson, Speir, Stevenson, Stuart, Thomson and Young.[310] The Probate Records of South Carolina dating from 1670 do not contain any wills of Scots before the year 1709. One, however, exists in New York, proved on 16 August 1693, and for a James Gilchrist, a planter in Berkley County,

309 See A S Salley jr, *Warrants for Land in South Carolina, 1672-1711*, Baltimore, Maryland, 1998
310 NRS.CC8.8.83

SCOTTISH TRADE WITH
COLONIAL CHARLESTON, 1683-1783

Carolina. Probably the first Scots merchant to settle in what is now South Carolina was a John Alexander, listed among the testaments confirmed with the Commissariat of Edinburgh.[311] This John Alexander is known to have been the son of Robert Alexander, the Clerk of Session, and that he was in South Carolina by 1687 and died there in 1699. He was possibly the Covenanter of that name, who was transported to the colony in 1684, and who was granted land in the colony in both 1694 and 1695. He acted as executor for James Gilchrist in 1693, and in 1697 was appointed by Thomas Miller, the minister of Kirkliston, to collect debts, goods, books, merchandise and rent due by residents in South Carolina.[312] John Alexander was the forerunner of the many Scottish merchants who were to settle in Charleston during the eighteenth century, and who, along with their descendants, were to become prominent merchants and planters of the colony of South Carolina in the coming century.

The political union of Scotland and England in 1707 enabled Scottish merchants and shipmasters to trade directly and without restrictions, with the former English colonies in America. Before this date, with only a few exceptions, direct trade was illegal under the English Navigation Acts, although these regulations were often flouted both by the Scots and the colonists in America. Although the trading of goods was banned by these Acts, there was no restriction on the movement of people. Since economic links were never entirely severed, it is reasonable to suppose that trading ships landed a few people as well as goods, and laid the foundations of future settlement by Scots.

311 South Carolina State Archives, (hereafter SCSA), *Records of the Secretary of the Province of South Carolina, 1692-1721.*
312 See Appendix

SCOTTISH TRADE WITH
COLONIAL CHARLESTON, 1683-1783

In the eighteenth century, Scots settlement began in South Carolina, with a steady trickle of merchants, planters, professionals, tradesmen, former soldiers and indentured servants. There is no source either in Charleston or in Scotland which identifies the names of contemporary migrant Scots, but some idea of the level of Scottish immigration can be obtained from land grants. An Appendix lists those bearing Scottish surnames, and these formed a large percentage of those awarded land grants in 1737.[313] It must be recognised, however, that it is possible that some of these individuals were from Ulster rather than Scotland, and others may have been born in America. In 1739 the Lieutenant Governor of South Carolina set aside land along the Santee River for an anticipated influx from Scotland which, in the event, did not happen. This may be explained by the fact that South Carolina was a less attractive destination when compared to North Carolina, because of the latter's bending the rules and providing financial help as outlined above. The significant numbers settling in North Carolina were for a large part from the county of Argyll.[314] At around the same time Lachlan Campbell, a land speculator, was promised a land grant in upper New York on the basis of bringing in immigrants, and though he successfully recruited from Islay and elsewhere in Argyllshire for this New York Colony, there was some delay in this promise being fulfilled.[315] Many Highlanders went to Georgia as a result of a

313 See Duane Meyer, *The Highland Scots of North Carolina, 1732-1776,* Chapel Hill, North Carolina, 1978, pp. 59-
314 See Robert A A McGeachy, 'Captain Lauchlin Campbell and Early Argyllshire Emigration to New York', *Northern Scotland,* Volume 19, Aberdeen, Scotland, 1999, pp. 21-46
315 TNA.CO5.670; Dobson, *Scottish Emigration,* pp 118-121; See Anthony W Parker, *Scottish Highlanders in Colonial Georgia. The Recruitment, Emigration and Settlement at Darien, 1735-1776',* Chapel Hill, North Carolina, 1978 passim

SCOTTISH TRADE WITH
COLONIAL CHARLESTON, 1683-1783

recruiting campaign in Inverness-shire, which was instigated by the Trustees of Georgia, who wished to find soldier-settlers for their frontier lands.[316]   It is of interest to note that all these Highland settlements were situated on the frontier between the English settlements and the potentially hostile Indians, French, and Spanish, and it might be surmised that those who sought to bring in Highlanders, viewed them as militia and positioned them to defend frontiers.   In Georgia this fact was stated at the time of recruitment, but in the case of the other colonies the Highlanders did not find out the precariousness of their settlement until after they had arrived.

Emigration from the Lowlands of Scotland in the eighteenth century did not necessarily mean it was from a Scottish port.   Many travelled via London or another English port as registers of the ports of London, Liverpool and Bristol illustrate.[317]   After the Union of the Parliaments of Scotland and England in 1707, it took some time for Scottish shipmasters to develop trade links with South Carolina but when they did, emigration was part of the enterprise, and a handful of records exist giving details of early indentured servants sailing directly from Scottish shores.   Some are manuscripts, but at least one is a printed pro-forma document.   Found among the Campbell of Barcaldine Muniments is the indenture of William Campbell, son of Hugh Campbell a tenant in Argyll, who contracted with John McLeod a resident of Edinburgh on 31 January 1737, to serve him or his assignees in Carolina for four years, during which time he was to be provided with all necessary clothes, meat, drink, washing, lodging, according to the custom of the

---

316 for example, Middlesex Guildhall, Westminster, Quarter Session Records, 1683-1684
317 NRS, Campbell of Barcaldine Muniments, GD170.3339

SCOTTISH TRADE WITH
COLONIAL CHARLESTON, 1683-1783

said Plantation.[318]   Possibly the only known indenture agreement extant in South Carolina relating to a Scot lies among the Charleston County Miscellaneous Records.   This contract was recorded in Charleston on 18 January 1729 having been written in Glasgow the previous 5 September.   In it, David Swinton, a tobacco spinner and snuff maker in Glasgow, agreed to serve Robert Paterson, a merchant in Glasgow, or his assignees, in any of His Majesty's Plantations in America for five years, certified by Walter Stirling, a Glasgow magistrate, confirming that it was a voluntary agreement.[319]

The use of printed indentureship forms in Scotland is referred to in a case brought before the High Court of the Admiralty of Scotland in 1757.   In 1753 a group of Edinburgh merchants had sent a cargo from Leith to Charleston and, as part of the evidence in a later court case held in 1757, there exists 'The Accompt of Expenses for indenting servants for going to Carolina'[320] which shows that six printed indenture forms cost a total of three shillings and nine pence.   The 'Accompt' also indicates that some of the emigrants were recruited from among the prisoners of the Canongait Tolbooth.   The total cost of forty one pounds, sixteen shillings and three and a half pence Sterling includes that of advertising for servants, purchasing the necessary indentureship

318 Charleston Public Library, Charleston County Miscellaneous Records,1
319 NRS.AC7.49.1304
320 see A. R. Ekirch, 'The Transportation of Scottish Criminals to America during the Eighteenth Century', *The Journal of British Studies, Volume 24,* Chicago, Illinois, 1985, pp.366-374; David Dobson, *Directory of Scots Banished to the American Plantations, 1650-1775,* Baltimore, Maryland, 1983; Peter Wilson Coldham, *Emigrants in Chains. A Social History of Forced Emigration to the Americas of Felons, Destitute Children, Political and Religious Non-Conformists, Vagabonds, Beggars and other Undesirables, 1607-1776,* Baltimore, Maryland, 1992

forms, feeding and accommodating prisoners prior to shipment, and transporting them to the docks of Newhaven, Midlothian.

Prisons in Scotland had, since the mid seventeenth century, been a source of emigrants for the colonies, and some felons banished to the American Plantations were temporarily imprisoned until a skipper was found to take them to America. Other prisoners occasionally volunteered to go to the colonies as indentured servants rather than remain in jail.[321] The indentured servant scheme, therefore, enabled a number of poor people to cross the Atlantic and settle there, but some individuals absconded from their masters long before completing the terms of their contracts, often due to having endured ill treatment. As valuable assets, who had had their passage paid by their master in return for their period of indentureship, much effort was expended in tracking down these runaways and returning them to their master's service. Advertisements were placed in local newspapers such as the Virginia Gazette, the Maryland Gazette, or the South Carolina Gazette. Every copy of these publications of the period carried advertisements for indentured servants or slaves who have absconded, examples being:

> ...'Isabel Shaw, middle size, well set round visage, she had on a deep green camblet gown and a black hat, she was born in Glasgow but speaks indifferent good English and is about nineteen years of age, absconded from Joseph Dapson, tailor in Middle Street, Charleston'.[322]

321 *SCGaz*.16.2.1734
322 *SCGaz*.14.7.1733

SCOTTISH TRADE WITH
COLONIAL CHARLESTON, 1683-1783

>...'Runaway from Captain Thomas Baillie, a servant man
named Robert Broke, aged about twenty-five years, and speaks
broad Scots.   Whoever apprehends the aid servant, to be
brought to James Smallwood in Charleston, shall have a £5
reward'.[323]

Servants were often recruited for their specific skills and
advertisements, such as this example, would appear in the newspapers
in Scotland:

>'Wanted to go to Grenada.   A cartwright and a blacksmith,
properly qualified in their respective trades, who will meet with
good encouragement by applying to Adam Duncan, lint-dresser
in the Gallowgate.   They must be speedy in their application as
the gentleman they are to serve intends they should go out in
the first fleet from London.'[324]

The skilled worker recruited directly was not sold in the same manner
as the usual indentured servants.   Like them, they would have been
required to work for a period of time for their master to repay their
passage, but would not have been auctioned off at the colonial arrival
port of arrival in the same manner as Africans who were bound for
slavery.   A merchant skipper from Leith, Andrew Cowan, advertised
in 1753 that he had for sale:

>'...an assortment of Scots manufactures, including saddles,
mahogany desks, wigs, books, bibles, good red wine, mustard,

323 *Aberdeen Journal*, No 1619, 1.1779
324 *SCGaz*.16.11.1753

barley and coal, at his store. And also several tradesmen of good character, under four-year indentures, among whom are joiners, house carpenters, shipwrights. Any person inclined to purchase any may have them on trial before he makes a bargain. NB merchantable rice, pitch, tar, turpentine, mahogany, deerskin, beaver, or indigo will be taken in payment at market prices provided it be mentioned at making the bargain.'[325]

The first major migration of Scots to the American colonies in the eighteenth century was a group of Jacobites prisoners, transported involuntarily in the wake of the failure of the Jacobite Rising of 1715.[326] These had risen in rebellion against the House of Hanover, with the aim of replacing King George with James Stuart of the House of Stuart to the throne of Great Britain. Supporters of the Jacobite cause were to be found throughout the British Isles, but by far the greatest numbers were in Scotland. This was for a variety of reasons including nationalism and religion. Those who took up arms in support of the Jacobite cause came largely from the conservative, Episcopalian north east, between Perth and Aberdeen, and the Catholic clans of the Highlands.[327] Pockets of supporters came also from the Lowlands of Scotland, from those who hoped that a return of the Stuarts would see a return of their previous influence, or a repeal of laws which they found to their disadvantage. Much of the population of northern England,

[325] See Dobson, *Banished Scots*, passim
326 See David Dobson, *Jacobites of the '15,* Aberdeen, Scotland, 1993
327 Cecil Headlam, *Calendar of State Papers, America and West Indies, 1716,* London, 1930; *Calendar of Treasury Books, 1716,* London, England, 1958

SCOTTISH TRADE WITH
COLONIAL CHARLESTON, 1683-1783

particularly Northumberland and Lancashire, had remained Catholic or at least were High Anglicans, and for wished to see the return of a Stuart king for reasons of religion. The Scottish campaign culminated in the indecisive Battle of Sheriffmuir on 13 November 1715, with both sides claiming victory. On the same day the Jacobites surrendered after the Siege of Preston, marking also the end of the English campaign. The Jacobite army which fought at Preston, Lancashire, contained a substantial number of Scots as well as men from northern England. Prisoners from both these battles were tried in England, and faced either execution or transportation. Of the latter, around 600 prisoners were sent to the colonies to work as indentured servants, and 185 of these arrived in South Carolina, aboard the Wakefield and the Susannah out of Liverpool in the Spring of 1716.[328]

As might be expected, a high proportion of these Jacobite transportees were both Highland and Lowland Scots and, as transportees, they had no choice but to sign indentureship forms, enabling them to be sold on arrival. They brought with them a range of skills useful to the development of the colonial economy. After their period of indentureship, their exile precluded a return to their native land, and although very few records verify this, it is believed that most stayed as on settlers in the Carolinas. Among those transported on the Susannah in 1716 were John Crockett, later a merchant in Charleston, Thomas Guild, from Glamis, later a planter in Colleton County, South Carolina, and James Johnston from Aberdeen, who settled in New Windsor, South Carolina and died there in 1744.[329] Of those transported on the

328 probate South Carolina, 1759, 1737, 1744; Aberdeen Burgh Archives, Aberdeen Proprinquity Book, Volume 3, folio 122
329 Dobson, *Scottish Emigration*, 118

SCOTTISH TRADE WITH
COLONIAL CHARLESTON, 1683-1783

<u>Wakefield</u> many were Highlanders who had fought at Preston under Brigadier William Macintosh of Borlum. Most of Borlum's men were originally from Inverness-shire, and this created an early link between Inverness and the American South. Twenty years later, when settlers with martial skills were needed in neighbouring Georgia, all were recruited from the areas in and around Inverness.[330]

A native of Inverness-shire is mentioned in the South Carolina Probate Records which holds the testament of Myles Macintosh from Delarish, dated 26 March 1729. As Macintosh was not among the Jacobite transportees, it might be assumed that he emigrated there voluntarily, perhaps encouraged by fellow countrymen who had arrived in 1716. A copy of his testament also was entered in the Sheriff Court Books of Inverness [331] on 8 March 1728 and it reveals his executors in Charleston were Andrew Allen, William McKenzie and Duncan McQueen. Allen was a burgess and guilds-brother of Glasgow, as well as a member of the St Andrews Society of Charleston, and Mackenzie and McQueen had arrived in Charleston as Jacobite transportees.[332] Myles Macintosh's widow in Delarish, Inverness-shire, Margaret McBean, in an assignation dated 20 December 1734, described her late husband as '*sometime tenant in Kellochie, thereafter an Indian trader in Charleston.*' A number of Scots are known to have become involved in various aspects of the Indian trade during and after the colonial

330 NRS.SC9.55.6.257
331 *Calendar of Treasury Books, Volume XXXI* ,London, England, 1960, fo.205
332 Charleston Public Library, Charleston County Inventories, Volume 60, fo.196

period. These Indian traders exchanged manufactured goods for Indian deerskins, which were to become a major component of the export trade of contemporary South Carolina.

Another Highlander who became established in South Carolina was Daniel McGregor whose inventory, dated February 1724, lists among his assets eleven Negro slaves and their four children, as well as six horses, fifty head of cattle, guns, tools and domestic goods, altogether valued at £2,131.[333]

As mentioned, contrary to popular belief, not all Jacobites had their origin in the Highlands of Scotland. Part of the Jacobite army that was captured after the Siege of Preston in 1715 had been raised in south-east Scotland,[334] and therefore many of the transportees had their origins in the Lowlands. This fact may explain why Charleston merchants bearing surnames from the Lothians and Borders were found in South Carolina in the 1720s and 1730s. Some Jacobite transportees of 1716 became merchants and founding members of the St Andrews Society of Charleston when it was established in 1729, and this would indicate they had achieved economic and social success there.[335] Others despatched from in chains from Liverpool to the Chesapeake belonged to minor gentry families from the south east of Scotland; men such as Francis Home of Wedderburn,[336] whose cousin Alexander

333 see David Dobson, *Jacobites of the '15,* Aberdeen, 1993, passim
334 See Appendix
335 Calendar of Virginia State Papers, Volume I, Richmond, Virginia, p. 185; Cecil Headlam, *Calendar of State Papers, America and the West Indies, 1716,* London, England, 1930, p. 310; Calendar of Treasury Books, Volume 31, London, England, 1958, p.208
336 Thomas Lane Ormiston, *Ormistons of Teviotdale,* Exeter, England, 1951, p. 91

SCOTTISH TRADE WITH
COLONIAL CHARLESTON, 1683-1783

Spotswood was Governor of Virginia at the time.   Home had administered his estate in Berwickshire, and on arrival in Virginia, he transferred these skills his cousin's estate. He also encouraged friends and relatives to move from Scotland to Virginia and among those who came were George Home, a surveyor.[337]   Unfortunately, there is no evidential documentation to show that a similar pattern as above happened in Charleston, but it would seem reasonable to assume that it did.

Since the slaves of the colony provided all the manual labor required, the demand was for skilled labor.   The economy of South Carolina reflected that of Barbados, an island in the Caribbean from which many of the original settlers came.   It was a plantation economy which utilised the labor of slaves, first the Native American, then African. The diseases which whites brought with them killed many of the Native Americans, and those who survived illness were able to escape enslavement with relative ease.   African slaves were first brought to the colony of South Carolina from the West Indies, then, as demand increased, directly from the continent of Africa.   In the labor market, the demand was for skilled or semi-skilled Europeans.   Craftsmen and tradesmen of all types as well as physicians and other professional people were encouraged to immigrate.   Disease also threatened whites in the colony; unused as they were to the conditions of a semi-tropical climate, and the relatively high death rate among the white colonists added to the constant requirement for skilled labor.   Most whites lived

337 See Appendix

SCOTTISH TRADE WITH
COLONIAL CHARLESTON, 1683-1783

in the towns of Charleston, Georgetown and other settlements.   On the plantations, apart from the planter and his family and a handful of white overseers, the majority of people were black.

South Carolina was, therefore, not a major destination for emigrants from Scotland but it did offer opportunities for people with specialised skills.   One such group were surgeons and physicians.   Scotland, especially the Medical School of Edinburgh University was producing far more physicians than the country could absorb, and as a result these doctors and surgeons sought opportunities elsewhere.   They joined the East India Company, relocated to England, or looked west, to the new American colonies.   In the colonial period, it is believed that about 150 Scottish medical graduates settled in the American colonies, of whom, 21 surgeons and physicians have been identified as practicing in Charleston and in South Carolina before the outbreak of the American Revolution in 1776.[338]   At the same time, over one hundred Americans left the colonies to study medicine in Scotland.   Being a relatively affluent colony, from a total number of 102 American medical students, 18 were from South Carolina.[339]

The skills which the American colonies required were not limited to the professions, and security against the Indians, French and Spanish or an uprising by slaves, demanded that a number of able bodied soldiers be recruited to defend the colony.   For this reason the colonial government

338 William R Brock, *Scotus Americanus. A Survey of the Sources for links between Scotland and America in the 18th century*, Edinburgh, Scotland, 1980, p. 118; T M Devine, *Scotland's Empire, 1600-1815*, London, England, 2003, pp 165-166
339 *Journal of the Commons House of Assembly* (hereafter JCHA), Volume V, fo.363

would occasionally offer bounties to those who successfully encouraged male servants from the British Isles. Some Jacobite rebels who were landed in 1716 were purchased by the government for employment as soldiers. On 1 August 1716 the Deputy Governor told the Commons House of Assembly that because he considered attacks by Indians on the colony to be imminent, he had bought *"thirty of the Highland Scots rebels at Thirty Pounds per head and would have taken more if he had the funds.'*[340] Three days later the Commons passed an act providing money to buy a further thirty two white servants, presumably more Jacobites. In 1717 payment was made *'the sume of one hundred and sixty pounds to Robert Gilcrest for his own and his man'sservice to the Public in his late Journey to and from the Cherikees'*[341]

In 1726, in order to keep down defence costs, the Assembly proposed that they should encourage *'Captain Stewart, or some other such person'*[342] be encouraged to bring over a number of indentured servants to man the forts. They offered him £40 to £50 for each person who would indent for four years. Captain Stewart was to *'be obliged to produce proper certificates from the Mayor of Bristol that they [his immigrants] are not convicts ...''*[343] The authorities were clearly attempting to control or prevent numbers of felons being imported, but in spite of this, two years later Stewart had among his immigrants eighteen men and six women who had been sentenced to seven years

340 JCHA.V, fos.153-158
341 JCHA.VII.fos.76-391
342 JCHA.VII.fos.76-391
343 PCR.1727-1729, fo.253

for felony.[344]   In 1712 the same Council passed a law imposing a fine
of £25 on those who imported felons from Great Britain.   One of the
few shiploads of felons from Scotland were aboard the John and Robert
of Gourock, master Thomas Clark, sailing on 23 October 1728 from
Greenock bound for South Carolina with twenty-eight convicts taken
from the jails of Glasgow and Edinburgh.[345]   Relatively few felons
were banished from Scotland to colonial America, perhaps only
approximately four hundred in total, most of whom were petty
criminals.   In comparison, during the colonial period nearly fifty
thousand convicts were shipped from England to America, and over
thirteen thousand despatched from Ireland.[346] Ordinary criminal
transportees from Scotland were greatly outnumbered by the religious
and political: rebel Covenanters and Jacobites exiled to the American
Plantations.[347]   The reason why England transported far more felons
than did Scotland was because Scots law protected prisoners guilty of
civil crimes from transportation.   While rebels could be transported
without restriction, ordinary criminals had to agree or volunteer to be
shipped in chains to the colonies and there to work for several years as
indentured servants, and it was the case that many Scots prisoners
considered working as indentured servants preferable to serving long

344 *Edinburgh Evening Courant*, No 559
345 See Peter Wilson Coldham, *British Emigrants in Bondage*, Baltimore, Maryland, 2004
346 See David Dobson, *Directory of Scots Banished to the American Plantations, 1650-1775,*
Baltimore, Maryland, 1983
347 Peter Wilson Coldham, *Emigrants in Chains, A Social History of Forced Emigration to the
Americas of Felons, Destitute Children, Political and Religious Non-Conformists, Vagabonds,
Beggars and other Undesirables, 1607-1776,* Baltimore, Maryland, 1992, p. 89

prison terms.   In 1766 Scots Law was changed to be in line with the established English practice and then Scottish courts began also to deport felons to the American Plantations.[348]

In 1717 Sir Robert Montgomerie of Skelmorlie, son of one of the Undertakers of the Scots Carolina Company, published his *Discourse Concerning the Designed Establishment of a New Colony to the South of Carolina in the Most Delightful Country of the Universe.*[349] Skelmorlie was proposing the formation of a new colony lying to the south of the existing boundary of Carolina, between the Savannah and Altamaha Rivers.   Such a plan required further encroachment on territory claimed by Spain and was bound to be resisted by the Spanish who had already mounted intermittent attacks on the southern settlements of Carolina. Montgomerie's plan included the development of an agricultural economy which would supply Great Britain with products such as silk, wine, olives, almonds, currents and raisons, up to then coming from countries around the Mediterranean.   'Margravate of Azelia,' the name given to Montgomerie's proposed colony, was never created, but the underlying ideas were incorporated into plans for the development of Georgia in the 1730s.

Georgia was established as a private Proprietary colony in 1732 and remained so until 1752 when it reverted to the direct control of the King of Great Britain, and it remained a Royal colony until the time of the American Revolution. During this colonial period Georgia had strong links with South Carolina, with Charleston being the centre of economic and social activity. The first emigrant ship that left England bound for Georgia was the Ann, sailing on 17 November 1732 from

---

348 Robert Montgomerie, *A Discourse Concerning the Designed Establishment of a New Colony to the South of Carolina in the Most Delightful Country of the Universe,* London, England, 1717

SCOTTISH TRADE WITH
COLONIAL CHARLESTON, 1683-1783

Gravesend with one hundred and fifteen passengers of forty family groups and a number of individuals. It arrived at Charleston on 13 January 1733 before disembarking at Beaufort, South Carolina en route for Georgia, where they arrived on 1 February 1733. Among this pioneer group of emigrants were people bearing the Scots surnames Gordon, Muir, Christie, Scott and Cameron, which may indicate a number of two-stage migrants,[350] that is people who had moved to London seeking their fortune and not finding it there, moved on to the colonies. Shortly afterwards, Georgia was attracting emigrants directly from Scotland, and this from two distinct groups and localities. Lowland farmers and merchants settled for the most part in the vicinity of Savannah, and Highlanders, recruited in the main to defend the colony from Spanish incursions, were settled about thirty miles south of Savannah at a place called Darien, otherwise known as New Inverness. [351]

The first party of Lowland settlers left Leith aboard the <u>Hope of Inverkeithing</u> in March 1734, arriving in Charleston on 17 May 1734 en route for Georgia.[352] The first party of Highlanders bound for Georgia left Inverness on the <u>Prince of Wales</u> on 21 October 1735 and sailed directly there, arriving at Tybee Roads in January 1736.[353] Most

349 *See* E Merton Coulter and Albert B. Saye, *A List of the Early Settlers of Georgia,* Baltimore, Maryland, 1983, *passim*
350 David Dobson, *Scottish Emigration to Colonial America, 1607-1785,* Athens, Georgia, 2004, pp. 115-121
351 TNA.CO5.509; *SCGaz*.1.5.1734
352 *Caledonian Mercury,* No 5902, dated 19.10.1759
353 TNA.CO5.670

SCOTTISH TRADE WITH
COLONIAL CHARLESTON, 1683-1783

Lowlanders settled along the Savannah and Ogeechee Rivers where they set about developing farms or plantations. The Trustees for Georgia were against slavery, and this meant that the costs of the settler's produce was uncompetitive with that of the unpaid slave labor of neighboring colonies; a fact which caused many to abandon their land in Georgia and moved north to South Carolina where black slaves could be used without restriction both on plantations and in the towns.

More settlers were needed to farm the lands and develop the economy in other ways, and during the eighteenth-century advertisements were placed in Scottish newspapers to encourage recruitment of emigrants for South Carolina:[354]

> 'These are to give notice to all tradesmen and others that incline to go abroad as servants or otherwise to His Majesty's colony of South Carolina, that Captain James Craigie, commander of the <u>Allan</u> galley now lying in Leith Road, and bound for the said colony may be spoke with at the Exchange Coffee House in Edinburgh any week day betwixt two and three in the afternoon and the whole forenoon at the Coffee House in Leith where he will give all due encouragement to such as incline to go with him. The ship will sail with all convenient speed.'

Merchants, who often had a share of the vessels which plied trade between Scotland and the colonies, sent manufactured goods west, and encouraged passengers to take up any space that was available. An example of such an advertisement appeared in the Caledonian Mercury, published in Edinburgh:

354 *Edinburgh Evening Courant*, No 506, 25.6.1728

SCOTTISH TRADE WITH
COLONIAL CHARLESTON, 1683-1783

'For Charleston, South Carolina, To sail the end of October from Borrowstoneness, the ship Industry, two hundred tons, mounting six carriage guns, is now ready to take in goods. Any intending to ship goods or take passage by her will please apply to John and Robert Cowan, merchants there, who will also give proper encouragement to tradesmen choosing to come under indentures to live at Charleston. NB Any gentlemen in Leith or Edinburgh who have goods to send in freight will have them brought from Leith to the ship free.'[355]

In the case of felons, the shipmaster or merchant received payment for the passage from the government, and, as with normal indentureship, on arrival an additional payment would be received for the sale of the indentureship contract. A felon's indentureship usually lasted longer than others and this between seven to fourteen years, after which he was free to settle in the colonies but was not at liberty to return to Great Britain. Some, who travelled as a regular volunteer for indentureship, became felons by jumping ship as soon as it docked in Charleston. One such was Henry Lawson, a tailor, who absconded from the Industry, master Hercules Angus, when it arrived in Charleston from Bo'ness in January 1759.[356] This particular ship is the one above which advertised for passengers as well as goods. Evidence of indentured servants is to be found in various sources, one being probate records. In the South

355 Caledonian Mercury, #5902, 19 October 1759
356 *SCGaz*, No 1329
357 Charleston Public Library, South Carolina Probate Court Records, 1736-1739, fos.299-300

178

SCOTTISH TRADE WITH
COLONIAL CHARLESTON, 1683-1783

Carolina Probate Court Records[357] the estate of Thomas Lynch, a Carolina Probate Court Records[358] planter, includes as assets:

> 'One servant Alexander Agnen {Agnew?} and wife, for one year's service, £50, one boy James McDonal, for 5 years £50, one Gilbert Guthrie, for three and a half years, £35, one David Guthrie, for two and a half years, £40, and one Robert Jones, two and a half years, £40.'

The surnames suggest that these indentured servants were probably of Scots origin, although it is possible that they came from Ireland, which was one of the two major sources of immigrants to America during the eighteenth century. Although most vessels bound for Charleston sailed from the Clyde or the Forth, some left from Dundee and Orkney. In December 1732, the snow <u>Jerviswood</u>, master Thomas Baillie, arrived in Charleston from Orkney with a cargo of salt and twelve servants.[359] Thomas Baillie was a member of the Baillie of Jerviswood family from the Scottish Borders. His brother John, a merchant in Edinburgh, had already been granted four hundred acres in the newly established colony of Georgia and the servants voyaging on the <u>Jerviswood</u> may well have been destined for Georgia and the Baillie plantation. Thomas himself was granted five hundred acres in Georgia in 1735, and, at a later date, more Baillies followed from Scotland. The family became a prominent one among the Scots merchants and planters in colonial Georgia, but owing to their allegiance to the Crown during the American War of Independence, some found it expedient to return to Scotland, or to relocate to the West Indies after 1783.[360] The case of the Baillies

358 *SCGaz*, No 51
359 TNA.AO12.101.94; AO12.74.101
360 See Dobson, *Scottish Emigration,* pp. 140-141

179

illustrates how an initial trading voyage could lead to settlement and subsequent chain migration.

Migration was once more boosted after the failure of the Jacobite Rebellion in 1746. This resulted in the involuntary transportation of nearly one thousand men, women and children to colonial America, where they were sold off as indentured servants, and as exiles, never allowed to return to Great Britain. These transportees settled the colonies of the Chesapeake and the West Indies, and were put to work on sugar or tobacco plantations. It is notable that none can be found to have worked on the rice or indigo plantations of South Carolina. Macdonells from Inverness-shire. This was a Roman Catholic family, which had given active support to the Jacobite cause and who, with many of their clansmen, found it expedient to leave Scotland for upper New York in 1773.[361] The Jacobite family of Ogilvie of Auchiries in Aberdeenshire was another which had supported of the Stuarts for generations, culminating in their participation at Culloden. William Ogilvie fled to Virginia after 1746 and died there in 1750. His twin brother John, a physician, took refuge in St Eustatia, in the Dutch West Indies. In 1744, James Ogilvie, another brother, became a merchant in Charleston and on his death in 1750 his business was taken over by Charles, yet another brother, who in 1761 moved to London leaving his plantations in South Carolina to be cared for by his nephew George Ogilvie. This George Ogilvie was a Loyalist who chose to return home in 1778 during the American Revolution. A kinsman of the Ogilvie

361 See Aberdeen University Library, Ogilvie-Forbes of Boyndlie Papers, MS2740; Barbara De Wolfe, *Discoveries of America, Personal Accounts of British Emigrants to North America during the Revolutionary Era,* Cambridge, England, 1997, pp. 187-206

family, one Alexander Cumine from Aberdeenshire, also emigrated to South Carolina where he became a merchant and later a schoolmaster in Beaufort before he too, as a Loyalist, in 1783 felt compelled to remove to Kingston, Jamaica.[362]

Episcopal clergymen generally supported the House of Stuart and the Jacobite cause, and they also found it beneficial to emigrate because of the diminishing opportunities to minister to congregations in Scotland. This had been a factor of their choosing the new world since the hasty departure of King James VII from London to France in 1689.   James Blair, once a clergyman in Banffshire, settled in Virginia around 1690 and attained fame as the Commissary of Virginia and co-founder of the College of William and Mary.[363]   Alexander Baron, a student in 1745 at King's College, Aberdeen, who probably had Jacobite sympathies, left for South Carolina in 1748 to work as a schoolmaster, and later as an Episcopal minister of St Helen's parish until his death in 1759.[364] Dr David Oliphant of Edinburgh was another professional man and active Jacobite who took refuge in South Carolina, settling in Charleston to set up in partnership with Dr John Murray and Dr John Linning, another two Scots.[365]

362 NRS.RD2.59.439; P J Anderson, *The Officers and Graduates of King's College, Aberdeen, Volume II* Aberdeen, Scotland, 1893, p. 234; Michael Olmert, *The Official Guide to Colonial Williamsburg,* Williamsburg, Virginia, 1997, p. 92
363 Old Scots Church Gravestone, Charleston, South Carolina;TNA.AO13.90.60
364 NRS.RD3.235.265
365 NRS.RH2.4.561/20; See *The Scots Magazine*, Volume XXII, April, 1760, Edinburgh, Scotland, p.211

SCOTTISH TRADE WITH
COLONIAL CHARLESTON, 1683-1783

France's support for Scotland in the Jacobite cause was in part an attempt to weaken the military effectiveness of the British army by diverting regiments from the continent to Scotland. The Seven Years War, 1756-1763, which followed the crushing of the Jacobites could be hailed as perhaps the first global conflict involving the continents of Asia, America and Europe. In America it was known as the French and Indian War, beginning in 1755 and ending in 1760, and in South Carolina a related campaign was known as the Cherokee War, and this occurred between 1760 and 1761. In order to defend British interests, the government found it necessary to recruit heavily thoughout the land to raise new regiments, and to this end they turned their attention to the remnants of the clan system in the devastated Scottish Highlands. Two of these new regiments, the 77th [Montgomery's Highlanders] and the 78th [Fraser's Highlanders], went on to play a significant role in North America in both defence and subsequent settlement, and in South Carolina the prominent fighting regiments were the 1st [Royal Scots] and the 77th Regiment, commonly called the Montgomery's Highlanders.[366]

The peace which followed these wars saw a great expansion in land for settlement. This in turn caused it to be more attractive for immigration, and as this which increased rapidly the economy of the American colonies began to flourish. The removal of the threat of French imperialist aggression, together with their Spanish and Indian allies, enabled them to push the frontiers westward. At the same time, Great Britain had taken Canada for the British Empire from the French, as well as several French West Indian islands and Spanish Florida. The

366 J. Revill, A Compilation of the Original Lists of Protestant Immigrants to South Carolina, 1763-1773, Columbia, South Carolina, 1939, p. 113

182

next step was to populate these territories with loyal subjects. Since land was made available free, or at a nominal price, in these new colonies they were soon attracting speculators, investors and settlers from the existing Thirteen Colonies and from the British Isles.

There seems to have been a steady trickle of emigrants from Scotland bound for South Carolina.   Little evidence for this exists in Scottish sources, but the colonial land records show the names of some of these people. The South Carolina Council Journal contains petitions from recently arrived immigrants who request land grants. For example, on 30 May 1768 a group of men, heads of households, petitioned for and were each granted 100 acres between the Savannah and Saludy Rivers. These twelve men, all Protestants, had arrived from Great Britain on the snow Kinnoull, master Alexander Alexander, in 1768.[367]   The Kinnoull is a vessel known to have voyaged with regularity between Leith and Charleston between 1766 and 1771.[368]

More immigrants had their passage paid for them.   These were the substantial numbers of soldiers which the British government had recruited throughout the British Isles for service in America during the period of the war gave many a taste for life in this new land, and many chose to remain behind at the end of hostilities.[369]   These soldiers wished to avail themselves of the land offered, an opportunity they

368 David Dobson, *Ships from Scotland to America, 1628-1828, Volume II,* Baltimore, Maryland, p. 94
369 For example, soldiers of the 78th [Fraser's Highlanders] Regiment discharged in Canada in October 1763, in Public Archives of Canada, R/G4.C2.Volume 1.

SCOTTISH TRADE WITH
COLONIAL CHARLESTON, 1683-1783

would be unlikely to have at home.   It was the government, however, which gained most advantage.   They avoided the cost of transporting the men back across the Atlantic to Europe; and more importantly, they could now settle experienced fighting men in strategic locations, particularly on the frontier, and be able to call on them for military service in time of conflict.   This policy was aimed at combating Indian incursions, but in the course of events supplied the British Crown with many of the Loyalist soldiers who fought in the American Revolutionary War.

The majority of former soldiers were settled on land grants in the former French colonies, especially Quebec, and also in the Mohawk Valley of Upper New York, some of these becoming tradesmen or merchants in colonial ports.   Letters sent home by soldiers during and after the French and Indian war stimulated more interest in emigration to America, which contributed to the rise in the numbers of immigrants, notably from the Highlands of Scotland.   The decade or so after the Peace of Paris, dated 1763, witnessed the highest level of emigration to British settlements of the colonial period.

While many of the demobilised soldiers opted to settle in the northern colonies, some chose to settle in the South, travelling along The Great Wagon Road.   They were joined in far larger numbers by the Scotch-Irish and Germans, which were the two major groups of immigrants at this period.   Arriving to collect colonial produce, especially flax-seed and timber, Irish ships disembarked linen, general provisions and indentured servants.   German immigrants, who generally boarded ships in Rotterdam, also landed in Philadelphia, the main port of entry in America.   The Great Wagon Road was the main route south.   From Philadelphia, it wound though Pennsylvania, Maryland, the Shenandoah Valley, the Carolinian Piedmont, and ended in Augusta.

SCOTTISH TRADE WITH
COLONIAL CHARLESTON, 1683-1783

The oaths of loyalty to the Crown taken by the former officers and men who went on to settle in America after 1763 meant that they could be recalled for duty, and this is exactly what occurred at the outbreak of the American Revolution in 1776. These men formed the nucleus of Loyalist units raised, units such as the King's Royal Regiment of New York and the 84th [Royal Highland Emigrant] Regiment. The collection of documents known as the Loyalist Claims, dating from around 1783, identify a number of Scots who had settled in the colonies after the French and Indian War and who had been recalled to the colors in 1776.[370] Among those who had settled in South Carolina was John Chisholm, a native of Ross-shire, who is shown to have fought in the 77th [Montgomery's Highlanders] Regiment in America, later settling in Camden, South Carolina, as a merchant. During the Revolutionary War, he acted as a guide to the 64th Regiment, before moving to Kingston, Jamaica.[371] Another was William Geekie from Arbroath, Angus. Geekie was discharged from the Royal Navy in 1763 and settled as a planter at Goose Creek, near Charleston. During the American War of Independence, he again served in the Royal Navy and afterwards returned home to Scotland.[372]

The decade following the end of the French and Indian War of 1755-1763, which effectively ended in 1760 with the French defeat, saw a phenomenal rise in the level of emigration from Great Britain to Colonial America. Such were the numbers emigrating, that in 1773 an alarmed British Government ordered the Boards of Customs in England

370 See Peter Wilson Coldham, *American Migrations, 1765-1799*, Baltimore, 2000
371 TNA.AO12.49.417
372 TNA.AO12.50.138

SCOTTISH TRADE WITH
COLONIAL CHARLESTON, 1683-1783

and in Scotland to keep records of those leaving the country. Customs officials at every port in Great Britain were required to note the names of those travelling, their ages, occupations, former places of residence, destinations and reasons for leaving. The contemporary Irish Parliament did not order a such a register be kept of emigrants from Ireland; a fact much regretted by emigration historians today. These official port records, collectively known as the Register of Emigrants 1773-1774, [373] though incomplete, are the only record extant of a nationwide survey of emigration from Great Britain during the American colonial period. In total, nine thousand three hundred and sixty-four emigrants were identified as leaving an English or Scottish port for the American colonies, and show that nearly four-thousand in number were Scots. One hundred and three emigrants were bound for South Carolina, but of these, only twenty-two were Scots.[374] One of the vessels, the <u>Countess of Dumfries of Ayr</u>, sailed from Greenock with seventeen passengers including six farmers, four merchants, a joiner, a weaver, a shoemaker, and a tailor, all from the Lowlands. [375] The other vessel, the <u>Jamaica Packet of Burntisland</u>, left Kirkcaldy with five passengers bound for Charleston.[376] All of these passengers came from the burgh of Dundee; two were joiners, one a laborer, and one a servant. This same vessel, described in Janet Schaw's Journal of a

373 TNA.T47.12
374 TNA.T47.12
375 TNA T47.12
376 E W Andrews (ed), *Journal of a Lady of Quality:Being the narrative of a Journey from Scotland to the West Indies, North Carolina, and Portugal in the years 1774 to 1776,* New Haven, Connecticut, 1922

SCOTTISH TRADE WITH
COLONIAL CHARLESTON, 1683-1783

Lady of Quality,[377] had a further fifteen Scots emigrants bound for Wilmington, North Carolina.

The Register of Emigrants for the period 1773-1774 was analysed by Bernard Bailyn, who published his findings which established that South Carolina was far less popular with Scottish emigrants than were the neighboring colonies of North Carolina and Georgia.   Bailyn categorised emigrants under different groups.   Under 'destinations of people travelling in families' he found that 405 Scots went to North Carolina, 110 went to Georgia, and only 2 went to South Carolina.[376] In total, during this time only 22 Scots emigrated to South Carolina, while by comparison, 1076 moved to North Carolina, and 198 went to Georgia.   As a percentage of the total Scots emigrants, 0.6% settled in South Carolina, 27.8% settled in North Carolina, and 5.1% settled in Georgia.[377] It can be seen, therefore, that South Carolina was not a popular destination for Scots emigrants at this time, and one of the reasons must have included the fact that the colonial authorities there provided no financial assistance to immigrants from the Highlands while neighboring North Carolina did.   Another reason would have been that South Carolina had no demand for unskilled or semi-skilled immigrants because all such work was carried out by slaves.

376 Bernard Bailyn, *Voyagers to the West. A Passage in the Peopling of America on the Eve of the Revolution,* New York, New York, 1986, pp210-211
377 ibid, Voyagers, pp. 206

SCOTTISH TRADE WITH
COLONIAL CHARLESTON, 1683-1783

By the close of the colonial period the Scots had become well established in South Carolina and Charleston in particular, some achieving governorship of the colony. One of the most successful governors of South Carolina was James Glen from Linlithgow,[378] and the last to hold this office was also a Scot, Lord William Campbell.[379] The unfortunate timing of his arrival, however, on the eve of the American Revolution, caused his tenure to be very brief. Among the merchant classes and physicians Scots were especially prominent, but they could be found among all the trades and professions. In rural areas, Scots were planters and Indian traders. Many were connected through bonds of blood and business and the networks were cemented by the existence of the Presbyterian Church, the St Andrew's Society [380] the Masonic Lodge; all which also linked them to the more numerous Ulster Scots otherwise known as the Scotch-Irish. A considerable number of South Carolina Scots took up the Loyalist cause in 1776, and when the town of Charleston fell to the Americans, many of these Loyalists fled to St Augustine, East Florida, and from there to Nova Scotia, the Bahamas, the West Indies, London, or home to Scotland.[381] Some who had left South Carolina in 1783 returned, and trading links with Scotland were restored, as was emigration. In 1784 and 1785 newspapers in Glasgow were again promoting passages available to America. The Glasgow Mercury, in June 1784, advertised that the ship the <u>Wilmington</u>, master James Harvie, was in Greenock bound for Charleston, South Carolina, and Wilmington, North Carolina.

378 ibid.p206
379. NRS.NRAS.#03336; NRS.GD215; NRS.GD45.2.44; NRS.GD30
380. TNA.AO12.101.141
381 see Coldham, *American Migrations*, pp.654-751

SCOTTISH TRADE WITH
COLONIAL CHARLESTON, 1683-1783

'...passengers wanted, house and ship-carpenters, block-makers, blacksmiths, coopers, bricklayers and tailors, willing to indent will meet with good encouragement.'[382]

Despite the hostility which had existed during the period of the American War of Independence, the world of commerce reasserted itself without delay. Emigration patterns, however, had changed, and the focus of Scottish, especially Highland, emigration turned to Canada.

[383] *Glasgow Mercury,* Volume XII, #605.246

SCOTTISH TRADE WITH
COLONIAL CHARLESTON, 1683-1783

CHAPTER FIVE

SCOTS MERCHANTS OF CHARLESTON
AND THE TRANSATLANTIC SLAVE TRADE

One of the single most important aspects of transatlantic commerce in
the colonial period was the slave trade.   The following pages will
address the extent to which Scottish companies and individuals were
involved in this trade in human beings, and will examine the question
of whether their involvement was direct or in an ancillary role.   It will
consider how far Scots participated in each of the main activities of the
slave trade, the collection and selection of African natives from the
coasts of Africa, their shipment across the Atlantic to the colonies and
their subsequent sale to slave owners.   Particular attention will be given
to the contribution of Scots in South Carolina to this branch of
contemporary commerce and details will be given outlining the amount
and type of evidence which exists to establish the extent to which
colonial Charleston Scots were involved in slavery.

The origins of transatlantic slavery

The Atlantic Slave Trade had its origin in the European demand for
sugar.   By the late fifteenth century the Portuguese had begun to
develop sugar plantations in their recently acquired territories of the
Azores, the Canary Islands, the Cape Verde Islands, and Madeira.   The
planting, cultivation and harvesting of sugar cane is very labor
intensive, and to solve the problem of labor shortages Portuguese
planters started to import Africans as slave labor.   During the sixteenth
century, the Portuguese expanded the growing of sugar into plantations

191

SCOTTISH TRADE WITH
COLONIAL CHARLESTON, 1683-1783

in Brazil, and they were followed by the Spanish in the islands such as Hispaniola and elsewhere in the Americas. As the demand increased, the Spanish also solved their labor problems in the same manner as the Portuguese had done. When the English, French and Dutch first occupied the islands in the West Indies and territory on the mainland of South America their intention was first to produce tobacco, but within a short period they had exhausted the soil and turned to the growing and cultivation of sugar. Following the examples of the Portuguese and Spanish, their labor shortage solution was to obtain more slaves, now easily acquired from the African continent.

It has been calculated that from the fifteenth century through to the nineteenth, possibly as many as 13 million slaves were transported across the Atlantic Ocean, of which only about six percent were at this time destined for the North American mainland, the rest for the Caribbean area and Latin America. By the seventeenth century ships from all over western Europe were engaged in obtaining and shipping those destined for slavery on plantations in the Americas. These African men, women and children came mainly from an area lying between Senegal in the north to Angola in the south. Usually supplied by local factors working for investors in slavery who ranged from ship-owners to merchant companies, these people were exchanged for a wide range of goods, especially such as European produced textiles and metal wares.

The Royal African Company was founded in 1672 by Charles II as an English chartered company with the monopoly of trade between Africa and England and its colonies, ending by an act of Parliament in 1698, which then enabled other English entrepreneurs and existing traders to enter the market legally.[383] The Royal African

SCOTTISH TRADE WITH
COLONIAL CHARLESTON, 1683-1783

Company's raison d'etre was to transport slaves to Carolina from Barbados, where settlers had used them extensively in the sugar plantations. In the first decade of the Carolina colony, there is evidence that many settlers had owned both native Indian and black slaves.384 It is therefore the case that from the very beginning, the institution of slavery existed in the colony, growing to enormous proportions during the Royal period.   The black population almost immediately outnumbered the white, and it was a fact that Charleston's slave trade was the largest and most widely developed in all the thirteen colonies, with its factors and merchants buying and selling slaves throughout the Western Hemisphere.384

The great majority of black slaves were employed in agriculture, particularly in the production of rice and tobacco.   Rice was grown in the Low Country of South Carolina where the wet conditions were ideal, while tobacco cultivation was mainly in the vicinity of Chesapeake Bay. Consequently, the greatest concentrations of African slaves were to be found in these two regions.   A might higher labor force was required for the rice industry, and therefore many more slaves were brought into the port of Charleston than into the ports of Virginia. A recent study claims that in the period 1700 to 1790, a total of 77,650 Africans was landed in Virginia compared to 110,900 landed in South Carolina.385 The fact that blacks soon greatly outnumbered their white masters became an increasing concern among the white colonial authorities of the Carolinas by the late seventeenth century.   The expanding plantations, however continued to demand more slaves, and

384 Robin Blackburn, *The Making of New World Slavery,* London, England, 1997, p.254
385 William L Ramsay, 'All and Singular The Slaves', in *Money, Power, and Trade,* Jack P Greene, Rosemary Brana-Shute and Randy Sparks [Eds.], Columbia, S.C., 2001, pp166-180

SCOTTISH TRADE WITH
COLONIAL CHARLESTON, 1683-1783

these mainly were got from markets at the port of Charleston.

Replacements were also demanded owing to the high death rate of slaves owing to the cruel realities of their life, and their low childbirth rates. In an attempt to address the insecurity felt by the whites by their race being greatly outnumbered by negroes, in 1698 the Colonial Council passed the 'Act for the Encouragement of the Importation of White Servants', which stated:

> "Whereas the great number of Negroes which of late have been imported into the colony may endanger the safety thereof if speedy care not be taken and encouragement given for the importation of white servants ..."

The act went on to state the desire that for every six male Negro slaves over the age of sixteen years there should be one white servant.

A report by the Governor and Council of South Carolina to the Board of Trade in 1709 gives facts and figures. It established that there were 9,580 people in the colony including 1,800 negro male slaves, 1,100 negro female slaves, 1,200 negro children slaves, 500 Indian male slaves, 600 Indian female slaves, and 300 Indian slave children. More than half the population were classed as slaves. By the 1720s, the South Carolinian swamplands were being converted to rice-fields and, as a consequence, the number of Negro slaves being imported rose from two hundred and fifteen in the year 30 September 1721 to 29 September 1722, to one thousand, seven hundred and fifty-one between 30 September 1725 and 29 September 1726. [386]

The Westminster Parliament's economic policies also caused a sudden growth in the slave population of South Carolina and Charleston's

---

[386] TNA.CO5.387.130

thriving market in slaves. The two most significant laws which
impacted on the economy of South Carolina were firstly, in 1748 the
introduction of a subsidy on indigo, and secondly the removal of the
duty on rice imports into Great Britain in 1767. The high demand for
these products stimulated the colony's economy; the first increased the
prosperity of indigo planters, and the second doubled within five years
the profit of rice planters. As a direct consequence of this legislation
the numbers of imported Negro slaves soared.

The physical demands made of workers in the fields prohibited the use,
even if it could be found, of significant immigrant white labor. Some
Africans sold into slavery had useful knowledge and skills in the
growing of rice, providing planters with an ideally experienced work
force, as well as a free one. In addition, African slaves were seen to be
exceptionally qualified for the punishing work required to produce
large quantities of rice and indigo, and they, unlike white workers,
could be considered expendable and replaceable when the work killed
them, as it usually did within a few short years. Whites, even
indentured servants, could not be worked to death in this fashion, nor
could they be so readily replaced.

In addition to the vast numbers of slaves used to work the plantations,
some were also found necessary in urban centres such as Charleston.
The town's increasingly affluent craftsmen bought slaves to be trained
in industrial skills, such as metal working or wood-working. Slaves
who had acquired such skills would then achieve high prices when sold
on or engender good profits for their owner if hired out. Many female
slaves were put to work on domestic duties. The easy availability and

SCOTTISH TRADE WITH
COLONIAL CHARLESTON, 1683-1783

minimal cost of enslaved black men and women discouraged the immigration of skilled craftsmen and other whites from Europe and the northern colonies, and therefore the benefit of easy access of imported slave labor was at the cost of discouraging an increase of white immigrants to colony. South Carolina had become a slave society almost totally dependent on a continuous flow of black slaves from the West Indies and Africa.387

Direct Scottish Involvement
In the 1630s the recently formed Scottish Guinea Company despatched a couple of vessels, the Golden Lion and the St Andrew, to the Gulf of Guinea off West Africa. There is, however, no evidence that the masters of these ships participated in the slave trade, and the known facts show them to have been involved in trading European merchandise for gold and silver.388 During the seventeenth century, however, it is clear that Scottish seafarers served aboard English and possibly Dutch vessels, which did engage in the slave trade. These included individuals such as Alexander Christie from Kinghorn who died on the Pineapple in Guinea 389; William Elder, a mariner who died

---

387 see S. Max Edelson, 'Affiliation without Affinity. Skilled Slaves in Eighteenth Century South Carolina, in *Money, Trade, and Power,* ibid, pp217-255
388 Robin Law, *The First Scottish Guinea Company, 1634-1639,* 'Scottish Historical Review, Vol. LXXVI, 2, October 1997, Edinburgh, fos.185-202; David Dobson, *Scottish Emigration to Colonial America, 1607-1785, Athens, Georgia, 1994, p33*
389 TNA. Prerogative Court of Canterbury, probate 1687

on the Eakin bound for Guinea 390; James Skeed, from Dunbar, mariner on the Samuel and Margaret died at Guinea 391; and Alexander Stormonth, a shipmaster on the Guinea coast. 392

The earliest mention of direct Scottish involvement in the shipping of native Africans 393 concerns a slave ship being organised by officers of the Bank of Scotland together with the London-Scottish firm of Michael Kincaid and James Foulkes in 1695. The Company of Scotland Trading to Africa and the Indies, better known as the Darien Company, had been established in the same year. In addition to its well- known attempt to establish a trading colony at Darien on the Isthmus of Panama which ended in failure in 1700, a few years earlier this company was briefly was active in the Africa trade. In 1699-1700, its vessel, the African Merchant, returned from West Africa with gold, ivory, and rice. The following year, in 1701, the company sent two ships, the Speedy Return and the Content to east Africa and Madagascar, and these voyages were, without doubt, partly committed to the slave trade. However, the company lost money on this venture when to the slaves obtained were lost alongside the ships themselves, after attack by pirates.394

Before the Union of 1707, possibly, the last known slaving voyage financed from Scotland occurred in 1705 or 1706. The testament of Robert Richardson shows him to have been a merchant in Leith and

---

390 TNA.PCC.probate 1700
391 TNA.PCC.probate 1700
392 NRS. Testament, Commisariat of Edinburgh, 1767
393 Thomas, *The Slave Trade,* pp204-205
394 P Hair and R Law, ''The English in Western Africa to 1700' in Nicolas Canny [ed]. *The Origins of Empire,* Oxford, England, 2001, pp 258-259

owner of one-twelfth part of the vessel, the Two Brothers. Richardson sailed on this vessel to Guinea, from where the ship was bound for the West Indies and returning via Holland in 1706. The testament shows him to have died on the voyage.395

Evidently there were some in Scotland who considered the advantages of entering the African trade, and by implication the transatlantic slave trade, early in the post-Union era. On several occasions between 1709–1711 the Convention of Royal Burghs in Scotland petitioned Parliament at Westminster opposing the restoration of the monopoly of the Royal African Company, which it had lost in 1698.396 In this they succeeded, and the petition for restoration was rejected by Parliament resulting in the opening up of the African trade to all parties within Great Britain.

Within the following few years, merchants in Glasgow began, albeit on a small scale, to despatch ships to Guinea. Much of the evidence for this comes from the contemporary records of the High Court of the Admiralty of Scotland. A trial of pirates held before the court in 1719 refers to several vessels, including some Scottish ones, which were plundered by the pirates at Guinea. Among the Scottish ships involved was one named the Loyalty of Glasgow, another commanded by a Mr Auchenleck, and a third under the command of a Captain Graham.

395 NRS.CC8.8.83/25
396 see *Journal of the Houe of Commons,* xvi, 1709 and 1711

SCOTTISH TRADE WITH
COLONIAL CHARLESTON, 1683-1783

There were also a number of ships with Scots crew members, such as the Eagle of New York, Captain McIntosh, and the Edward and Sarah of Barbados, Captain James Nisbet. 397

Probably the best documented slaving voyage originating in Scotland is the Hannover of Glasgow, sailing in 1719-1720. 398   Details also derive largely from the records of the High Court of the Admiralty of Scotland. 399   The Hannover sailed from the Clyde to Guinea where it loaded slaves which were to be sold or exchanged for sugar in the West Indies.   The supercargo, Alexander Horsburgh, was instructed to purchase gold and 'elephants teeth' in Guinea, as well as slaves.   One hundred and thirty- five Negro slaves were embarked in Guinea but only eighty-seven in total were sold in Barbados, Nevis and St Kitts. The pursuers, Glasgow merchants who had financed the voyage, claimed that Horsburgh had failed to explain the discrepancy in the number of slaves loaded and the number subsequently sold.

Another case held before the Admiralty Court pertained to the voyage of the Loyalty of Glasgow 400 in 1718-1719.   This vessel sailed from Glasgow via Liverpool and Rotterdam, where it loaded trade goods supplied by the local Scots factor John Carstairs, bound for Guinea, where it was to obtain slaves for sale in the West Indies or in Virginia.

397 NRS.AC16/1
398 Eric J Graham and Sue Mowat, 'The Slaving Voyage of the Hannover of Port Glasgow, 1719-1720', *History Scotland, Vol.3, no.2,* Edinburgh, Scotland, 2003, pp 26-34
399 NRS.AC7.33.433-583
400 NRS.AC7.25.946-975

SCOTTISH TRADE WITH
COLONIAL CHARLESTON, 1683-1783

Fifty slaves were marketed in Barbados by Alexander Dundas, a resident Scottish factor, but on its return voyage to Glasgow the ship was taken by pirates.

The port of Montrose on the east coast of Scotland, was also for a short time involved in the slave trade, a fact is borne out by the records of the High Court of the Admiralty and from a charter party, (shipmaster's contract with the merchants), kept in Montrose Museum. Evidently Thomas Douglas and a group of Montrose merchants despatched ships to Guinea in search of slaves in the mid-eighteenth century. In a court case held in 1754 it was revealed that the snow, St George of Montrose, master Richard Hartley, sailed to Guinea where Hartley purchased three hundred negroes which he later sold in Antigua at £30 each.[401] Douglas sent five vessels, the Potomac Merchant, the Neptune, the St George, the Montrose, and the Delight of Dundee from Montrose [402] on slaving voyages during the 1750s. To put this in proportion, around the same time, in 1749 alone, Liverpool sent 70, London sent 8, and Bristol sent 50. [403] The method of operations was set out in charter parties. In the case of the Potomac Merchant, the skipper Richard Hartley was required to sail from Montrose via Newcastle to Holland to obtain the necessary trade goods, then to West Africa to exchange these goods for slaves and other 'goods,' which were to be exchanged in the Caribbean for sugar or in Virginia for tobacco, and be brought back to Montrose. The port book of South Potomac, Virginia, records

401 NRS.AC7.46.51-62
402 NRS.E504.24.3
403 Thomas, *Slave Trade*, p.264

200

the arrival of the <u>Potomac Merchant of Montrose</u> and its cargo of '*One hundred and ninety-seven passengers from Africa*' on 6 July 1752.[404] The Aberdeen Journal of December 1752 noted the arrival in Montrose of the said ship with a cargo of colonial produce including '*gold dust and elephants' teeth*.'.[405] Montrose's participation in the Slave Trade was, however, short-lived, because it could not compete with ports such as Liverpool who had the advantage in being able to participate in this trade more efficiently and profitably.

There is evidence of an attempt to send a vessel from the Highlands on a voyage to Guinea in 1763 which seems to have been abandoned. According to the records of the Vice Admiralty Court of Argyll, seamen had been recruited in the vicinity of Campbeltown to man the <u>Christian of Campbeltown</u> on a voyage via London bound for Guinea. However, the crew largely deserted as warrants were issued for their arrest in October 1763.[406]

Direct participation of Scots in the African slave trade can therefore be seen to be small scale when compared to the ports of Liverpool and Bristol, and almost all of the relatively few voyages occurred during the eighteenth century.

Scots resident in Guinea and elsewhere in West Africa

During the seventeenth-century the various European companies trading with Africa began to establish permanent trading stations,

404 Walter Minchinton, Celia White, and Peter Wilson, [eds] *The Virginia Slave Trade Statistics, 1698-1775,* Richmond, Virginia, 1984
405 *Aberdeen Journal, no.258*
406 NRS.AC20.2.20

known as 'factories' along the coast of West Africa. These centers were under the management of factors sent from Europe to represent companies in negotiations with local merchants and local chiefs, and to sreadiness for the arrival of the company's next ship. The first of these permE trading stations was constructed near Accra by the Portuguese, and named Sao Jorge da Mina, otherwise known as Elmina Castle. From the 1660s, the main factory of the Royal African Company of England was at Cape Coast Castle. A number of Scots were among settlements, and some can be identified from their testaments confirmed with the Commissariat of Edinburgh. Donald Clark was a merchant in Senegal,[407] Francis Robertson, was a surgeon at Cape Coast Castle[408], James Scott was also at Cape Coast Castle [409], and James Skinner was Governor of Fort James on the River Gambia.[410] A few of these Scots who worked on the west coast of Africa were admitted as honorary burgesses of various burghs, possibly to admitted as a burgess of Montrose in 1776.[411] Others, such as Dr Francis Duff in Whydah, Guinea, 1738, appear in contemporary correspondence or records.[412]

One of the most active of the British companies engaged in slaving on the west coast of Africa during the eighteenth century was the London based firm of Grant, Oswald and Company. Although located in

407 NRS. Testament, 1779, Edinburgh
408 NRS. Testament, 1763, Edinburgh
409 NRS. Testament, 1775, Edinburgh
410 NRS. Testament, 1772, Edinburgh
411 Angus Archives, Montrose Burgess Roll
412 Aberdeen University, ms997.6.2.22

SCOTTISH TRADE WITH
COLONIAL CHARLESTON, 1683-1783

London, the majority of its partners were Scots entrepreneurs with mercantile experience and connections in the American colonies. In 1748, this recently formed company purchased Bance Island in Sierra Leone, a fort and trading post which had originally been owned by the Royal Africa Company but abandoned by them in 1728. Later it had been bought by a London based slave merchant, George Fryer, who subsequently disposed of his interest to Richard Oswald on behalf of Grant, Oswald and Company. These London based merchants were Richard Oswald, Augustus Boyd, John Boyd, Alexander Grant, John Mill, and John Sargent jr.[413] David Hancock writes:

> 'The Scots connection was the strongest of all bonds. Between 1751 and 1773 …it appears that a quarter [of the employees at Bance Island] were born in Scotland or to Scots parents. Scots ties certainly influenced the selection of agents and clerks. From 1748 to 1776 there were thirteen agents, Melvin, Staple, McLeod, McLeish, Stephens, Aird, James, Tweed, Stirling, Teise, Knight, Davidson and McIntosh, nine were Scots. The agent John Aird and the clerk John Bowman were sons of prominent Glasgow merchants who Oswald had known in the 1730s and 1740s.'[414]

Personal connection was important in the recruitment of employees, and especially those intended for promotion. John Aird, who was sent to Bance Island as a clerk in 1754 and later became manager, was known to Oswald through their connections in Glasgow. James Low

---

413   see David Hancok, *Citizens of the World, London Merchants and the Integration of the British Atlantic Community, 1735-1785,* Cambridge, England, 1995
414   ibid, p194

had worked for the Grants of Monymusk prior to going to London in 1761, where he was recruited by Alexander Grant to work at Bance Island. [415]

Between 1748 and 1784 Grant, Oswald and Company shipped nearly thirteen thousand African slaves from Bance Island in Sierra Leone to destinations in South Carolina, Georgia, St Kitts and Grenada, mostly on their ships the Betsey, the Bance Island, the Nancy, the Africa, the Rockhall, and the King George.[416] Among the Naval Officer's accounts for the port of Charleston [417] are entries which confirm that consignments of slaves sent from Bance Island arrived in Charleston. For example, on 10 July 1758 the Betsey of London, an eighty-ton snow, master Robert Deas, owned by Richard Oswald, Alexander ntwo hundred and twenty slaves.

It is clear, therefore, that a Scottish trading network engaged primarily in the transatlantic slave trade was active on the west coast of Africa. In the case of Grant, Oswald and Company, although the firm was based in London, the leading partners were Scots and some of the capital would have originated in Scotland. On Bance Island a high proportion of the European staff was Scottish and some of the shipmasters employed were also of Scots origin. Scots were therefore represented at every level of the slave trade.

The Middle Passage

While the direct involvement of known Scots ships in the transatlantic

415 NRS.GD345.1180
416 Hancock, Citizens, p.205
417 TNA.CO5.508-510

slave trade was minimal, totalling perhaps thirty voyages, there is evidence to support the claim that Scots seafarers served aboard ships trading between Africa and America. It is also likely that vessels from Scotland, involved in the Triangular Trade between Scotland, the West Indies and North America, carried slaves on the leg of the journey between the West Indies and the thirteen colonies. This is certainly the situation found in Virginia, where of a total of twelve Scottish registered ships that arrived in Virginia with slaves, prior to the American War of Independence, eleven had brought slaves from the West Indies and one brought a Negro slave from Scotland.[418]

The Slave Trade created a demand for surgeons and physicians both at sea and on land. The surgeon was on board a slave ship was one of the senior officers, and carried out essential duties, these being to assist in the selection of healthy Africans before they were taken for the Atlantic passage, thus attempting to ensure that as many as possible reached the ports of Charleston, Port Royal in Jamaica, Bridgetown in Barbados, or whichever port they were to be disembarked, is as healthy a condition and marketable state as possible. In the slave colonies of the Caribbean and the American mainland there were surgeons and physicians who serviced the needs of the planters, the slavers, and, within limitations, the slaves. Scots surgeons who served English slave ships were John Strachan from Dundee, who died on the <u>Samuel and Margaret</u> at Guinea before 1700, [419] and Charles Hamilton, a surgeon from Balderston, West Lothian, who died on the brig <u>Swallow</u> at Guinea by 1695.[420] Dr

---

418 Minchinton, *Virginia Slave Trade Statistics,* passim
419 TNA.PCC.probate, 1700
420 TNA.PCC.probate, 1695

SCOTTISH TRADE WITH
COLONIAL CHARLESTON, 1683-1783

William Houston, a medical graduate of St Andrews and Leyden worked for a period in the 1730s as a surgeon on the <u>Don Carlos</u>, a South Sea Company vessel operating in the Caribbean.421 As a result of the Treaty of Utrecht in 1713, The South Sea Company had succeeded in obtaining the asiento, the contract to supply 4,800 slaves annually to the Spanish colonists. 422

Letters from Scots mariners engaged in the Slave Trade are very rare, but one was found in the Glasgow Archives, written by a William Colhoun.   He wrote home from Senegal in July 1770 stating that he was mate on board a vessel bound for the Potochan River, Virginia, with 150 slaves.   Several months later, in October 1770, he wrote from Oxford, Maryland, confirming his arrival there.423

The earliest link between Scots and the Slave Trade into Charleston is documented in a complaint made to the Privy Council Colonial in June 1700.   In July of 1697 George Peers and other merchants in Barbados sent a sloop, the <u>Turtle</u>, master Robert Cunningham, from Barbados with a cargo of sugar, rum, molasses and Negro slaves to Charleston for sale.   On her arrival on 14 August 1697 a naval officer, Jonathan Amory, seized the ship and cargo on the basis that Cunningham was a Scot and therefore contravening the Navigation Acts.424

Overall, the best single source of information on Scottish overseas trade for the American colonial period lies in the Customs and Excise port books.   These books list every import and export, origin and destination of voyage, together with information on the shipmaster, the vessel, and

421 D. Dobson, *Scots in Georgia and the Deep South, 1735-1845,*Baltimore, Maryland, 2000, p82
422 Thomas, *The Slave Trade,* pp235-242
423 Glasgow City Archives, TD301.6
424 W L Grant, *Acts of the Privy Council, Colonial, Vol.II, 1680-1720,* Hereford, England, 1910

SCOTTISH TRADE WITH
COLONIAL CHARLESTON, 1683-1783

the merchants involved. Dating from 1742, this source is almost definitive, but prior to that date there is no single source of information available. Newspapers of the period provide the occasional item which suggests a possible slaving voyage, for example the Caledonian Mercury 425 reported the departure of the Elizabeth of Greenock, master James Hastie, from Greenock via Belfast and the Isle of May bound for Carolina in 1741. The Isle of May, (Ilha Maio) is one of the Cape Verde Islands, and was noted for its slave market, therefore the Elizabeth may well have embarked slaves there bound for the market in Charleston. This certainly seems to have been the practice of some Scots vessels bound for American ports via the West Indies.

For Scottish ships entering the port of Charleston, probably the best sources which can be used to identify a Scottish element among the seafarers engaged in the slave trade are the colonial Port-books and the South Carolina Gazette. Among the arrival entries of the Charleston Port-books 426 is one dated 20 June 1727, stating:

> "...the Glasgow of South Carolina, a seventy- ton square-sterned ship, with a sixteen man crew, six guns, master William Warden, owners Andrew Allen and Charles Hill, Plantation built during 1725, registered in South Carolina on 13 January 1725, arrived from Guinea with a cargo of one hundred and seventy seven negroes." 427

The South Carolina Gazette carried advertisements promoting the sale of recently imported sales. For example, the issue of 17 May 1734 states that slaves were to be sold by Cleland and Wallace aboard the

425 Caledonian Mercury, #3366
426 TNA.CO5.508-510
427 TNA.CO5.509

207

SCOTTISH TRADE WITH
COLONIAL CHARLESTON, 1683-1783

London Frigate, master John Sutherland.   Both of the above sources clearly demonstrate that Scots or men of Scots origin were involved in the Charleston slave trade in the capacity of ships captains, ship-owners, and merchants.   All the vessels arriving in Charleston in the colonial period which seem to have a Scottish link have been extracted from the South Carolina Gazette and from the Port Books and have been listed .   A Scottish link is defined as being a Scots ship, a ship having a skipper with a Scots surname, Scottish surnames of ship owners, or ships carrying a cargo which is sold by merchants bearing Scots surnames.   All the men listed are believed to be Scots or of Scottish origin.   This criteria, though loose, is the only method which can give an indication of the level of Scottish participation in the slave trade.   It will be seen that some vessels have been registered in British and others in colonial ports.   Of the forty-five shipmasters identified, two thirds had Scots surnames, and only four can be seen to have made more than one such voyage.   John Carruthers completed three, and William Warden, William Gordon and John Sutherland completed two each. Ashore, few of those selling the slaves in the marketplace can be identified as to their origin.   Some of the human cargoes of these slave ships were picked up in Africa, and some in the West Indies.   Thirty-three ships arrived in Charleston from Africa, twenty from the West Indies, and one unspecified.   African locations included Angola, Guinea, Senegal, Gambia, Sierra Leone, the Windward and the Gold Coasts.   In the West Indies, slaves were collected from Barbados, Antigua, Jamaica, St Croix, Montserrat and St Kitts.   The ports of registration of these thirty-three ships were in the main English and colonial, with only one ship from Scotland, the Barbary of Leith in

208

1730. This ship, master Samuel Scollay, landed seven negro slaves in Charleston in June 1730, having brought them from Barbados. There is no evidence of any Scots ship bringing slaves directly from Africa to South Carolina, and this pattern also seems also to be the case in Virginia.428   Virginia Slave Statistics, 1698-1775, identifies only ten Scottish ships landing slaves in Virginia during the colonial period. Five had brought slaves from Barbados, two from Antigua, and one from St Kitts, but none from Africa.   Notably, in 1716 the Friendship of Leith, master Walter Flett, brought one Negro slave to Virginia from Scotland.

Scots merchants selling slaves in South Carolina

As the Scots were very prominent among the merchants of Charleston, there can be little doubt that they were as involved in the Slave Trade as they were in any other 'cargo' passing through the harbour of Charleston.   Evidence to support this comes from the pages of the local newspaper, the South Carolina Gazette, which was used to advertise forthcoming sales of slaves imported from Africa and the West Indies. Those firms which have been identified as marketing the imported slaves, some of whom having a Scottish connection are: Cleland and Wallace; Robertson, Jamieson and Company; John Forbes and Company; Kennan and Campbell; Robert Pringle and Company; McKenzie and Michie; W. Glen; Woodrop and Cathcart; Inglis, Lloyd and Company, also Torrans, Pouag and Company. W. R. Higgins 429 has identified hundreds of those who ran the Charleston side of the business.   Nearly four hundred of the names on the list are of Scottish

428 Minchinton, Virginia Slave Statistics, *passim*
429 W R Higgins, 'Charleston Merchants and Factors dealing in the External Negro Trade, 1735-1775'. *The South Carolina Historical Magazine,* Vol.65, Charleston, 1964, pp.205-217

SCOTTISH TRADE WITH
COLONIAL CHARLESTON, 1683-1783

origin, although the men were not necessarily natives of Scotland. The most active firm was that of Austin and Laurens (Laurens being of Huguenot origin), which was involved in selling slaves imported on forty-five voyages between 1751 and 1758. John Simpson and Company was responsible for marketing thirteen shiploads of African slaves brought into Charleston between 1771 and 1774. It is obvious that the largest consignments arrived directly from Africa, and the largest cargo was three hundred and eighty slaves brought from Angola aboard the London of London, master J. Sutherland, in 1736. The smallest number, totalling three, arrived in Charleston from Antigua on the Dorothy of London, master William Douglas.

The following are examples of contemporary advertisements from the pages of the *South Carolina Gazette:*

"June 5, 1749 "This day arrived from the Windward Coast of Africa the Hector, Captain Peter Bostock, with a choice parcel of young healthy slaves; to be sold by the subscribers in Charles Town, the 20th instant, credit will be given till the first of January next, giving security if required. John Mackenzie and Kenneth and Benjamin Michie. Great Abatement will be made for ready money."

"February 23, 1765 "On 7 March, seventy slaves from the West Indies on the Prudence, Captain Thomas Farmer, by William Kirby at Messrs Woodrup and Cathcart on the Bay ... being the prime picked out of a large cargo. NB indigo will be taken in payment."

SCOTTISH TRADE WITH
COLONIAL CHARLESTON, 1683-1783

As a matter of interest, among these seventy slaves there is believed to be included the celebrated Olaudah Equiano, alias Gustavus Vassa.[430] Equiano was born in the Igbo village of Essaka in the region of Benin, West Africa, and after being kidnapped and surviving the passage to the American colonies, he was purchased by a British naval officer and taken to England as a personal servant. During this time he was taught to read, and as a sailor was part of several major battles of the Seven Years War. After this he was sold to a slave trader bound for the West Indies who employed him as a clerk, and with the money earned in this way he was able to purchase his freedom and return to London. In 1773 he took part in Captain Phipps search for the North East passage to India, and in 1777 he settled in London where he wrote 'The Interesting Narrative of the Life of Olaudah Equiano or Gustavus Vasa the African.' His final years were committed to working for the abolition of slavery.

The contemporary Naval Officer's Accounts provide a record of Charleston's shipping from 1712 onwards, giving details of the ship and its cargo but none of the selling agents. However, this source does provide the names of the ship-owners who would have, to some extent, organised and possibly financed the voyage as can be ascertained from the following two examples.

> "Glasgow of South Carolina, eighty tons, master William Warden. owners Francis Borland and Andrew Allan, with six negroes from Barbados, date of arrival 13 August 1734."[431]

430 Olaudah Equino, *The Interesting Narrative of the Life of Olaudah Equino, or Gustavus Vassa, the African,* London, England, 1789
431 TNA.CO5.509

SCOTTISH TRADE WITH
COLONIAL CHARLESTON, 1683-1783

All of the above individuals are known to have been Scots residents of Charleston, and the six slaves mentioned were brought back from a trading voyage to Barbados, an island with which Charleston merchants had built strong economic links. The next example suggests that the shipmaster and the owner are either Scots or of Scots origin, and again illustrates the networking that has been established among the Scots communities throughout the American colonies:

> "Rebecca of Jamaica, master Robert Craig, owner Duncan McWalter of Jamaica, with nine negroes from Jamaica, 2 May 1764." [432]

Scots slave-owners in South Carolina

As South Carolina was, without doubt, a society and economy built upon slavery, it is inevitable that the majority of the Scots living there, owned slaves. Ownership can be identified to a limited extent from the surviving wills and inventories of the white population outlined below. The currency quoted is South Carolina pounds.[433]

The inventory of the goods, chattels, rights and credits of Daniel MacGregor compiled by his executor on 27 February 1724 includes *'seven negro men valued at £1100 (ranging from £60 to £230) and four negro women with two boys and two girls valued at £530.'* To put these values in perspective, four riding horses would be worth £125, and one mare and colt worth £30. MacGregor's assets were worth a total of £2131 South Carolina currency, of which slaves were valued at £1630 SC, or roughly three quarters of the total.

432 TNA.CO5.509
433 Charleston Public Library, *Charleston Wills, Inventories and Miscellaneous Documents,* Volume 60

SCOTTISH TRADE WITH
COLONIAL CHARLESTON, 1683-1783

The inventory of Alexander Michie, merchant in St Michael's parish, dated 1st November 1774 includes: Sarah, a mulatto woman with her two girls £800; John, a mulatto boy £300; George, a young mulatto child, £50; and Tom, a negro boy valued at £350 The total value of slaves his slaves was £1500, and his other assets amounted to £837.7.3. The inventory of Dr Archibald McNeill, dated 4 July 1774 show his assets to total £28,275.5. He owned fifty-four named slaves worth in total £20,540. These slaves varied in value from £800 (Hector) to £10 (Old Jack).

In the Charleston Public Library, as well as testamentary evidence there exist a number of commercial documents recording the purchase or sale of slaves by people of Scottish, and other origins. The above mentioned source also contains such documents, for example the following Bill of Sale dated 1 November 1769:

> "William Jenkins, late of Jamaica, but then of Charlestown, Berkley County, South Carolina, sold to John Bowman, late of Glasgow, four negro slaves, namely Esther and her two sons, John and Terismond, and her daughter, Kiturah, for £700, South Carolina currency."

Another Bill of Sale dated 31 March 1729 documents

> "John Blake, planter in Berkley County, South Carolina, sold to Alexander Nisbett, a merchant in Charleston, two Negro men, one Negro or mulatto woman, a Negro boy and three girls, for £995 South Carolina currency. The document was witnessed by Walter Nisbett and Hugh Campbell." [434]

434 Charleston Public Library, *Charleston County Miscellaneous Records, 1727-1729*

SCOTTISH TRADE WITH
COLONIAL CHARLESTON, 1683-1783

The 1751 Account Book of Austin and Laurens, show two Scots to be leading merchants of Charleston. 435   Austin originated in Perth, and his partner, Laurens was a Huguenot. Page 307 of the Account Book records the individuals to whom slaves were sold in that year, and this includes a number of Scots.   It can be seen that on 4 July 1751, a Dr John Linning purchased two male slaves; *"payable per bond given this date, due on 1 November 1751 with interest £300."*   Dr Linning was a physician from Dundee who died in Charleston in 1760.436

George Seaman, a successful Scots merchant who was prominent in Charleston, died in 1769.   His will, proved in London on 24 July 1769, reveals that he owned two hundred and twenty-four slaves to work in his three plantations in South Carolina and his town house in Charleston.437

Although the economy of South Carolina was very much dependent on slavery, it would appear that not every individual or family were slave-owners.   The evidence for this is based on the Loyalist Claims of the immediate post-war era.   Slaves were deemed to be assets, whose loss due to their support of the Loyalist cause during the American Revolution, could be claimed for in reparations from the British government.   An inspection of the approximately 600 Loyalist Claims from former residents of South Carolina is notable for its lack of slaves on inventories of losses.438   Around a quarter of claimants bore

435 South Carolina Historical Society MS
436 W R Brock, *Scotus Americanus,* Edinburgh, Scotland, 1982, p.115
437 TNA.PCC.1769
438 see P W Coldham, *American Migrations, 1765-1799,* Baltimore, Md., 2000, pp.654-751

SCOTTISH TRADE WITH
COLONIAL CHARLESTON, 1683-1783

surnames which indicate a Scottish origin, though some may have arrived from Ulster. Of these, only forty-one made a claim for the property in the form of lost slaves. Collectively, these 'Scottish' slave-owners registered ownership of 738 black slaves. Breaking down the claims, it is seen that most owned only a handful of slaves each, with a small proportion of plantation owners making up the numbers. Charles and George Ogilvie of the Auchiries family in Aberdeenshire owned one hundred and thirteen, and seventy slaves respectively.[439]   In only in a small number of instances was there a clue as to the particular skills of slaves. Of these, Thomas Creighton, who had a bakery in Queen Street, Charleston, claimed for three negro bakers,[440] and John Imrie, from Dundee, who worked as a shipwright in Charleston from 1761 to1776, claimed for a Negro shipwright.[441]   There were four Negro shoemakers, one carpenter, and one cooper listed amongst the Loyalist Claims.

As can be seen, therefore, the town of Charleston functioned as the main slave market in the Thirteen Colonies. Large cargoes of slaves often arrived at the port directly from Africa as well as smaller consignments from the West Indies. Charleston slave markets were the almost exclusive source of labor for planters throughout the American South from the colonial period to well into the nineteenth century. There were, however, some planters who chose to bypass the local market and bought directly from merchants in the West Indies. For example, a branch of the family of Murray of Murraythwaite was established in

439 TNA.AO12.48.63, etc., TNA.AO12.51.227, etc.
440 TNA.AO12.3.341, etc.
441 TNA.AO12.3.252, etc

SCOTTISH TRADE WITH
COLONIAL CHARLESTON, 1683-1783

South Carolina around mid-century, where John and James functioned as physicians and planters. Their letter-book survives for the period 1756 to 1758, and it reveals that the Murrays were importing Negro slaves from Antigua to staff their plantation in South Carolina. In January 1756, they wrote to Andrew Smart, a partner of the firm Smart and Walker in Antigua, requesting that he purchase fifteen to twenty negroes and despatch them to the Murray's new plantation in South Carolina. Interestingly, the transaction was to be financed through a bill of exchange drawn on Robert Scott at the Jamaica Coffee House in London.442

A notable, and admirable exception to this practice of using Negros as slave labor in the early colonial period was the colony of Georgia. Founded in 1732, it had from its inception an anti-slavery policy. This colony had been set up in order that the poor of London could establish a new and better life. In 1735, in an effort to avoid the encroachment of the use of slaves it prohibited the practice by law, through "An Act for rendering the Colony of Georgia more defencible by Prohibiting the Importation and use of Black Slaves or Negroes". Sadly, these high ideals gave way in the face economic forces as planters of the colony of Georgia were unable to compete on price with those of neighboring South Carolina who used slave labor. Some early settlers abandoned Georgia and moved north to South Carolina where they could use slaves. Among these were a group of Lowland Scots who had settled in the neighborhood of Josephstown.443 William Stirling444 was a merchant from Glasgow who settled in Georgia in 1734 as a planter on

442 NRS.GD219.290
443 Dobson, *Scottish Emigration,* 117
444 TNA.CO5.668; CO5.670.128

SCOTTISH TRADE WITH
COLONIAL CHARLESTON, 1683-1783

the Ogychee; Joseph Wardrop, 445 a carpenter from Edinburgh, had received a land grant in Georgia, and Patrick Tailfer 446 was a surgeon from Edinburgh who settled on the river Neuse in Georgia before moving to Charleston. Those who stayed included Highland Scots who had settled around Darien, Georgia, and who very much opposed slavery. On 3 January 1739, John Mackintosh Bain and seventeen other Highland freeholders of Darien, alias New Inverness, petitioned the Trustees of Georgia, demanding that slavery not be introduced, describing the practice as *'shocking to human nature'*.447 Despite opposing pressures to introduce slavery, the Trustees maintained their original policy until 1750, just prior to the colony being taken over by the Crown. After this date, Georgia was to become a major market for the slave merchants of Charleston.

Conclusion

It is clear, therefore, that Scots were active at each and every stage of the Transatlantic Slave Trade. They were involved in financing voyages, manning ships, supplying ships, staffing African trading posts, buying, selling, and final utilisation of slaves. Taking Scottish surnames as evidence, it can be implied that those of Scottish origin were, relatively speaking, more heavily involved in the slave trade than those belonging to other ethnic groups in South Carolina. It has been shown that the direct participation of Scottish based companies operating in the transportation of slaves turns out to be small, with a maximum of thirty voyages leaving Scotland.448 This compares to

445 TNA.CO5.670.128; CO5.668; CO5.668.107
446 TNA.CO5.668; CO5.670.106
447 H H Jackson, 'The Darien Anti Slavery Policy of 1739 and the Georgia Plan'; *William and Mary Quarterly, 3ʳᵈ series,* Vol.31, Williamsburg, Virginia; A W Parker, *Scottish Highlander in Colonial Georgia,* Athens, Georgia, 1997, appendix 3.

SCOTTISH TRADE WITH
COLONIAL CHARLESTON, 1683-1783

approximately two thousand from Bristol alone before 1800. The Scots, therefore, can be shown to have had considerably more than an ancillary role in the selection, collection, and transportation of slaves, providing also the agents in factories on the African coast and sailors aboard largely English and colonial ships. Only in the final stage of the slavery chain, the sale in slave markets, were they significant.

SCOTTISH TRADE WITH
COLONIAL CHARLESTON, 1683-1783

CHAPTER SIX

MERCHANTS TRADING BETWEEN
SCOTLAND AND CHARLESTON

In this chapter an attempt will be made to identify the Scottish merchants who were resident in Charleston and the ways in which they integrated within society there through such media as the church, the Masonic Lodge and the St Andrews Society.   This thesis seeks to provide evidence of a Scottish network which links Scots to their compatriots in Scotland, elsewhere in the American or West Indian colonies, the Atlantic Islands, Africa, and possibly European ports. The methods by which trade was promoted will also be examined, as will the degree to which trade between Scotland and Charleston was continuous or intermittent.   All these details will be compared to the known patterns of trade between Scotland and the Chesapeake region. Firstly, however, the general development of the economy will be described.

On 24 March 1663, Charles II of England granted to eight men, known as the Lord Proprietors, who, though residing in England, speculated in lands in the New World.   This particular grant referred to the regions later known as North and South Carolina and part of Georgia.   By 1670, the port of Charleston had been established, and between then and the outbreak of the American Revolution in 1776 this minor settlement had expanded to become the major port of the American South.   As a major entrepot, it had developed links with all the major

SCOTTISH TRADE WITH
COLONIAL CHARLESTON, 1683-1783

ports along the Atlantic coast of American as well as with the Caribbean, Europe and Africa.448

Charleston exported goods which had been produced in the surrounding regions included the South Carolinian produce of deerskins, timber, rice and indigo, as well as other American colonial goods such as sugar, tobacco, mahogany and rum. Imported goods from Britain were manufactured commodities, especially textiles and metal-ware and included also provisions such as soap, herring, ale, coal and luxury items.

Another important import for the colony via Charleston was, of course, slaves from Africa. Initially slaves arrived by way of the West Indies, but soon the Carolinians were sending ships directly to Africa to be loaded with human cargo for work on their expanding plantations.449

The economy of Carolina in the seventeenth century depended largely on stock-raising and the deer trade. Cattle and pigs were slaughtered and their salted carcasses exported to the West Indies. Deerskins were obtained through trading with the Indian tribes of the interior, and these formed the staple trade with Britain. Rice, which had been introduced in the late seventeenth century from Africa, was extensively farmed and this, and the growing of indigo from approximately 1740 for use in fabric dye, became the prime produce of the eighteenth century. The

448 R C Nash, 'The Organisation of Trade and Finance in the Atlantic Economy, Jack P Greene, Rsemary Brana-Shute, and Randy J Sparks, [eds], *Money, Trade, and Power, The Evolution of Colonial South Carolina's Plantation Society*,Columbia, S.C., 2001. p.93,
449 Jennifer L Morgan, 'This is Mines', Slavery and Reproduction in Colonial Barbados and South Carolina, ibid, p.199

220

demand for indigo grew alongside the rapidly expanding British textile industry and rice found a market throughout much of Western Europe. From the planter's viewpoint, these were excellent crops, in that they required different growing environments and grew in different seasons. Since their cultivation was labor intensive, the demand for slaves grew in proportion with the European demand for these products.[450]

By the middle of the eighteenth century the plantation economy of South Carolina was generating considerable wealth for the white planter class.   Wealthier planters began to turn their attention to aesthetics and the building of substantial properties began.   Town houses in Charleston and large plantation houses required to be furnished, and in turn, this generated a demand for all sorts of consumer luxury goods which had to be brought from Europe.   In addition to the increase in import of goods, the expanding economy was seen to offer good opportunities to European craftsmen who began to arrive in the colony as settlers.   These craftsmen set up their own businesses and increased the range of merchants in the town of Charleston.   By the eve of the American Revolution, the profits that were being generated by the demand for what the colony could produce, together with the cheapness of its production, caused the elite of Charleston to become far richer that their counterparts in any other colonial town on the Chesapeake, and even richer than the northern cities of New York and Boston.[451] Including slaves, by 1775 the population of Charleston had grown to approximately 12,000. While Charleston was the main English settlement, the Scots had established a base at Stuartstown, South Carolina, approximately twenty miles to the south in the area of

450 Robert M Weir, 'Shaftesbury's Darling: British Settlement in The Carolinas at the Close of the Seventeenth Century', ibid, pp.387-389
451 see Edward Pearson, 'Planters Full of Money', ibid, passim

221

SCOTTISH TRADE WITH
COLONIAL CHARLESTON, 1683-1783

Port Royal which replaced an earlier Spanish settlement.452   Until recent recently it had been thought by historians that this colony was founded by Covenanters fleeing from oppression in Scotland, but recent research claims that although the settlement had Covenanting sympathies, Stuartstown owed its existence to the Carolina Company, a group of Scots landowners and merchants who sought to expand trade with the New World.453   My research would support this claim, as examination of the ships' cargoes bound for Stuartstown as listed in the Scottish Port Books cannot be explained as being solely for the use of the travelling passengers and crews.   Take, for example, the cargo of the Pelican of Glasgow, master James Gibson, which sailed from Glasgow bound for Charleston in June 1684, carrying pack-cloth, linen, worsted, shoes, hats, thread, gloves, knitting, stockings, plaiding, iron work, woollens, gird buckles, furniture, aqua vitae, nails, loaf sugar, and fingram. 454 The Charles of Glasgow, master John Murray, which sailed to Carolina in August of the same year, carried shoes, linen, gloves, hats, coal, buttons, pack-cloth, stockings, and worsteds.455 The James of Ayr, master David Ferguson, sailing from Ayr bound for Carolina in August 1684 had on board textiles, stockings, hats, shoes, gloves, pipes, knives, thread buttons, hair coverings, blankets and brandy.456   It is clear from the records that this range of goods formed the backbone of Scottish exports to South Carolina for the coming

452 see maps
453 Linda G Fryer, Documents Relating to the Formation of the Carolina Company in Scotland, 1682, *South Carolina Historical Magazine,* Vol.99/2, Charleston, S.C., 1998, PP.110-134
454 NRS.E72.19.9
455 NRS.E72.19.9
456 NRS.E72.3.13

SCOTTISH TRADE WITH
COLONIAL CHARLESTON, 1683-1783

century and is evidence that trade was at the heart of Scottish involvement from the very beginning. In 1685 George Muschamp, the Customs Collector in Carolina, wrote that the Scots:

> 'are evidently able to undersell the English, their goods being much coarser or slighter, which will serve for servants wear and will be sure to go off [sell], they being cheap so that an Englishman must go away infreighted or sell to vast disadvantage'.[457]

This niche market for cheap and inferior textiles was one that the Scots exploited during the eighteenth century, especially among poor colonists and slave owners. Direct trade between Scotland and Carolina dates from 1684 and the merchants in Scotland who participated then were Thomas Weir, William Rowan, William Hamilton, William Dunlop, Thomas Crawford, Jonathan Haggons, and George Lyon in Glasgow,[458] David Ferguson in Ayr, [459] and James Dundas and Robert Malloch in Edinburgh.[460] While most of them were involved in trading a range of Scottish goods, especially textiles, Malloch shipped prisoners taken from the jails of Edinburgh to sell as indentured servants.

The attempt to establish a trading colony at Stuartstown was, however, short-lived, and within a couple of years of its foundation the settlement was over-run and completely destroyed by the Spanish from St Augustine, at the time the capital of East Florida. Those Scots who survived fled to Charleston and for the most part there they remained.[461]

457 T. Keith, 'Scottish Trade with the Plantations before 1707', *Scottish Historical Review,* Vol,6, 1908-1909, Edinburgh, p.37
458 NRS.E72.19.9
459 NRS.E72.15.28
460 NRS.E72.3.13
461 D. Dobson, *Scottish Emigration to Colonial America, 1607-1785,* Athens, Ga., 1994, p.65

SCOTTISH TRADE WITH
COLONIAL CHARLESTON, 1683-1783

A number of refugees from the failed colony of Darien in Panama settled also arrived in Charleston in 1700 and in this way the Scottish presence in the English colony grew.462   Few of these original Scots inhabitants of Charleston are known to have been merchants.   Those who were included John Alexander from Edinburgh, from 1688 until his death in 1699, 463 George Fullarton from Ayrshire who died by 1708,464 and John Stuart from Edinburgh, with his sons, John and Charles, prior to the date of 1718.465

As there is no evidence of shipping links between Scotland and the Carolinas between the years 1690 to 1712, it has to be assumed that these merchants obtained their supplies and found their markets elsewhere, presumably in London.   John Alexander is known to have had dealings with Alexander Laing, a Scots merchant in London.466 Alexander is also known to have sent at least one consignment of deerskins to Bristol. 467 Other than during a short period around 1684, the English Navigation Acts would have outlawed any direct trade between Scotland and Carolinas, inhibiting the development of shipping links.   This changed at the Union of Parliaments in 1707, when all trade bans were lifted on Scottish trade with the former English colonies.   All colonies were now to be regarded as British and free trade was established.

Principally involved in this trans-Atlantic trade was the merchant.   This term cannot be accurately defined by its modern usage.   In the colonies

462 ibid
463 NRS.RD2.82.203; GD393.79; probate 15 January 1700 S.C.
464 probate 3 January 1709 S.C.
465 NRS.CC8.8.87
466 NRS.CC8.8.83
467 see Charleston County Wills and Miscellaneous Records, 1694-1704

SCOTTISH TRADE WITH
COLONIAL CHARLESTON, 1683-1783

a merchant might act as factor for both exporter and importer; be a self-employed entrepreneur importer and exporter; be a retailer or wholesaler, or a mixture of all these things. They might begin as an Indian trader, and as their wealth accumulated, open a store, and from that move to import and export on their own behalf. Very few merchants in the colonies received the formal type of training which they would have benefited from in contemporary Scotland, where potential merchants were required to serve a period of apprenticeship under other established merchants. George Seaman (1705-1769), the son of a baker burgess of Leith, served his merchant apprenticeship in Edinburgh under the merchant burgess Charles Crokatt, before being admitted as a burgess and guilds-brother of Edinburgh.[468] Both George Seaman and Charles Crokatt became prominent merchants in Charleston in due course.

In Scotland, a prospective merchant would, during his five-year apprenticeship be required to have trained in book-keeping, arithmetic, mercantile law, business practice, and sometimes a foreign language such as Dutch or French. Business education in colonial Charleston in 1735 was partly supplied through the efforts of the schoolteachers, Corbet and Buchanan, who established a boarding school teaching Latin and Greek, arithmetic and mercantile accounting.[469]

Another possible Scot providing education during this early period was John Graham, whose school was advertised in 1758 as being next to the Scotch Meeting House. There he taught '*the three Rs, Surveying and*

468 C B Boog-Watson, *Register of Edinburgh Apprentices, 1701-1755*, Edinburgh, 1929, p.65; *The Roll of Edinburgh Burgesses and Guilds-brethrne, 1701-1841*, Edinburgh, 1930, p.181
469 South Carolina Gazette #54

SCOTTISH TRADE WITH
COLONIAL CHARLESTON, 1683-1783

Navigation'.470 Educational facilities in colonial South Carolina were, as would be expected at an early stage of development. Recognising this, one enterprising Scot, Robert Dobson, MA, is seen attempting to recruit students for his Glasgow school, by advertising for pupils in the colonial press, offering instruction in English, Latin, French, Writing, Geography, Drawing, Dancing, Arithmetic, Book-keeping and Geometry *'all useful to mechanics, merchants, scholars and statesmen. A celebrated university is at hand for such pupils as may be intended for any of the learned professions.'*471

Although before 1725 there is little evidence of the presence of Scottish merchants in Charleston, the transportation of Jacobite prisoners to Charleston in 1716 had brought men with a variety of skills. The colonial authorities found use for many of the Highlanders by employing them to defend the frontier region against hostile Indian and Spanish incursions.472 Because of their contact with the Indians, many later became Indian traders, and these men would bring deerskins traded with the Indians for other supplies, into Charleston. It may well be the case that these Indian traders preferred to deal with Scots merchants, and in this way founded early trading networks.

There is evidence that more Scots were becoming merchants in Charleston and South Carolina from the 1720s, and this may have been due to the fact that members of landed families from south-east Scotland were among the Jacobites exiled to South Carolina. The Jacobite army which invaded England in 1715 was comprised of Highlanders from around Inverness, under Mackintosh of Borlum, and Scottish gentlemen with their retainers from south-east Scotland.

470 S.C.Gaz#1261
471 Maryland Gazette #1209, 10 November 1768
472 Journal of the Commons House of Assembly, Vol.V, p.363

SCOTTISH TRADE WITH
COLONIAL CHARLESTON, 1683-1783

Merchant surnames indicating Lowland Scots of south-east origin appear ten years later in Charleston, among them the names Pringle, Nisbet and Crocket, and this would seem to hint at chain migration. One Jacobite family from south east Scotland with a *"continuous loyalty to the Stuart cause ...a striking feature of the Nisbet family'* was the Nisbets.[473] This family was represented among the Jacobites of 1716 and 1746 who were transported as prisoners to the colonies, and soon others of that name emigrated there. [474]

It seems safe to assume that transported educated men who knew how to do business would have been on the lookout for opportunities to increase their wealth. Their links at home would have provided a ready-made network for trade and finance, and the rapid expansion of the Scottish mercantile presence suggests that money for investment was available alongside mercantile experience. The trading networks can be shown to link Charleston with not only Scotland and London, but also Spain, Portugal, the eastern Atlantic islands, the Caribbean, the mainland colonies and Africa. Networks were also extended and strengthened through marriages and by social connections.

Social life began to take on the appearance and trappings of home, with the presence of the Presbyterian community dating from the seventeenth century and particularly the founding of the First (Scots) Presbyterian Church in Charleston in 1731,[475] and also the early

473 R C Nesbitt, *Nisbet of that Ilk,* London, 1941, p.43
474 D. Dobson, *The Original Scots Colonists of Early America, 1612-1783,* Baltimore, Maryland, 1988, pp.263-264
475 George Howe, *History of the Presbyterian Church in South Carolina,* Columbia, 1870
476 G S Draffen *Scottish Masonic Records, 1736-1950,* Edinburgh, 1950, p.12,

SCOTTISH TRADE WITH
COLONIAL CHARLESTON, 1683-1783

establishment of a Scottish-rite Masonic Lodge established in 1737 and chartered as the Lodge Union Kilwinning, Charleston, in 1759.[476] Charleston residents also formed a St Andrew's Society in 1729 [477], and all these institutions would have contributed to the strengthening of bonds between the Scottish families. It seems likely that the common religious denomination encouraged marriages of those of Scots descent within the colony, and examples of this are on record. Robert Pringle, who had arrived in Charleston during 1734, was married within a year to Jane Allan, daughter of Andrew Allan, a prosperous Scots merchant in the town.[478] Marriages between Scots with links to different colonies were also occurring, as in the case of William Keith, son of Dr William Keith in Charleston, and Jean Moodie, daughter of James Moodie in Jamaica, who married in Edinburgh in 1769 and returned to the Charleston in September that year.[479]

Marriage was the quickest and easiest way for a newly arrived Scottish merchant to advance in business. By marrying either the daughter or widow of a local merchant the recently arrived colonist would not only make kinship links and acquaintances, but also potential customers or suppliers. Individually and collectively Scottish merchants in Charleston and the other colonies provided a network which offered both support and opportunity to the new Scots immigrant and the established Scottish merchant alike.

It was also the case that some Scots merchants residing in Charleston at the period, who had married in Scotland, left wives and children in Scotland and returned to South Carolina alone. Generally speaking, while the northern colonies of New England and the Middle Colonies

477 see appendix
478 see W B Edgar, *The Letter Book of Robert Pringle, 1742-1745*, Columbia, S.C., 1972
479 F J Grant, *Register of Marriages in Edinburgh, 1751-1800*, Edinburgh, 1922, p.391;
S.C.Gaz.28 September 1769

228

SCOTTISH TRADE WITH
COLONIAL CHARLESTON, 1683-1783

attracted families from Scotland, men unaccompanied by wives or families settled the West Indies and to a lesser extent in the Lower South. In Charleston the picture was mixed, with some wives and children accompanying the men to the settlement and others staying at home. It is likely that the very hot climate of the southern colony and the tropical diseases found encountered there, discouraged some. Records indicated a high level of mortality of white settlers in the Lower South and the islands of the Caribbean. William Dunlop from Ayrshire, who was, for a short time, a planter in Stuartstown near Charleston in 1684, probably knew of this unattractive aspect of colonial life when he arrived unaccompanied by his wife Sarah Carstares.430

One of the earliest Scottish merchant families in business in Charleston was the Nisbets of Dean. This was a landowning family from the neighborhood of Edinburgh who grasped the economic opportunities offered to Scots in the American colonies under the Treaty of Union between Scotland and England of 1707. They may have been encouraged to consider Charleston as a place in which to invest or establish a business, by acquaintances among the Jacobites from south-east Scotland who had first appeared in Charleston in 1716 as indentured servants exiled to the colonies after the first uprising.

Sir John Nisbet of Dean, the head of the family, remained in Edinburgh and acted as financier to the enterprise, and by 1721 his brother, Robert, had arrived in Charleston and was working for Alexander Nisbet, presumably a relative. A well-documented case brought before the

430 C H Lesser, South Carolina Begins; The Records of a Proprietory Colony, 1663-1721, Columbia, S.C., 1995, p.145

SCOTTISH TRADE WITH
COLONIAL CHARLESTON, 1683-1783

High Court of the Admiralty of Scotland involving the Nisbets, illustrates how transatlantic trade between Scotland and South Carolina was carried out at this time.431

The court records show that on 2 January 1732 John Lyon and Hew Milliken, merchants in Glasgow, commissioned the Charleston merchant, Alexander Nisbet, to sell their cargo of cloth, sugar, and claret put aboard the vessel The Euphemia.   At the same time they contracted with him to buy tar, pitch, turpentine, and rice for the return shipment back to Port Glasgow.   According to the accounts supplied by Nisbet to the High Court of the Admiralty he took nearly a year to sell the consignment in relatively small quantities to retailers and possibly planters in and around Charleston.   The gross sales, mostly credit, amounted to £2589.1s.4d, payable by bills of exchange to be settled within a few months.   Alexander Nisbet is also seen to have operated as a factor on behalf of overseas merchants, as the same record shows him to have transported goods for the Charleston merchants Richard Sinclair and Hugh Campbell, originally from Scotland, to their store on the Cape Fear River, North Carolina.   Part of the consignment for these Cape Fear merchants were six Negro slaves.

Other Nisbets sought their fortunes as merchants and planters during the mid-eighteenth century in the West Indies.   Robert Nisbet of Greenholm,432 George Nisbet of Cairnhill, 433 and James Nisbet of Letham 434 settled in Jamaica, and Walter and James Nisbet in Nevis,435

431 NRS.AC9.6455
432 R C Nesbitt, *Nisbet of that Ilk,* London, 1941, p.208
433 NRS.RD2.238/1.940
434 Nesbitt, *Nisbet*p.208
435 NRS.CC8.......8.108; V L Oliver, *Monumentla Inscriptions of the British West Indies,* Dorchester, England, 1927, p.97

230

SCOTTISH TRADE WITH
COLONIAL CHARLESTON, 1683-1783

David and Robert Nisbet in St Kitts.436 The latter, Robert Nisbet, who died 29 September 1740 437 had connections with the Glasgow merchant David Nisbet, and is seen to have been first in Nevis where is brother Walter is also documented, before moving to St Kitts. Another Nisbet, John, eldest son of George Nisbet of Cairnhill, Lanarkshire settled as a planter on Belisle Estate, Jamaica before 1784.438

The Pringles are another prominent family of Scots descent found in both Charleston and in the West Indian islands of Jamaica, Dominica and St Kitts. The published letter book of Robert Pringle, partly in book form 439 and partly in a journal, 440 also provides insight into the area of Scottish connections and trading links of a Charleston-based Scots merchant.

After serving an apprenticeship under Humphrey Hill, a London merchant trading with the West Indies, Robert Pringle settled in Charleston during 1725, taking up employment as a factor for various British and colonial firms. His brother, Andrew, was for some time master of a merchant ship before becoming a London merchant, but the two did not seem to have business interests in common. In Charleston, Robert Pringle was in partnership with a James Reid, probably a Scot, in the Guinea Trade, otherwise known as the Slave Trade, between Robert Pringle was in partnership with a James Reid, probably a Scot, in the Guinea Trade, otherwise known as the Slave Trade, between

436 National Library of Scotland. Ms8793/4
437 NRS.CC8.8.108
438 NRS.RD2.238/1.940
439 W B Edgar, *Letter Book of Robert Pringle, 1737-1742,* Columbia, S.C., 1972
440 *South Carolina Historical Magazine,* Vol.XXV, Charleston, 1924

1740 and 1742, when his partner changed to George Inglis.   His correspondents over the years appear to have been almost exclusively Scots or those of Scots origin, but who were resident everywhere in the British Atlantic World, except Scotland.441   These included John Erving and Alexander Forsyth, both merchants in Boston; James Henderson in New York; Alexander McKenzie in Virginia; Alexander Grant in Rhode Island; Hugh Pringle in Belfast; Stewart and Ferguson in London; Alexander Andrew in Rotterdam; Charles Campbell in Gibraltar; James Archibald in Oporto; Robert Scott in Madeira, and many others in the West Indies and the American South.   Profits from trade were invested in plantations, enabling the family to diversify its economic base at the same time as vertically integrating its business interests.

The first involuntary immigrants were joined in the 1730s by more Highlanders, recruited from the Inverness area to guard the frontiers of the new colony of Georgia.   These included Archibald and Lauchlan MacBean who began trading with Indians there at this time.442 Ludovic Grant, was an Indian trader among the Cherokees from 1724 until around 1750.443   Daniel Clark worked as an Indian trader in Augusta and then turns up in Charleston.444 One of the most successful Highlanders in the Indian trade was Lachlan McGillivray 445 who rose

441 ibid, passim
442 E Merton Coulter & Albert B Saye, *A List of the Early Settlers of Georgia*, Baltimore, Maryland, 1983, p.83
443 Charleston Probate Court Book, 1754-1758, P.31
444 Probate 1757 SC
445 A W Parker, *Scottish Highlanders in Colonial Georgia, The Recruitment, Emigration, and Settlement at Darien, 1735-1748*, Athens, Georgia, 1997, pp.97-98

SCOTTISH TRADE WITH
COLONIAL CHARLESTON, 1683-1783

from being a pack-horseman to becoming a member of HM Council for Georgia.

The Indian trade was not the prerogative of Highlanders alone and among the Lowland Scots were William Struthers from Alva who worked as an Indian trader in Augusta from around 1760 [446] and Alexander Fyffe from Dundee who was the son of James Fyffe of Dron and brother of John Fyffe, a merchant in Dundee who traded with Charleston.[447] This Alexander Fyfe announced in the South Carolina Gazette of 11 July 1761 the opening of a store in Savannah for the Indian trade, *'deerskins or cash taken'*.[448] He died in Charleston in May 1766.[449] John Gordon was settled as a merchant in Charleston during the 1740s, and between 1759 and 1773 he was probably the major exporter of deerskins in the city, later moving to East Florida.[449] Panton, Leslie and Company was one of the biggest firms involved in the Indian trade in the American South, and both Panton and Leslie were Scots from the north-east. John Leslie [1749-1803] was born in Morayshire, and William Panton [1742-1801] in Aberdeenshire.[450] Originally operating in Savannah, Georgia, the firm found it expedient to move to St Augustine during the American Revolution. When the Spanish regained East Florida from the British in 1783 they permitted Panton, Leslie and Company to remain in St Augustine. It's established trading practices with the surrounding Indians was extremely valuable to the local economy, and its removal would have

446 TNA.CO5.648.E68

447 W R Brock, *Scotus Americanus,* Edinburgh, 1982, p.29

448 S.C.Gaz#1407

449 Georgia Gazette, Vol.1/1; probate 1766, Georgia

450 W S Coker & T D Watson, *Indian Traders of the South Eastern Spanish Borderlands,* Gainesville, Florida, 1986

had dire economic consequences for Spanish Florida. Of equal importance was the firm's good relationship with the Indians, which contributed to maintaining security and stability within the colony, a fact which the Spanish recognised. 451

Scots entering the Indian trade later in the eighteenth century, had an advantage over other ethnic groups, in that a considerable number of government posts were in the hands of fellow Scots who gave them their support: men such as John Stuart, the Superintendent of Indian Affairs in the Southern District of America from 1762, or his secretary William Ogilvy, from Angus, between 1764 and 1776.452

However, despite the prominence of the Scots among the Indian traders and deerskin merchants, very little trade was in this product was done with Scotland, possibly only a score of consignments during the colonial era.453

Scottish Merchants Trading with Charleston

Leith and Greenock were the main Scottish ports trading with Charleston during the colonial period. The following represents a decennial sample of exports taken from the Exchequer records detailing the cargoes sent from these two ports to South Carolina between the years 1745 - 1775. These records provide details on those merchants exporting goods to the colony of South Carolina. There would appear, from the port of Leith records of the years 1745 and 1755 that few individual merchants traded repeatedly with Charleston, the only

451 ibid
452 TNA.AO12.51.146; AO12.47.141
453 NRS.E504, series, passim

merchant's name which is seen duplicated in these records is that of George Anderson, who sent one cargo of tallow candles and another of handkerchiefs. From the table below it will be seen that many merchants were involved in sending a large variety of goods. The data from Greenock paints a similar picture. However, the merchants of Greenock which do appear in the records are almost all names which also were active in the tobacco trade with the Chesapeake. Trade with Charleston seems to have been relatively small-scale from these two ports, with no more than two vessels leaving either port in any one of the sample years.

Table 6/1
Leith merchants exporting to South Carolina

1745	1755
Magdalene	**Endeavour**
	(1st Voyage)
Hugh Clerk	William Bellfor
John Greenlees	David Graham
Robert Greenlees	John Morrison
David Somervail	Robert Moody
David Deas	David Loch
George Anderson	
Alexander Learmonth	**Endeavour**
Mercury	
Charles Mayne	[2nd voyage]
James Strachan	George Anderson J
Robert Grant	McCulloch & Todd
John Hay	
John Graham	

SCOTTISH TRADE WITH
COLONIAL CHARLESTON, 1683-1783

1765

Jean of Ely
Robert Scott Moncrieff
John Smith

Bachelors of Leith
John Farquhar
Sheriff and Guthrie
Robert Mundell
James Strachan
Robert Grant
John Hay
John Graham

1775

George of Leith
John Hutton
Alexander Scott
William Stoddart
JamesLindsay
Edward Corbett
John Fairbairn
Hugh Cheap

Table 6/2
Greenock Merchants exporting to South Carolina

1745

Robert of Greenock
Robert Donald
James Peadie
James Smelie
Archibald & John Coates
Richard & Alex.Oswald
George Murdoch
Gabriel Mathie

1755

Catherine
John Glasford
Alexander Buchanan
William Watson
George Kippen
Robert Gilmour

SCOTTISH TRADE WITH
COLONIAL CHARLESTON, 1683-1783

Alex Porterfield	**Rebecca**
James Andrews	Robert Gilmour
Robert Gilmour	Alex. Buchanan

The variety of merchants trading from the port of Leith and Greenock differs from the situation found in Dundee, where the same merchants traded on a regular basis. Between 1753 and 1773 the port of Dundee despatched on average one vessel to Charleston each year. Each westward bound vessel carried a wide range of products, some of which were manufactured locally, with the rest coming from either elsewhere in Scotland or abroad.[378]

Duncan Campbell, the son of Duncan Campbell, the minister of Rosneath, and his wife Elizabeth Shaw, was a merchant in Edinburgh trading with Charleston around the middle of the eighteenth century, and had a varied commercial career. Starting off as a Glasgow merchant, he is subsequently to be found in New York in 1726, the following year in Kingston, Jamaica, in London during the 1740s, and then to Edinburgh. This travelling man may have been a member of the St Andrew's Society of Charleston in 1730, as this name appears on their records. Campbell married Janet Black, daughter of the merchant Alexander Black, in Edinburgh in 1739, and settled in Edinburgh around 1750. From this Edinburgh base he became established as a merchant importing indigo from the colony of South Carolina, which he then processed in his workshop in the Grassmarket for supply to Scotland's burgeoning textile industry. Documents indicate that Campbell had links with Robert Cumming, an Episcopal clergyman in

---

[378] NRS.E504.11.3-8, passim

the vicinity of Charleston, who seems to have supplied shipments of indigo on a small scale around 1750. For some undisclosed reason Excise officers saw fit to raid Campbell's workshop in the Grassmarket and closed for a month during which time they removed unspecified articles. As Duncan Campbell seems to have been the sole manufacturer and merchant of indigo in the city, such an interruption of supply may well have had implications for the local textile industry.[379]

On 14 September 1753, the Customs Collector in Dundee wrote to the Board of Customs advising them that the <u>Mercury of Dundee</u>, a 160 ton square-sterned ship, master Robert Stirling, had arrived from Amsterdam with timber for Dundee. In addition it carried three hogsheads of brandy, six hogsheads of gin, eight casks of currants, one box of diaper, and eighty cases of empty bottles for onward shipment to Madeira, and '*Fifteen bales and two trunks of bounty linen, one box of British printed linen, four casks, three trunks, four bundles and two cloak-bags whereof the shoes, saddles and other leather manufactures*' were for Carolina.[380] Other commodities which were shipped from Dundee were beer and linen from Danzig, wine from Spain and Madeira, glass-bottles from Holland, and drinking glasses from Newcastle. Locally produced goods included textiles, particularly linen-wares, soap, leather-ware, especially saddles and shoes, ironmongery, sailcloth, books and nails. Linen came from Renfrewshire, coal from Alloa and Bo'ness, snuff from Aberdeen, beer from Edinburgh, and glass-bottles from Leith. These widely varied cargoes were supplied by individual merchants or partnerships, mostly

[379] NRS.RD2.28.11.1707; NRS.RH15.59; J. Scott, (ed.), *Fasti Ecclesiae Scoticanae,*, Edinburgh, Scotland, 1915-, Volume 3, fo.363
380 NRS.CE70.1.3

SCOTTISH TRADE WITH
COLONIAL CHARLESTON, 1683-1783

based in Dundee, some regularly sending consignments to Charleston. The firm of Smith, Strachan and Company of Dundee exported in 1756, 1757, 1759, 1760 and 1763; John Rankine, merchant of Dundee, in 1770, 1772, 1773, and 1775, while James Fotheringham, another Dundonian, only appears as a freighter to Charleston on one occasion.[381]

Some firms based around the Forth opted to use Dundee as a port of export despite the existing shipping links that existed with South Carolina from local ports. Among these were the Edinburgh Glasshouse Company which annually, between the years 1761 and 1765 sent regular consignments of glass-bottles, and the Edinburgh brewers, John Milne and Hugh Bell, who each sent ale from their breweries in the Pleasants. On the return voyage from Charleston the cargo of rice would be dropped off mainly at Lisbon and Amsterdam, and the rest including deerskins, indigo and timber, together with lemons, oranges, almonds, cork, salt, wine loaded in Lisbon would arrive in Dundee. [382] It seems clear from the above that the port of Dundee was successfully exporting goods brought from the Baltic, Spain, Portugal, the Netherlands and England, as well as those locally produced, to South Carolina during the late colonial period.

Marketing in South Carolina

The South Carolina Gazette, started in 1732, was the only newspaper published in Charleston, and its columns provide an insight into how the Scottish merchants there promoted and distributed their imported wares and also give an indication how they obtained the raw materials they exported to Europe. Established shopkeepers would advertise a

[381] NRS.E504.11.3-8
[382] NRS.E504.11; NRS.CE70.1.3,4,5

wide range of commodities imported from the British Isles and ports
visited by vessels en route, such as Madeira.   Issue Number Seventy-
nine of this newspaper announced that the brigantine Betty, master
Robert Boyd had arrived from Glasgow on 14 July 1733:

> 'To be sold at Captain R. Austin's on the Bay, choice claret
> imported on the Betty from Glasgow, Scotch coal at £4 per
> chaldron on board the said brigantine lying at the wharf, and
> good Madeira wine, by Alexander Nisbet'.

These advertisements show that the Scots merchants did not rely solely
on Scottish suppliers, but goods were also shipped from other ports,
especially London.   Robert Pringle advertised on 11 May 1734:
*'Hollands, calicos, hose, shoes, tea, pipes, saddles, ironware, sugar,
etc, just imported on the Happy Gilbert, master J. Paul, from London'*

Evidence of family networks are can be seen by newspaper
advertisements in which goods are transferred between people of the
same surname, for instance Andrew Pringle, master of the Susannah,
arrived from Madeira with wine which was subsequently sold by Robert
Pringle.[383]   James Seaman, master of the Davie, docked in Charleston
with goods from London which were later sold by the firm Crokatt and
Seaman.[384]

Imported goods could, however, be sold directly off newly arrived
vessels, as seen from the local newspaper, the *South Carolina Gazette*.
One, dated 7 January 1751 announces:

> 'Cargo imported on the ship Industry from Leith and Lisbon,
> Cowan, wines, ales, threads, gingham, and Sheffield wares,

[383] SCGaz No 51
[383] SCGaz No 89

grates, olive oil, sold on board ship at Mollen wharf, will take rice in payment'.

The bartering of goods was not uncommon, and may also often have been the method of payment for indentured servants. This certainly was certainly the case in November 1753 when Andrew Cowan advertised:

'An assortment of Scots manufactures including saddles, mahogany desks, wigs, books, bibles, good red wine, mustard, barley, coal, and at his store has to dispose of several tradesmen of good character, under four year indentures, among whom are joiners, house carpenters, shipwrights. Any person inclined to purchase any may have them on trial before he makes a bargain. NB merchantable rice, pitch, tar, turpentine, mahogany, deerskin, beaver, or indigo will be taken in payment at market prices'.

Probably one of the earliest stores in rural South Carolina was established by Charleston-based Scots in 1723.[385] In that year Alexander Kinloch and Alexander Nisbet became partners in a store at Redbank with an initial capital amount of six thousand pounds. The following year Walter Nisbet, a merchant in Berkley County, joined this partnership.

Some of the stock of manufactured goods sold at Redbank may well have been supplied by William Robertson a merchant in Edinburgh, as a bill of exchange was issued in his favor in 1724, drawn on Sir John Nisbet of Dean. Ten years later Robertson was still supplying the

---

[385] NRS. Tods, Murray and Jamieson Collection, GD237.1.153

Nisbets in Charleston, which suggests a regular but unrecorded shipping link from Leith.[386] On the other hand, it may be that the goods were sent from Leith to London for shipment to Charleston. Robert Nisbet, brother of Sir John Nisbet of Dean, was indentured as an apprentice merchant under Alexander Nisbet, merchant in Charleston, on 15 June 1721 and was soon active in their stores at Charleston and at Redbank. [387]

The Scots merchants of colonial Charleston differed from those on the Chesapeake in a number of ways. The most obvious variation was that while the Tobacco Lords of Glasgow dominated the Scottish merchant community in Virginia and Maryland, this pattern was not repeated in Charleston. Merchants from both the east and west coast of Scotland were well represented in South Carolina, indeed the majority may well have come from the eastern lowlands. Merchants in Glasgow could trade with the Chesapeake more efficiently because of its west coast geographical location. The Clyde based merchants capitalised on their great advantage of access to the quickest route between Britain and the Chesapeake, enabling them to make the most effective use of their financial, material and human resources and enjoy both absolute and comparative advantage over the control of this trade. The store system on the Chesapeake, which the Glasgow tobacco merchants developed, reduced the turn-around time of their vessels, and added to the overall efficiency of the operation. Another variation that existed between the two regions was that while the trade between Scotland and the Chesapeake was mainly vessels shuttling back and forward, the Charleston trade was more of a triangular trade with shipping trading

<hr>

[386] NRS.GD237.1.153/31
387 NRS.GD237.1.153/29

between Charleston, Europe especially Iberia, and Scotland, details of which was considered in an earlier chapter.

Chief factors controlled the networks established by different companies of Glasgow tobacco merchants. In Virginia and Maryland these factors were based in the major towns of Norfolk and Alexandria, Virginia. In South Carolina there were no equivalent agents controlling trade although some individual Charleston merchants had subsidiary stores in parts of South Carolina or Georgia, or had direct links with the Indian traders of the interior who supplied deerskins. The destinations of colonial produce exported from the Chesapeake were also different from that exported from Charleston. Under the Navigation Acts, all colonial produce had to be shipped to a British port in the first instance, and this certainly happened in the case of tobacco where much of it was bound for Glasgow, where it was processed before being re-exported to European markets, creating jobs and wealth in and around Clyde ports in the process. However, the rice, indigo, timber and deerskins shipped from colonial Charleston, even on Scottish vessels, largely went directly to their ultimate markets. This meant, of course, that there was not the same creation of jobs and wealth associated with the trade from this port.

The reason ships were able to by-pass Scotland was that introduction of Mediterranean Passes.[388] Under the Navigation Acts, ships leaving American colonial ports were required to call in at any port in Great Britain before delivering cargo of colonial produce to continental destinations. This increased costs and also postponed delivery times, which collectively made the commodities less competitive in the

---

[388] T. M. Devine, *The Tobacco Lords. A Study of the Tobacco Merchants of Glasgow and their Trading Activities, 1740-90*, Edinburgh, 1975, p.13

SCOTTISH TRADE WITH
COLONIAL CHARLESTON, 1683-1783

European market. Carolinian rice was therefore at a disadvantage with rice brought from the French or Spanish colonies. To overcome this problem the British government introduced the system of Mediterranean Passes under which ships carrying colonial produce, except tobacco, were allowed to sail directly to ports south of Cape Finisterre. Shipmasters before leaving their home ports would obtain a Mediterranean Pass from the local Collector of Customs and returned it having delivered their cargo to ports in Iberia or Italy. In Scotland the issue of such licenses was under the jurisdiction of the Board of Customs in Edinburgh. Rice would allowed to be shipped directly to the markets of Spain and Portugal, while many of the ships with cargo which did require to comply with the Navigations Acts called in at English Channel ports, such as Cowes, to fulfil the terms of the Acts before proceeding to the markets of northern Europe, especially Rotterdam.

The regular shuttle operating to and fro between the Clyde and the Chesapeake was not the same as the trade routes of South Carolina where a triangular route was followed. If Mediterranean passes were used the route was: Scotland to Charleston, Charleston to Iberia, Iberia to Scotland. When not using this pass, the ships sailed either directly between Scotland and Charleston, returning via Cowes to Rotterdam, and from there directly to Scotland or indirectly via a north European port to Scotland. While the Clyde-Chesapeake axis operated quite simply as far as cargoes out and in were concerned, the Carolina trade was more complex involving more ports and varied cargoes. The trade routes out from Charleston were for this reason less cost efficient than the Clyde-Chesapeake run and the Scottish merchant firms trading with the Chesapeake may have been larger organisations than those trading

SCOTTISH TRADE WITH
COLONIAL CHARLESTON, 1683-1783

with Charleston as they operated numerous stores throughout the
Chesapeake whereas with commerce concentrated largely in Charleston
a fewer retail and wholesale outlets were required.

Finance

Emigrants to Charleston intending to follow a mercantile career had
either to arrive with sufficient capital to establish a business or they had
to have credit with major merchant houses in London or elsewhere in
Great Britain.   Some younger members of the landed or mercantile
families of Scotland seem to have had little problem in financing their
mercantile adventures. J. Russell Snapp refers to Charles Ogilvie, from
Aberdeenshire, who went to London in 1751 to raise capital or credit
before emigrating to South Carolina.[389]   In London, Ogilvie met
Charles and James Crokatt, two Scots who had previously been
merchants in Charleston before to returning to the British Isles and
establishing their business in London. The Crokatts provided Ogilvie
with the necessary introductions to enable him to raise the credit he
sought and together with funds raised from his family, Ogilvie was then
able to become established as a merchant in Charleston and began his
involvement in the Scottish trading network which ranged throughout
the British Atlantic world.

In every link of this network, merchants sought not only to diversify the
variety of products in which they traded, but also supplied the finance
or credit essential to the continued growth of commence, both domestic

[389] J Russell Snapp, *John Stuart and the Struggle for Empire on the Southern Frontier,* Baton
Rouge, Louisiana, 1990, pp. 22-24

and international.   To facilitate this flow of funds, often merchants would discount bills of exchange.   The following advertisement appeared in the Edinburgh Evening Courant in July 1730, inserted by James Blair, Saltmarket, Glasgow, in which he offered to deal with: 'persons who have occasion to buy or sell bills of exchange, or want to borrow, or have money to lend on interest, or have any sort of goods to sell, or want to buy any kinds of goods, or who want to buy sugarhouse notes, or other good bills, or desire to have such notes or bills discounted, or who want to have policies signed, or incline to underwrite policies in ships or goods'.[390]

Once a merchant in Charleston had arranged credit with a merchant house or bank in Great Britain, he was then in a position to issue bills of exchange.   To pay for imports, the Charlestonian would hand over a bill of exchange to the shipmaster or supercargo (a term used for a merchant's agent aboard ship) in exchange for the wares.   This document was an instruction to the banker or merchant in the British Isles with whom the Carolina merchant had established credit, to pay to a named party or assignee a specific sum of money on a fixed or determinable future date.   These bills of exchange were always post-dated, and had the advantage to the colonial merchant of enabling him to sell the goods bought and receive payment from his customers before the date of settlement.   When the exporting merchant had in his possession the bill of exchange, he could either wait until the due date for payment in full, or he could discount the bill with a bank or money merchant, the amount of discount depending on the current rates of interest, together with the creditworthiness of the issuer of the bill.

[390] Robert Chambers, *The Domestic Annals of Scotland, Volume 3,* Edinburgh, Scotland, 1861, p. 577

SCOTTISH TRADE WITH
COLONIAL CHARLESTON, 1683-1783

This system of payment was also in use within the colonies themselves, alongside payment in cash and produce.[391]

Merchants fulfilled many of the financial roles later provided by the increasing emergence of banks. During the seventeenth century only a limited amount of banking services were available in Scotland, mostly provided by the Edinburgh goldsmiths. This was to change around the beginning of the eighteenth century, when the Bank of Scotland opened its doors in 1695, and the Royal Bank of Scotland in 1727. In addition to this there were a small number of local country banks and some merchants who also acted as bankers. The most prominent of the merchant firms which also provided banking services was the British Linen Company, founded 1746. Driven by demand, the second half of the eighteenth century saw a rapid expansion throughout Scotland of merchant-bankers and bill-discounters as well as local banks. In Glasgow, the Ship Bank was founded in 1749, the Thistle Bank was founded in 1761, and the Arms Bank was founded in 1750. It was due to the significant interest in the Virginian and West Indian trades that these banks were established by local merchants, and they were largely committed to the financing of port facilities and providing credit for merchant houses and colonial planters. It can be seen, therefore, that towards the end of our period Scottish merchants, at home and abroad, had a relatively good banking system in place to provide the financial support necessary for development of all sorts, and it seems likely since they were financing the tobacco and merchants, that they were also making funds available to those merchants who were expanding their interests in Charleston. Although the availability of credit greatly

[391] R. C. Nash, 'The Organisation of Trade and Finance in the Atlantic Economy', J. P. Greene, R. Brana-Shute, and R. J. Sparks, (eds), Money Trade, and Power, The Evolution of Colonial South Carolina's Plantation Society, Columbia, South Carolina, p.84

SCOTTISH TRADE WITH
COLONIAL CHARLESTON, 1683-1783

improved the business community's ability to expand, the system was not without its casualties. In 1772 the collapse of the Douglas, Heron and Company, bankers in Ayr caused a major financial panic at the time and a consequential drop in land values. Since many Bank owners were also landowners, their need to pay creditors required the sale of land. Their financial problems caused a fall in land prices, and a knock on effect of widespread unemployment which in turn increased the number of emigrants to America, shortly before the outbreak of the American War of Independence.[392]

The far less developed access to funding in Charleston than that of contemporary Scotland caused residents to be more dependent upon each other and Scots did come to the aid of their countrymen in times of need. In 1752, John Crokatt, the Scottish merchant in Charleston, provided financial aid to a shipwrecked Scottish mariner, master Robert Wardroper. In 1751 his two hundred ton ship the Newmarket of London, was bound from Jamaica to London when it became severely damaged in a storm and was forced to seek refuge in Beaufort, South Carolina. Wardroper, a Dundonian, was able to raise the necessary finance to repair his ship through John Crokatt, whose family had links with Dundee. However, it has to be said that Crokatt later found it necessary to take legal action in the High Court of the Admiralty of England to recover his loan.[393]

---

[392] T M Devine, *Scotland's Empire, 1600-1815,* London, 2003, p. 113
[393] TNA.HCA.15.60

SCOTTISH TRADE WITH COLONIAL CHARLESTON, 1683-1783

Networking

Networking was not a new concept. The expansion of business depends on credit and therefore on trust. Trust in one's compatriots, especially relatives and friends, or one's co-religionists, is one of the most natural practices in a business community and therefore is the foundation of commercial networking. Networking occurs when individuals in a community, large or small, establish economic or social links. The founders of the Scottish transatlantic networks were the Scots based on islands in the eastern Atlantic Ocean, the Azores, Madeira, the Canaries, possibly as early as the fifteenth century, and these acted as intermediaries between English and Spanish merchants during periods of hostilities between these nations. John Drummond from Perth, claiming to be a nephew of Robert III, settled on Funchal, Madeira, and his descendants spread to the Azores. William Crawford and William Ray, 'Englishmen', were operating in Madeira in the 1640s, while Henry Criton, was an 'English' merchant on Funchal during the 1680s.[394] Another Scot, Walter Mowbray, was in Spain and in the Canary Islands around 1600 [395], and John Cross, a merchant from Glasgow, was a factor on the Canary Islands from 1695 to 1703.[396]

From these small beginnings, networking expanded as the seventeenth century progressed to incorporate Scots factors and merchants based all around the North Atlantic. In London, from 1670 John Foulis, and James his son, were prominent Scottish merchants active in overseas

---

[394] T B Duncan, *Atlantic Islands Madeira, The Azores and the Cape Verde Islands in Seventeenth Century Commerce and Navigation,* Chicago, Illinois, 1972, pp. 55-56
[395] Calendar of State Papers, Scotland, Volume II, London, England, 1858
[396] NRS.PC2.28.271; also see L. de Alberti and A. B. Wallis-Chapman, *English Merchants and the Spanish Inquisition in the Canaries,* London, 1912

trade, and members of a Scottish mercantile group.[397] Andrew Russell, a merchant from Stirling who settled in Rotterdam, was at the centre of another Scottish network linking the Baltic, the North Sea, the Bay of Biscay, to Surinam, New York, and New England, in the late seventeenth century.[398] Some networks are based on religious denomination as well as ethnic origins, as in the case of the Scots Quakers trading between Scotland, New Jersey, Pennsylvania and Barbados in the later seventeenth century. The establishment and development of a Scots network and an example of chain migration, which is likely to have been mirrored in South Carolina, is outlined in Angus Calder's account of the position in the contemporary colony of St Kitt's:

> 'Walter Tullideph, son of a Kirk minister, went out to Antigua about 1726 as a doctor. Several friends and relatives were already established in their professions there. He sold Scottish linen and other goods to the planters, carrying merchandise on his doctor's rounds. After ten years he married a widow who owned 63 slaves. After forty he had over 500 acres and 271 slaves. He brought in other Scots doctors, plantation managers, attorneys and lessees.'[399]

According to David Hancock,[400] nine of the top ten wine exporters of wine in Madeira during 1768 were British, controlling sixty three per

---

[397] See for example –TNA.HCA.Examinations, Volume 82, James Foulis and William Gordon versus the King, 9.11.1700, a case concerning an
infringement of the Navigation Acts by two Scots, the owner and skipper of a London ship trading with America
[398] NRS.RH15.106
[399] Angus Calder, *Revolutionary Empire, The Rise of the English-Speaking Empires from the Fifteenth Century to the 1780s*, London, 1981, p.426
[399] David Hancock, *The Early Modern Atlantic Economy*, Cambridge, England, 2000

cent of the exports, and of these, twenty-eight per cent were managed
by Scots. Some of this wine reached South Carolina either directly or
indirectly via Scottish and English ports. John Murray was one of the
Scots merchants of Charleston trading with Madeira, who, as stated
above, had links with the Scottish merchant Robert Scott of Madeira.
The Scots wine merchants of Madeira around 1768 included James and
John Murdoch, James Duff, Joseph Gillis, and Andrew Donaldson.

The St Andrew's Society of Charleston which was founded in 1729 was
the leading Scottish organisation in South Carolina. Its membership
largely comprised of Scots, and men of Scots origin. Between its date
of formation and the outbreak of the American War of Independence,
five hundred and five men were admitted to membership of the Society.
Although the records provide only the names and dates of admittance,
it has been possible to identify the occupations of one hundred and
eighty-seven, or approximately thirty-seven per cent, of the Society's
members. There were forty-nine merchants, sixteen colonial
administrators, twenty-nine shipmasters, seventeen physicians, four
planters, fifty military officers, one Cherokee chief, and twenty-one
with various occupations such as ministers and craftsmen. The vast
majority of members had Scottish surnames, as would be expected, but
based also on surnames, there were also ten Huguenots, sixteen English,
two Welsh, two Irish, two Dutch, one Jewish, and one Native American.
The impression is that most Scots of a professional level arriving in
Charleston, even on a temporary basis, applied for membership of the
Society, and included shipmasters and officers of the 77th Regiment of
Foot (Montgomery's Highlanders) who were stationed there during the
French and Indian War. It may be assumed that the existence of the St
Andrew's Society of Charleston was to some extent a centre of
networking of Scots in the colony of South Carolina, and in all

SCOTTISH TRADE WITH
COLONIAL CHARLESTON, 1683-1783

probability in the Lower South. The elite of the Scottish community in and around Charleston were members of the Society, and the majority of these were merchants.[401] The Society provided a forum in which the Scots could work, trade, exchange information, provide financial assistance, as well as socialise, to their mutual advantage.

By the outbreak of the American Revolution Masonic Lodges using the Scottish rite had also been established throughout the American colonies. These lodges were most numerous in Virginia where eight were located. Elsewhere on the North American mainland lodges could be found in Boston, Philadelphia, Florida, and Charleston. The Charleston Masonic Lodge was opened in 1759 and, like the St Andrews Society, would have been an important meeting place for Scots networking around the British Atlantic World, enabling recently arrived Scottish immigrants to quickly integrate with the local community and establish themselves within the colonial economy. By the 1760s Masonic Lodges, of the Scottish-rite, were also to be found in Jamaica, Antigua and St Kitts; all being islands with trading links to Charleston also to Scotland, and containing sizable Scottish populations.

Integration of Settlers

During the colonial period, over three hundred and thirty merchants bearing Scots surnames have been identified as being involved in businesses in Charleston or elsewhere in South Carolina.[402] It can be assumed that most were therefore either Scottish or the sons of Scots,

[401] See Appendix 6
[401] See Appendices 2, 6

although a number may have come from Ulster. Among these three hundred and thirty were eighty two established partnerships with one or more partner bearing a Scots name and the other partner having a surname indicating a different ethnic origin. Of these, as far as can be ascertained, based on surnames, there were fourteen partnership where one of the partners seems to have been of English origin; nine examples where there were Huguenot partners; one instance where the partner was of Dutch origin; and possibly one with a Jewish partner. From these figures can be seen the beginnings of the melting pot which America became.

Religious denomination enabled the Scots to choose to either integrate or to remain apart within colonial Charleston. As far as can be ascertained most, if not all, of the Scots found in South Carolina during the late seventeenth century and early eighteenth century were Presbyterians. In Stuartstown they had been served by William Dunlop as minister, and from 1700 in Charleston, by Archibald Stobo, a minister of the Church of Scotland who had arrived as a refugee from Darien. Appeals were made to the General Assembly for a supply of qualified ministers for South Carolina but there were not many volunteers. [403] Perhaps for this reason, before 1731 the Presbyterians in Charleston seem to have merged with their fellow Calvinists, the Congregationalists. Eventually, however, thirty Scottish families abandoned this arrangement to establish the First (Scots) Presbyterian Church of Charleston. During the colonial period it is likely that the bulk of its congregation were of Scots and Ulster origin, and the solidarity of its members would have provided an additional support network for the Scots community there.[404] Friendship bonds would

[403] NRS.CH1/2.24/1/fos.110-112; 24/2.fos.224-227; 32, fos.531-540
[403] Howe, *Presbyterian Church,* passim

SCOTTISH TRADE WITH
COLONIAL CHARLESTON, 1683-1783

have been forged between merchant families which in turn strengthened the trust required for the provision of credit, on which most commercial contracts were built.

At the same time there seem to have been a number of Scots Episcopalians in South Carolina, some no doubt among the Jacobite transportees and others among the local merchants. These latter would have come from the gentry of the north east of Scotland, as was the case with members of the Ogilvie of Auchiries family.[405] From Edinburgh, John Crockatt and David Deas are described as wardens of St Philips Episcopal Church in 1751. [406] In some outlying areas where there was a lack of choice, or of minister, it may have been the case that Scots joined other dominations, as did a substantial number of French Huguenots who became Anglicans. In the early years of the American colonies there was a shortage of Anglican priests. This fact encouraged Scottish Episcopal ministers and schoolmasters, who were unable to obtain employment in Scotland, to apply for positions as Anglican priests in South Carolina and other colonies. One Scottish Episcopal minister who resided in South Carolina between the years 1764-1777 was the Loyalist, Reverend Alexander Cumine, who during the Revolution moved on to Kingston, Jamaica.[407] The Reverend James Stuart, another Loyalist, served in Prince George's parish, South Carolina from 1771 – 1777. [408] The integration of some Scots within the Church of England, the Established Church in South Carolina since 1706, would no doubt have created familiarity and good faith among people of varying ethnic roots, in turn benefiting commercial interests within the merchant community.

[405] Aberdeen University Library, Special Collections, Ogilvie-Forbes of Boyndlie papers, ms2740/10/4-
[406] SCGaz No 883
[407] TNA.AO12.49.422
[408] TNA.AO12.50.375
254

SCOTTISH TRADE WITH
COLONIAL CHARLESTON, 1683-1783

Sojourners

A significant minority of those emigrating to the American colonies in the seventeenth and eighteenth centuries did not intend to stay there permanently. Rather, they intended to make their fortunes in the New World and then return home. There was a significant difference in immigration between the northern and southern colonies. As a rough rule of thumb, the northern colonies attracted families, which strongly indicated a commitment to resettlement. The climate in the north was more moderate, and diseases less prevalent. Climate and tropical disease were factors that unaccompanied men were willing to put up with if there was a chance to make a lot of money quickly, with the hope of returning home considerably richer than they left. The West Indies obviously fell into this category, and increasingly, the southern mainland colonies were introducing the plantation system where wealth could be generated at minimal cost using the same slavery system.

South Carolina was a plantation colony which had been settled by colonists from Barbados,[409] bringing with them the methods, attitudes and sojourning practices prevalent there. To some extent these methods were introduced in the Chesapeake also, where young Glasgow men were happy to take up employment as storekeepers or factors, which enabled them to set up in some style when they returned home. The practice in South Carolina seems to have been a hybrid between what the experience was in the Caribbean and that on the Chesapeake. Whereas in the Caribbean many went for the sole purpose of making a quick fortune and returning home, and immigrants to the northern colonies, for the most part, intended to settle permanently

---

[409] Warren Ripley, *Charles Towne, Birth of a City,* Charleston, South Carolina, 1970, p. 4

there, in the Lower South, those arriving included both sojourners and permanent settlers. In a way William Dunlop, leader of the Scots settlers in Stuartstown, could be considered as a sojourner although he had not made a fortune in South Carolina. On 26 March 1688 he wrote from South Carolina to Sir James Montgomerie of Skelmorlie:

> 'I am resolved to return within eight to ten months at latest to see you all, not that I am resolved to quit this country and our interests here but that I yield so far to the desires of my wife and other friends as to see Holland.'[410]

A number of gentry families who had fallen upon hard times, sent out their sons to make their fortunes in the colonies before returning to Scotland to restore the family to its rightful position in society. Having acquired economic success, some emigrants returned briefly to Scotland to marry, before returning to work in the colonies. John Stuart was a South Carolinian merchant from Leith, whose wife, Henrietta Burnett, died in Edinburgh in 1718. [411]

Those whose families lived with them in South Carolina found it necessary to send their children north or home to Britain for education. Robert Pringle sent his son, John Julius, to be educated at the College of Philadelphia, then to the Middle Temple in London. Dr Alexander Garden the botanist, sent his son Alexander to study medicine at Glasgow University in 1779. Among the Pringle/Garden Families Papers, 1701-1882, [412] is a letter written by Robert Pringle of

---

[410] NRS., Eglinton Muniments, GD3.5.778
[411] NRS.CC8.8.87
[411] South Carolina Historical Society, MS275/01/01

SCOTTISH TRADE WITH
COLONIAL CHARLESTON, 1683-1783

Symington from Balfour's Coffee House in Edinburgh, dated 4 March 1772, which was conveyed from Leith by Captain Alexander to Charleston. This letter reveals that the recipient, his nephew in South Carolina, intended to invest in property in Edinburgh and possibly improve the farm at Symington, indicating perhaps, that his nephew was intending to return to Scotland in the future. It also suggests that the writer's son had come back to Scotland from the College of Philadelphia. Robert Pringle himself had obviously returned to Scotland from South Carolina and other members of the family were in process of doing so. These men may well have been sojourners, although there is also the possibility that they anticipated the outbreak of the War of Independence and had decided to return home. Some Scots men found the limited opportunities in Charleston not to their liking, and can in due course be found in London, the center of commerce in the British Atlantic World. For instance, the merchant from Edinburgh, James Crockett, who settled in Charleston by the year 1730, had moved permanently to London by 1752.

Charleston was one of the richest cities of colonial America by the mid-eighteenth century and an attractive place to live. This was due to those who had made their fortunes in the plantations, building large and gracious townhouses and the increasing cultural aspects of the town. Although in the early period South Carolina, like the West Indies, may have attracted the sojourner, these may have been induced to settle permanently instead of returning to the British Isles. In addition, given that the 1763-1775 was the peak period of Scottish emigration to the American colonies, the outbreak of the American War of Independence only a few years later, with its subsequent Loyalist diaspora, the true level of intended permanent or sojourning residence in the Carolinas cannot easily be established in precise terms.

SCOTTISH TRADE WITH
COLONIAL CHARLESTON, 1683-1783

The Loyalist Diaspora

The American War of Independence started in 1776, and from 1780, Charleston was a British garrison, offering sanctuary to those with Loyalist leanings.   From the male population they recruited for the Crown forces.   The defeat at Yorktown, Virginia, in 1782, signalled the failure of the British in their attempt to control the Thirteen Colonies, and after this the British forces and the Loyalist community of South Carolina found it expedient to retreat to St Augustine, Florida. At the War's conclusion, the British Government was obliged to provide compensation for losses experienced by Loyalist settlers who had lost their assets owing to their support of the British.[413] In 1783, St Augustine was no longer a safe haven, and these Loyalists, together with those from the newly established United States of America, numbering approximately seventy thousand in total, were forced on to places such as Nova Scotia, Quebec, the West Indies, and the British Isles.   Many of these can be found in Government records, making claims for compensation through the American Claims Commission. This Commission had been established as a result of legislation passed in an Act of Parliament in 1783 which rationalised the existing arrangements for helping the Loyalists, and its aim was to establish established to examine claims presented by the Loyalists.   The documentation largely survives among the Audit Office papers in the Public Record Office in the form of two collections AO12 and AO13, the former mainly being minute books and Commissioners reports and the latter being documents supporting the claims.   Among the thousands of documents collectively known as the American Loyalist Claims, are those of five hundred and seventy-seven former residents

[413] Peter Wilson Coldham, *American Migrations, 1765-1799*, Baltimore, Maryland, 2000, pp. vii-xii

SCOTTISH TRADE WITH
COLONIAL CHARLESTON, 1683-1783

of South Carolina, which include nearly two hundred from Scots or people of Scots origin judging by their surnames.

One of these Loyalists was Thomas Inglis, who had been a merchant in Charleston since 1765, and a partner in the firm of Inglis Lloyd and Company dealing in the Guinea Trade [alias the Slave Trade]. In 1775 he had been a Militia Captain with the British forces, but resigned his commission when the Governor of South Carolina left the colony. In 1778 he refused to take the rebel oath which forced him to leave the colony. After a sojourn in the West Indies, he returned to mainland America in 1779 and joined the Loyalist forces in Georgia, reaching the rank of Lieutenant Colonel. By 1784 he had taken refuge in Kingston, Jamaica, which is where he filed his Loyalist Claim. For a moiety of eight hundred and seventeen acres on the Wando River, a lease of stores in Charleston, two thousand five hundred acres on Broad River, five hundred acres on Sandy River, one thousand acres in Thicketty Meadows, five hundred acres on the Altamaha River, rice taken by the American Army at Ogeechee in 1779, and debts due to him.[414]

Another Scots merchant who made a claim was Andrew Mackenzie, a clerk from Leith who emigrated to work for John Simpson and Company, a Scottish firm in Charleston. Mackenzie became a merchant in his own right and later was Captain of a Militia Regiment. By 1784 he was in London making a claim for one thousand acres on the Saluda River, two Negro men servants, and debts due to him.[415] The opportunity to make a Loyalist Claim was not without its problems.

[414] TNA.AO12.52.249, etc
[415] TNA.AO12.102.189

SCOTTISH TRADE WITH
COLONIAL CHARLESTON, 1683-1783

Although the Act authorising the scheme was passed in July 1783, it was not published in Quebec until October that year. Claims were to reach London by 25 March 1784, but claimants in Canada had only three weeks' notice before the last ship sailed for England that winter. Protests over this unreasonably short time period, when most would not have heard the details in time, lead to agreement of an extended closing date of 1 May 1786. Compensation claims were then also allowed to be assessed in either London or Canada, all being thoroughly scrutinised by the Commissioners in these places before being accepted or rejected.

A few ex-colonists returned to the former American colonies, some only temporarily to collect debts or other assets, but others attempted to reintegrate into the former colonial society and economy. One Scot, Alexander McKenzie, presumably a Loyalist, formerly in Charleston, is known to have attempted to settle in the Netherlands, possibly because of his Dutch wife and the indirect links that Charleston had with Rotterdam. With his wife Margareta Reitenbach and their two children, he left Charleston in 1776 bound for Rotterdam where they had hoped to settle. After applying to the minister of the Scots Kirk in the city he obtained a Permission Billet on 21 August 1776 to settle in Rotterdam. The Scots Kirk records show that his intention was soon to leave for London, and then return to North America.[416]

The departure of Loyalists from the Thirteen Colonies clearly had implications for the new United States of America. With the exodus of thousands of skilled craftsmen, merchants, planters and entrepreneurs, two important sectors of the South Carolinian economy,

---

[416] Records of the Scots Church in Rotterdam, MS No I.60

the fur trade and indigo planting suffered.   The partners of Panton, Leslie and Company mentioned above, were all Loyalists who been forced to leave after 1782.   Indigo production and exports were much reduced after the American Revolution owing to the fact initially production fell, then the British sought to keep imports within the British Empire.   In addition to that which could be got from the West Indies, it sanctioned the development of new indigo plantations by a group of men bearing Scottish names, in India.[417]   It is possible that those who were previously involved in the growing of indigo in the American colonies were the same as those who now set up in Bengal, as this group included a Hugh Baillie, a surname which was common among the Scots planters of colonial Georgia.

While the American War of Independence might have been expected to have ruined relationships between the British and the former colonies, much trading quickly re-established.   Some products could simply not be obtained elsewhere, particularly tobacco, and commercial interests prevailed.   While America's freedom from compliance with the Navigation Acts had very little impact on their economy, the same was not the case for British ports, manufacturers, and shipping.   However, imported goods to the United States, continued to be manufactured in Britain because of its technological lead in the manufacture of goods. The inclination to support the French economy could not be fulfilled because of their relative manufacturing inexpertise, and the fact France was itself soon in turmoil.

---

[417] India Office, O series, O/526, Private Europeans, Calcutta, 13 November 1804

SCOTTISH TRADE WITH
COLONIAL CHARLESTON, 1683-1783

CONCLUSION

Trade between Scotland and Charleston provided many benefits for all those concerned, creating and sustaining the economic growth of both societies. Planters and merchants in South Carolina were guaranteed an outlet for their produce which enabled them increasingly to enjoy a comfortable lifestyle, and manufacturers and merchants in Scotland were able to secure supplies of raw materials and foodstuffs from the Charleston area to be processed in the country for home consumption and export, as well as the trading which occurred en route. These enterprises brought profits and wealth to a country which until then was relatively impoverished. It was due in large part to the opening of trading opportunities with colonial markets such as South Carolina, that the Scottish manufacturing industry began a period of rapid expansion and diversification of range of products.

With the burgeoning population of the American colonies, companies, small and large, recognised and grasped the economic opportunities which this increasingly presented. Cargoes of indigo which were landed in Scottish ports were required for the textile industry which was expanding rapidly due to the increase, both domestic and colonial for its products. Prominent amongst the manufacturers of linen, was the British Linen Company, which, despite its name only operated in Scotland.

The infant Scottish iron industry was producing a range of goods to supply demand from the colonies, and regular consignments of cast iron-goods, such as grates, nails, tools and the like were in steady demand in America. The glass industry of Leith benefited from Spanish, Portuguese and Madeira wine being bottled in Scotland,

262

SCOTTISH TRADE WITH
COLONIAL CHARLESTON, 1683-1783

before onward dispatch to the American colonies. Additional quantities of beer were brewed for shipment to Charleston, which also increased the demand of glass bottles supplied by the glasswork companies of Edinburgh and Leith. Alongside the main industries grew ancillary industries, all occasioned by this expansion of transatlantic trade. Shipping was the key to all the development and growing wealth of the economies of both Scotland and Charleston, and vessels required maintenance. Naval stores was the ancillary industry of shipping, and the goods produced and distributed by ships chandlers grew with demand on both sides of the Atlantic, with the increase in sea traffic. As wealth grew there was an ever-increasing requirement for raw materials such as timber for the production of furniture. Tropical hardwood was ideal for this purpose, and craftsmen were eager to obtain supplies in order to fulfill their customers' requirements as the development of the New Town of Edinburgh grew apace. Mahogany, and other hardwood was grown in the Caribbean, and often shipped via the port of Charleston.

Profitable trading increased the wealth of both merchants in Scotland and South Carolina. This in turn stimulated demand for consumer goods on both sides of the Atlantic, and the knock on effect of this was to force the pace of industrialisation. The supply and demand of raw material and finished product caused the economies of both to expand and became increasingly interdependent.

This research has identified a wide range of commodities, mostly produced in Scotland, that were exported to Charleston for sale and use throughout a wide catchment area in the American South, the West Indies, and possibly Africa. As might be expected textiles, predominantly linens and woollens, formed a major component of

SCOTTISH TRADE WITH
COLONIAL CHARLESTON, 1683-1783

exports, together with metal work mainly from Scotland's iron industry. Surprising, so too did a large and regular amounts of coal. Other goods exported were small quantities of leather goods, apothecaries' wares, furniture, carpets, medicine, chaisse and horse iron, earthenware, glass bottles, ale, books, paper, and most surprisingly of all golf clubs and golf balls. Merchants in Charleston exported to Scotland and elsewhere a limited range of colonial products, some which originated in South Carolina, and others which came from the Caribbean. In the main, these were rice, indigo, timber, tar, turpentine, sugar, and deerskins. Much of the rice aboard Scots vessels was delivered en-route to dealers on the continent, especially Portugal.

This research has produced evidence which conflicts with the traditional view of Scotland's transatlantic connections of the colonial period. The belief that the Clyde ports, specifically Glasgow and Greenock, had an almost complete monopoly of trade with America during the seventeenth and eighteenth century is shown to be inaccurate. While it is true that trade with the tobacco colonies of Virginia and Maryland did for the most part use the west coast ports, this is not the case when trade between Scotland and Charleston, the pre-eminent port of the southern colonies is considered. The shipping evidence provided here in this publication, illustrates that the east coast ports sent as many vessels to Charleston in the Colonial Period as did those of the west coast of Scotland. Only additional research will show whether it was the case that the other major northern ports of Boston, New York, and Philadelphia followed the pattern of the tobacco traders or that of the more general trading studied here.

The numbers of people emigrating from Scotland to the American colonies only became significant after the end of the Seven Years War

264

SCOTTISH TRADE WITH
COLONIAL CHARLESTON, 1683-1783

in 1763. Although not a destination for the masses, it is clear from the evidence that Charleston did attract skilled artisans, physicians, craftsmen, and above all planters and merchants from Scotland. While many of these Scots became permanent residents in South Carolina, a number were clearly sojourners, who, having made their fortunes or for other reasons, intended to return home. The general trend, however, becomes confused in the dispersal of Loyalists in the aftermath of the American Revolution. Before this time, South Carolina had successfully managed to attract immigrants from Ireland and continental Europe through land grant incentives which were not offered to residents of Great Britain. Colonies such as neighboring North Carolina had attracted Highland emigrants by classifying them as 'foreign Protestants' in the years between the end of the French and Indian Wars in 1763, and the outbreak of the American War of Independence in 1776. Both before and after the Revolution, merchants of Charleston continued to actively recruit, transport, and settle immigrants in South Carolina, and these people and their families became consumers of the goods and services supplied by the same merchants.

One of the services offered by merchants in Charleston was the provision of slaves. The port of Charleston was the major port in the African Slave Trade, and this thesis clearly establishes that Scots, like all white merchants, were involved at every stage of this trade from the procurement of African men, women and children, their transportation on ships, their sale in the colony and their employment in the plantations of South Carolina and elsewhere.

Hitherto the only region of Colonial America that has been investigated in depth regarding economic links with Scotland has been the

265

SCOTTISH TRADE WITH
COLONIAL CHARLESTON, 1683-1783

Chesapeake which comprised the colonies of Chesapeake which comprised the colonies of Virginia and Maryland. This research now enables a comparison to be made between two adjoining colonial regions. The geography of South Carolina and the Chesapeake varies significantly and this had an effect on the types of trading carried out. Chesapeake Bay provided a sea route which penetrated into much of Virginia and Maryland, beyond which there were many navigable rivers flowing into the Bay. This, enabled vessels to sail deep into the colony, and trade directly with many of the individual ports, settlements and plantations. The ability of Scottish merchant vessels to anchor alongside tobacco plantation enabled a fast turnaround period thereby increasing profit. In South Carolina, the position was quite different as there were very few navigable rivers and those too shallow for vessels. Charleston and Georgetown were the only trading ports of the colony, and of the two, Charleston was by far the busiest during the colonial period. Cargoes of deerskins, rice, indigo, timber, and latterly cotton were brought to the market there for export. Although there were stores in rural South Carolina, they were centers for the collection of produce and distribution points for imported manufactured goods from Britain, not loading or unloading points as in the Chesapeake, and Indian routes through the back-country were used to transport goods to the port of Charleston and onwards to foreign markets.

The Scots merchants of Colonial Charleston differed from those on the Chesapeake in a number of ways. The most obvious was that while the Tobacco Lords of Glasgow dominated the Scottish merchant community in Virginia and Maryland, there was no equivalent situation in Charleston. Merchants from both the east and west coast of Scotland were well represented in South Carolina, while on the Chesapeake merchants from the west coast predominated. The Clyde-based

266

SCOTTISH TRADE WITH
COLONIAL CHARLESTON, 1683-1783

merchants capitalised on their geographical advantage of having the quickest route between Britain and the Chesapeake, their domination of the trade enabling them to make the most effective use of their financial, material and human resources. They helped develop a store system on the Chesapeake which reduced the turn-around time of their vessels, adding to the overall efficiency of the operation. Another difference between the traders to the Chesapeake and Charleston was that the former concentrated almost exclusively on a single product, tobacco, while the latter traded in a number of different commodities. The sea-routes followed also differed. Trade with Virginia and Maryland was a regular shuttle back and forth between there and the Clyde while that with South Carolina was often a triangular route which included Portugal.

Employees, known as chief factors, controlled the networks established by different companies of Glasgow tobacco merchants. In Virginia and Maryland these factors were based in the major towns of Norfolk and Alexandria, Virginia. In South Carolina, there were no equivalent agents controlling trade, although some individual Charleston merchants had subsidiary stores in parts of South Carolina or Georgia, or had direct links with the Indian traders of the interior who supplied deerskins. The destinations of colonial produce exported from the Chesapeake were also different from that exported from Charleston. Tobacco was bound for Glasgow, for processing and re-exporting to European markets, creating jobs and wealth in and around Clyde ports in the process. However, the rice, indigo, timber and deerskins shipped from colonial Charleston, even on Scottish vessels, largely went directly to their ultimate markets. This meant, of course, that there was not the same direct creation of jobs and wealth associated with the trade from this port.

267

SCOTTISH TRADE WITH
COLONIAL CHARLESTON, 1683-1783

The restrictions of the Navigation Acts had allowed Glasgow the opportunity to exploit its geographical advantages and its trade in tobacco became established. Exemptions, necessitating the issue of a Mediterranean pass, allowed Scotland to be by-passed, enabling a more economic triangular route to Scotland to the ships which traded with Charleston. Rice, for instance, which had a market on the continent, but not in Scotland, was allowed to be shipped directly to the markets of Iberia. It was the case, therefore, that the regular shuttle operating to and fro between the Clyde and the Chesapeake was not the same as the trade routes of Carolina where a triangular route was followed. When not using a Mediterranean pass, ships voyaged either directly between Scotland and Charleston, returning via Cowes to Rotterdam, and from there to Scotland, or variant. While the Clyde-Chesapeake axis operated quite simply as far as cargoes out and in was concerned, the Carolina trade was more circuitous, calling at more ports, and with varying cargoes. The trade routes out from Charleston were for this reason less cost efficient than the Clyde-Chesapeake merchants, and for this reason, perhaps, the Scottish merchant firms trading with the Chesapeake seem to have been much larger organisations than those trading with Charleston.

The goods traded had, of course, to be paid for, and the lack of currency to some extent held back the development of trade. As colonial authorities did not initially have the right to produce their own coinage, it being the prerogative of the London Mint, the early American colonial economy was disadvantaged by its scarcity. Local residents, as well as merchants of South Carolina were faced with problems arising through the lack of an acceptable medium of exchange. In order to alleviate this problem, a barter system was established in which specified commodities began to be used as money. Beaver pelts were one such used which had a fixed exchange rate against sterling. The limitations of this system were evident during times of a surplus or deficit of the item being bartered. Eventually the colony of South Carolina introduced a local currency which provided a standard medium of exchange for business transactions to proceed more quickly within the colony. Fluctuations in value between South Carolina pounds and the pound sterling and other colonial currencies, did give rise to difficulties, some of which resulted in cases brought before courts in Scotland. Many of the transactions that occurred between merchants in Charleston and those in Scotland did so through use of bills of exchange drawn on merchant bankers in London and in Scotland where banking services were reasonably advanced for the period.

Political unrest was another difficulty the colony of South Carolina had to deal with. For around 20 years, starting about 1765 an increasing number of American colonists who remained steadfastly loyal to the British Crown found it necessary to abandon their homes in the Thirteen Colonies and take refuge either in the British Isles or in some or other of the remaining British possessions in the Americas. It has been calculated that over seventy thousand people, termed Loyalist, resettled in Britain, Canada, the West Indies or elsewhere during this period. Records show some thirty thousand moved to Nova Scotia, seven thousand to Quebec, and three thousand to the West Indies and the British Isles. From the 1760s onwards Loyalists were increasingly being harassed in the colonies and some were enduring hardship and financial losses which show up in claims for compensation made following the Revolution. To begin with, the British government took

SCOTTISH TRADE WITH
COLONIAL CHARLESTON, 1683-1783

an ad-hoc approach to claims from subjects for losses experienced through rebel action, but in July 1783 an Act of Parliament was passed to formalize compensation claims, which continued until into the 1790s.

Not all Loyalists made claims for compensation but several thousand did so. In the case of South Carolina, the Commission received nearly six hundred claims, of which about a quarter was from people who were Scots or of Scottish origin. These claims provide variable data on the claimant, his or her occupation, occasionally their place of origin, and what losses they incurred through their support for the British during the American Revolution. Of those whose details point to their being of Scots origin, forty-eight had been planters, thirty-one merchants, three ministers, nine shipbuilders and mariners, nine physicians, fifteen civil-servants, two lawyers, seven miscellaneous tradesmen, and others with no specific occupation. Considering the many Scots shopkeepers and merchants in Charleston who have been identified, a substantial number of merchants either chose not to make Loyalist claims, or had supported the American cause.

As with other ethnic groups, the Scottish colonists in the Thirteen Colonies, both Highlanders and Lowlanders, had been divided over their attitude to American independence, but on balance they tended to be Loyalists. Since a significant number of Scots were merchants in the colonies they faced difficult options in 1783. Some returned to Great Britain, some moved to the colonies remaining under British control and some stayed and attempted to rebuild their businesses in the new republic. Of those who either remained in Charleston during the Revolution or returned there in its aftermath, it is possible to identify some through naturalization records. As early as 26 March 1784, the

SCOTTISH TRADE WITH
COLONIAL CHARLESTON, 1683-1783

South Carolina Legislature passed a statute concerning naturalization, quickly followed by another on 27 February 1788.   Residents and immigrants, wishing to establish their loyalty to the new republic generally opted to take up citizenship.   In 1783 a group of fifty merchants, of which more than half bore Scottish surnames successfully petitioned the General Assembly of South Carolina to become citizen of the United States.[418]   The South Carolina Citizenship Book dates from 1784 and the first four names thereon are Andrew Kerr, James Anderson, Adam Tunno, and Thomas Stewart,[419] all of whom are likely to have been Scottish.

The American War of Independence did not cause a complete breakdown in shipping links between Scotland and North America. During the period of war, although emigration was suspended, trade between Great Britain and the ports under British control continued, albeit certain of the cargoes were made to sustain the war effort.   With the post-war era had come a renewed period of trade and shipping between Scotland, especially the Clyde, and South Carolina.

The Scottish merchants of Charleston became established and thrived owing to a number of reasons.   Firstly, the Act of Union of 1707 enabled them to trade without restriction in and from the colony. Secondly, a Scottish presence in Charleston had existed from 1679 which meant that they were already established and more especially had maintained strong links through a Scottish network to other Scots throughout the American colonies, the West Indies, Africa, and Europe. This networking, forged by bonds of blood and business, was reinforced

[418] Brent Holcomb, *South Carolina Naturalisations, 1783-1850,* Baltimore, Maryland, 1985, p. 76
[418] Ibid p. 46

SCOTTISH TRADE WITH
COLONIAL CHARLESTON, 1683-1783

through the churches, the Masonic lodges, and St Andrews societies, all to be found around the British Atlantic World. The Scots merchants in the colonies were enterprising and participated in a number of profitable ventures. Success was aided by a strong Scottish based and owned merchant fleet, and financial services run in Scotland or by London based Scots. When the American Revolution impacted on daily life, some of the merchant community of Charleston who were of Scottish origin and of Loyalist sympathy chose to abandon South Carolina, but others remained or returned to run their businesses there despite changed conditions.

Appendix 1

Cases brought before the Court of Session in Edinburgh with links to South Carolina, 1739-1785

17 July 1739, Andrew Ross, clothier in Musselburgh, v. James and John Crockett and George Seaman, all merchants in Charleston, and Charles Crockett a merchant in Edinburgh, [NRS.CS16.1.69]

2 November 1739, 26 February 1740 John Ross of Blackhill and his wife Grizell, plus Charles Hay of Hopes and his wife Christian Ross, v. James and John Crockatt and George Seaman, all merchants in Charleston, plus Charles Crockatt a merchant in Edinburgh, [NRS.CS16.1.69]

11 July 1741, Reverend Mathew Reid of Prestonkirk v. Lord Elibank, James Crockatt of Charleston, and others. [NRS.CS161.69]

26 July 1743, Archibald Dunbar of Newton v. Alexander McGillivray merchant late of Carolina. [NRS.CS16.1.72]

22 November 1743, John Watson and others, merchants in South Carolina, v. Thomas Baillie of Charleston. [NRS.CS16.1.72]

SCOTTISH TRADE WITH
COLONIAL CHARLESTON, 1683-1783

20 December 1743, Margaret and Helen Baillie, daughters
of late Hugh Baillie, customs collector in Orkney, v
Thomas Baillie, a merchant in Charleston, eldest
son of the late Hugh Baillie. [NRS.CS16.1.72]

22 February 1745, John Watson, John Crockatt, Kenneth
Michie, and William Woodrop, merchants in
Charleston, v. Thomas Baillie merchant in
Charleston. [NRS.CS16.1.73]

19 November 1751, James Bull of Cronaster, Shetland, v.
Thomas Moubray eldest son of late Arthur Moubray
late surgeon in Carolina. [NRS.CS16.1.85, 88]

18 December 1754, John Crockett, merchant in
Charleston, v. Anna Jeffrey, Northwaterbridge, Pert,
Angus, [NRS.CS16.1.95]

8 March 1755, Farquhar McGillivray of Dalcrambie v.
Lauchlan McGillivray, merchant in Charleston,
eldest son of late William McGillivray, brother
german of Farquhar McGillivray of Drumnaglash.
[NRS.CS16.1.95]

3 July 1755, Jermyne Wright, sometime of South Carolina
now of London, and John Home of Charleston, v.
Robert Deas, merchant from Charleston now in
Leith, [NRS.CS16.1.95]

23 July 1756, Smith, a merchant in Bristol v. John Rowand
senior, merchant in Glasgow, and Rowand, Mills
and Rowand, merchants in Charleston.
[NRS.CS16.1.98]

274

SCOTTISH TRADE WITH
COLONIAL CHARLESTON, 1683-1783

22 December 1756, Lieutenant Lauchlan Shaw, of
Captain Demere's Independent Company, in South
Carolina, v. Captain Walter Stewart of General
Ferrill's Regiment. [NRS.CS16.1.99/131]

16 February 1757, George Carmichael and Company,
merchants in Glasgow, v. Rowand, Wills and
Rowan Company, merchants in Charleston.
[NRS.CS16.1.99/192]

17 July 1759, Andrew Ross, a clothier in Musselburgh, v.
James and John Crockat, also George Seaman,
merchants in Charleston, and Charles Crockat a
merchant in Edinburgh. [NRS.CS16.1.69]

16 January 1761, Reverend Patrick Keir in James Island,
South Carolina, v. Andrew Bennet of Balgonar,
[NRS.CS16.1.107]

19 June 1771, Trustees of Robert Crawford v. George
Ramsay, from Greenock then in Charleston, and
John Jamieson a merchant in Charleston.
[NRS.CS16.1.146/15]

31 July 1771, George Heriot, a planter in South Carolina,
v. John Heriot, sheriff clerk of Haddington,
[NRS.CS16.1.146/192]

10 February 1773, James Edmundstone and others v.
David Fleming, late merchant in Edinburgh, now in
South Carolina. [NRS.CS16.1.154/103]

275

SCOTTISH TRADE WITH
COLONIAL CHARLESTON, 1683-1783

9 July 1773, Mary Janet Boyd of Charleston, spinster only
child of the late Robert Boyd merchant in
Charleston, v. Kelly. [NRS.CS16.1.154/323]

2 February 1774, William Coke, a bookseller in Leith, v.
Robert Wills a bookseller in Charleston.
[NRS.CS16.1.157/285]

6 August 1774, Robert, Edward and Marion Corbet,
children of late James Corbet merchant and former
provost of Dumfries, and Thomas Irving, Receiver
General of HM Revenue in South Carolina,
husband to said Marion Corbet for his interest, v.
George Paton, innkeeper in Crawfordjohn, and
others. [NRS.CS16.1.161/182]

18 January 1775, Act nominating and appointing William
Walker, a writer in Edinburgh, to be factor loco
tutoris to James Burn only child of deceased John
Burn late of Charleston, and one of HM Council
there [NRS.CS16.1.161/343]

1 March 1775, Decreet in absence, Dr David Oliphant,
South Carolina, v. John Oliphant, eldest son of late
John Oliphant of Carpow, alias John, Lord Oliphant.
[NRS.CS16.1.165/40]

11 March 1775, Creditors of John Galt late merchant in
Edinburgh, v. James Skene, a physician in
Carolina, William Robert, a physician in South
Carolina, and others. [NRS.CS16.1.165/42]

SCOTTISH TRADE WITH
COLONIAL CHARLESTON, 1683-1783

5 July 1775, Ross of Pitcalnie v. David and John Deas, James and William Lennox, all merchants in Charleston. [NRS.CS16.1.165/157]

17 January 1776, John Tawse, a writer in Edinburgh, v. George Millar, a leather merchant in Edinburgh now in South Carolina, and others. [NRS.CS16.1.168/31]

4 July 1776, Janet Vair, widow of George Vair sometime of South Carolina, then in Edinburgh, v. Margaret Vair, daughter of said Janet and George Vair sometime of Carolina then in Edinburgh, and William Vair a peruke maker in Edinburgh, [NRS.CS16.1.168/317]

27 November 1776, Mrs Elizabeth Seaman, sister of late George Seaman a merchant in Charleston, v. John Deas, David Deas, James Lennox, and William Lennox, merchants in Charleston. [NRS.CS16.1.170/117]

30 June 1779, Alexander Mirrylees, a brewer from Leith then in South Carolina, son of John Mirrylees. [NRS.CS16.1.175]

8 February 1782, John Thomson in Jamaica, and Thomas Whitelaw, late of Jamaica now in Glasgow, partners in trade, V. John Thomson a blockmaker in Leith, Thomas McDonald Writer to the Signet, arrestees, and Robert McKenzie late of Charleston, principal debtor [NRS.CS17.1.1/61]

SCOTTISH TRADE WITH
COLONIAL CHARLESTON, 1683-1783

7 July 1784, David Smith of Methven v. Dr David Oliphant in South Carolina, brother of late John Oliphant of Bachilton, Lord Oliphant, and others. [NRS.CS17.1.3/204]

27 July 1785, Janet Salter v. Thomas Ogilvie, John Walker, late merchant in Dundee now in Charleston. [NRS.CS17.1.4/250]

SCOTTISH TRADE WITH
COLONIAL CHARLESTON, 1683-1783

APPENDIX 2

Scottish Merchants, Craftsmen, and Professionals in Colonial Charleston, 1675-1775

AFFLECK, THOMAS, born 1730 in Dunbar, a merchant in
        Prince William parish, SC, probate 1758 SC
AIKMAN, ALEXANDER, born in Bo'ness during 1755, a
        printer and publisher in Charleston by 1771, a Loyalist
        who moved to Jamaica, where he died in 1838.
        [GM.NS10.556]
ALEXANDER, ALEXANDER, shipmaster from Leith,
        property owner in Charleston and SC, husband of
        Elizabeth Murray, niece of John Murray judge in SC,
        Loyalist killed in Naval service in the Delaware in
        1777. [TNA.AO13.96.6]
ALEXANDER, JOHN, a merchant in Carolina, son of Robert
        Alexander of Blackhouse, died 1699, probate 1700 SC;
        executor Robert Alexander clerk of Session, testament
        confirmed 1707 in Edinburgh. [NRS.CC8.8.83]
ALLAN, ANDREW, a merchant in Charleston, was admitted
        as a Burgess and Guilds-brother of Glasgow in 1723;
        died 1735, his will links him to his son in law Robert
        Pringle, the Savage family, Robert Buchanan
        deceased; Rev. Archibald Stobo; John Fraser and John
        Allan, merchants of Charleston; Rev. Hugh Stewart of
        the Presbyterian Meeting House at Vanderhorst Creek
        near Charleston; sister Margaret in parish of Eastwood
        Renfrewshire.; Laurence Dinwiddie merchant in
        Glasgow; etc. Co-owner of the Glasgow of Carolina, a

30 ton sloop, trading from Charleston to Philadelphia,
Madeira, etc in 1719; co-owner of the <u>Glasgow of
South Carolina</u>, 70 tons, master William Warden,
which brought 177 negroes from Guinea arrived in
Charleston on 20 June 1727
[TNA.CO5.508/509][probate 1735 SC]

ANDERSON, GEORGE, a minister in Pon-Pon, SC, 1750,
son of Rev. George Anderson in Dunbog, Fife, died
1751. [NRS.RD3.211.77; CS17.1.23/100]

ANDERSON, HUGH, to Georgia in 1737 as Inspector General
of Public Gardens, moved to SC in 1739 as a teacher
of philosophy. [ESG#62]

ARMSTRONG, CHARLES, a planter in Berkely County, SC,
from 1709. [probate 1726 PCC]

AUSTIN, ADAM, born 1751, a merchant in Charleston, son of
Captain Joseph Austin of Kilspindie, Perthshire, 1782.
[NRS.SH]

BAIRD, ARCHIBALD, a planter in South Carolina, husband
of Winifred Irving, Georgetown, SC, will subscribed
on 20 January 1777, probate 11 March 1788 PCC;
[NLS.CH3837] [NRS.RS23.XXII.154]

BALFOUR, ANDREW, a merchant in Edinburgh, bought land
in St Andrew's parish, South Carolina, during 1741.
[SC Deeds, book W#469]

BALFOUR, ANDREW, born Edinburgh 1737, son of Andrew
Balfour and Margaret Robertson, a salt manufacturer
in Charleston, died 1782, testament confirmed 1783 in
Edinburgh [NRS.CC8.8.126]

BALFOUR, JOHN, born Edinburgh 1748, son of Andrew
Balfour of Braidwood and Margaret Robertson, a
merchant-planter on the Peedee River, South Carolina,
a Loyalist soldier, died in South Carolina during 1781,
testament confirmed 1783 in Edinburgh.
[NRS.CC8.8.126][TNA.AO12.48.238]

SCOTTISH TRADE WITH
COLONIAL CHARLESTON, 1683-1783

BALLINGALL, ROBERT, born in Scotland, a resident of St Bartholemew's parish, Charleston, Loyalist, JP and Colonel of Militia, Chief Magistrate, with 950 acres land in Port Royal. [TNA.AO12.48.254]

BANKS, CHARLES, from Ross-shire, a merchant in Charleston for 30 years, naturalised there 1788. [SC Citizenship Book]

BARON, ALEXANDER, born Aberdeen, educated at Marischal College, Aberdeen, in 1745, emigrated to South Carolina in 1748, a schoolmaster in Charleston, later an Episcopalian minister from 1753-1759, died in St Helena's parish, S.C., during 1759. [CCVC]

BARON, Dr ALEXANDER, born 1745, graduated MD at Edinburgh in 1768, a physician in Charleston ca1769-1777, a Loyalist, moved to St Augustine, East Florida, in 1782. [TNA.AO13.90.60]

BARRIE, JAMES, a merchant from Glasgow, in Charleston 1745. [GA.B10.15.7105]

BEGBIE, JAMES, a shipbuilder in Charleston, a Loyalist in 1776, settled in Kingston, Jamaica, losses incurred during the War of Independence included a new brigantine and a new schooner. [TNA.AO12.51.184]

BEGBIE, JOHN, a planter at Goose Creek, SC, probate 1738 SC

BELL, ANDREW, from Edinburgh, a blacksmith in Beaufort, probate 1753 SC

BERRIE, JAMES, from Glasgow, a merchant in Charleston around 1745 [GA.B10.15.7105]

BISSETT, WILLIAM, a tailor in Charleston, son of Kenneth Bissett a gentleman in Edinburgh, probate 1754 SC

BLACK, WILLIAM jr, possibly from Aberdeen, bought land on the Peedee River in 1759. [SC Deed book C3, #314]

SCOTTISH TRADE WITH
COLONIAL CHARLESTON, 1683-1783

BLAIR, ROBERT, a planter on the Pedee River, a Loyalist in 1776. [TNA.AO12.92.1A]

BLAIR, WADE, son of Rev. William and Lucy Blair in Inverness-shire, settled Craven County, probate 1763 SC

BOTHWELL, JOHN, from Aberdeen, a peruke maker in Charleston, probate 1777 SC

BOWMAN, JOHN, from Glasgow, in Charleston by 1 November 1769. [Charleston County, Misc. Rec. fo.172]

BRISBANE, ROBERT, born 1707, 3rd son of William Brisbane and Catherine Patterson in Glasgow, at Glasgow University, ca1723, a physician, to SC in 1733, co-founder of the Charleston Library Society in 1748, member of the St Andrews Society, died 1781. [SCHM.14.123]

BRISBANE, WILLIAM, born 1710, 4th son of William Brisbane and Catherine Paterson in Glasgow, at Glasgow University 1726, a surgeon, to SC during 1732, given land grants in 1738, a planter on Ashley River, died 1771. [SCHM.14.125]

BROWN, ARCHIBALD, a planter of 3160 acres, 12 miles from Camden and merchant in Charleston, a Loyalist and a militia officer, in St Augustine, Florida, by 1783. [TNA.AO12.92.5]

BUCHANAN, WILLIAM, son of John Buchanan jr a merchant in Glasgow, a planter in Granville County, given a land grant in 1737, probate 1758 SC

BULLOCH, JAMES, born Glasgow 1701, to Charleston 1728, married Jean Stobo 1729, a member of the St Andrew's Society of Charleston in 1730, died 1780. [SAS][SHR.1.416]

BURNETT, HENRIETTA, in Edinburgh, widow of John Stuart late a merchant in Carolina, died 1718, her testament refers to sons John and Charles Stuart merchants in Carolina, only sons of said John Stuart and Henrietta Burnett, confirmed 1718 in Edinburgh. [NRS.CC8.8.87]

BURT, PATRICK, born 1740 in Perth, settled in St Michael's, SC, testament confirmed 1775 in Edinburgh. [NRS.CC8.8.123]

CALDER, ROBERT, son of George Calder of Aswanley, a wigmaker and barber in Charleston by 1724. [NRS.GD44.43.16.128]

CAMERON, ALAN, to SC in 1773, with Dept of Indian Affairs in the Southern District, a Loyalist and soldier, moved to England. [TNA.AO12.56.10]

CAMERON, ALEXANDER, former Army officer who was granted land in 1763 in Granville County, Deputy Superintendent of Indian Affairs in Southern District 1765, Loyalist, died Savannah during 1781. [TNA.AO12.50.402]

CAMPBELL, ANDREW, a plantation overseer, owned 50 acres at Cannock's Creek, Craven Co., a Loyalist in 1776, returned home. [TNA.AO12.100.233]

CAMPBELL, COLIN, brother of Hugh Campbell of Lix, and also the brother in law of Lord William Campbell, had a large estate in SC, died in Charleston by 1778, Loyalist, had 400 acres Nelville Plantation, Campbeltown near Savannah; 2000 acres on Butcher's Island, 935 acres near Dorchester, 27 slaves. [TNA.AO12.52.192-200]

CAMPBELL, Lord WILLIAM, Governor of SC, arrived in June 1775, violently abused and insulted, when he took refuge on a warship his house was attacked and its contents sold, died in 1784. [TNA.AO12.101.141]

CASSELLS, HENRY, 250 acre land grant in Craven County, SC, during 1738 [TNA.CO5.398]

CASSELLS, JAMES, settled in SC for 25 years, planter of over 3000 acres, Loyalist , estate worth £6500 stg., 1000 acres on Peedee River, 1150 acres on Waccamaw Creek, 500 acres on Black River, 500 acres on Briton's Neck, house in Georgetown, settled in Leith by 1788. [TNA.AO12.13.127, 325]

CAW, DAVID, in Charleston, probate 1758 SC

CAW, THOMAS, a gentleman in Charleston, probate 1773 SC

CAW, THOMAS, from Carolina, graduated MD from Edinburgh University in 1769. [EMG#10]

CHALMERS, Dr LIONEL, born 1715, emigrated 1737, a physician in Charleston 1737-1777, graduated MD from St Andrews in 1756, had Robert Pringle jr as an apprentice. [SA]

CHEVAS, ALEXANDER, from Buchan, settled in America 1762, a planter on Rocky River, Long Cane Settlement, 96 District, Loyalist. [TNA.AO12.101.87]

CHISHOLM, JOHN, born in Ross-shire, a soldier of the 77th Regiment during the French and Indian War, then a merchant in Camden with 974 acres, Loyalist, moved to Kingston, Jamaica. [TNA.AO12.49.417]

CLARK, DANIEL, an Indian trader in Augusta, Georgia, later in Charleston, probate 1757 SC

CLELAND, JOHN, settled in Craven County, SC, a member of HM Council of SC 1740-1760, died 1760, probate 1760 SC

CLELAND, Dr WILLIAM, settled in SC by 1729, a member of the St Andrew's Society in 1730. [NRS.GD237.153.19][SAS]

COCHRANE, ROBERT, a furniture painter from Edinburgh, settled in Charleston in 1750. [NRS.AC10.323]

CRAWFORD, DANIEL, a member of the St Andrew's Society of Charleston in 1730, probate 1760 SC

CRAWFORD, DAVID, postmaster of South Carolina in 1746. [Charleston County Misc. Records #75a/131]

SCOTTISH TRADE WITH
COLONIAL CHARLESTON, 1683-1783

CROCKATT, JAMES, a merchant in Charleston; treasurer of
the St Andrew's Society of Charleston in 1730;
appointed a member of the Council of SC during 1738.
[SAS][NRS.CS16.1.69] [TNA.CO5.401.249]

CROCKATT, Dr JAMES, in SC, son of George Crockatt a
surgeon in Cupar Angus, Perthshire, 1763; died in
Winyaw, SC, 1765. [NRS.SH; RGS.107.106]

CROKATT, JOHN, merchant in Charleston, subscribed to his
will in Lisbon in 1738, which refers to his brother in
law John Jolly merchant in Edinburgh, brother James
Crockatt in Charleston; brother in law William
Woodrup; 'Margaret Strachan who has lived with
James Crockatt"; and his father Charles Crockatt in
Edinburgh, probate 1740 PCC

CROCKETT, JOHN, [possibly the Jacobite transported in
1716], a merchant in Charleston, son of Daniel
Crockett in Scotland, probate 1759 SC

CROCKETT and SEAMAN, merchants in Charleston, 1737.
supplied 10 pieces of osnaburgs or 1070 yards to
Thomas Causton agent in Savannah for the Trustees of
Georgia. [TNA.CO5/667/46-47][SPAWI.XLIV.86];
provisions and necessaries shipped to Crockett and
Seaman in Charleston sent on to Savannah
[TNA.CO5.640.229/232] [SPAWI.1738.511]; the
above osnaburgs were charged at £38.5.4
[TNA.CO5.667/101]; in August 1738, 62 parcels were
sent from London on the Minerva, Captain Nickleson,
to Crockett and Seaman for Trustees' representatives
in Savannah. [TNA.CO5.667.102D]

CUMINE, ALEXANDER, from Aberdeenshire, left Scotland
in October 1762 possibly via London on the
Nightingale to Charleston, arrived in Spring 1763,
initially employed in a merchant house then, in
February 1769, became a Latin schoolmaster in

Beaufort, Port Royal, a Loyalist, moved to Jamaica in
1777 a schoolmaster in Kingston. [TNA.AO12.49.422]

CUMING, ROBERT, settled in Charlestown by 1750, possibly
a clergyman [links with Duncan Campbell indigo
merchant in Edinburgh, see NRS.RH15/69]

CURRIE, WILLIAM, settled in SC 1772 as a merchant, a
Loyalist who was banished from Charleston, returned
home. [TNA.AO12.5.65]

DAVIDSON, GEORGE, to America 1767, a land conveyancer
in Charleston, Loyalist in 1776. [TNA.AO12.51.139]

DEAS, DAVID, born 1722, son of David Deas, a skipper in
Leith, and Catherine Dundas; to SC 1738 probably as a
book-keeper to Robert Pringle, a merchant in
Charleston, was admitted as a Burgess and Guilds-
brother of Edinburgh in 1764 by right of father, a
member of the Council of SC in 1771, died in
Charleston 1775. [NRS.RD3.224/1.630][JCTP]

DEAS, JOHN, born 1735, son of David Deas, skipper in Leith,
and Catherine Dundas, to SC in 1749, was admitted as
a Burgess and Guilds-brother of Edinburgh in 1769,
died in Charleston 1790, probate 1790 SC, a Loyalist
merchant in 1776. [TNA.AO12.73.129]

DEAS, WILLIAM, a landscape painter in SC, who was
admitted as a Burgess and Guilds-brother of Edinburgh
in 1769. [EBR]

DENHAM, THOMAS, to America 1774, owner of a trading
vessel in Charleston, Loyalist, later in Shelburne, Nova
Scotia. [TNA.AO13.25.138]

DICK, ALEXANDER, in SC, son of George Dick in Airth,
probate 1742 PCC

DICK, WALTER, born in Glasgow, to America, a journeyman
gunsmith and cutler in Charleston 1774, by 1775 had 2
journeymen and 1 apprentice, Loyalist.
[TNA.AO12.50.185]

SCOTTISH TRADE WITH
COLONIAL CHARLESTON, 1683-1783

DICKSON, ROBERT, a cooper in Charleston, 1768.
[NRS.GD219/318]

DOUGLAS, JOHN, planter near Charleston, partner with
George Torrance and Alexander Rose in managing a
distillery, Loyalist, died 1781. [TNA.AO12.100.75]

DRAYTON, CHARLES, in Carolina, graduated MD from
Edinburgh University in 1770. [EMG#10]

DUFF, ALEXANDER, possibly from Edinburgh, Loyalist, 200
acres and 190 lots in Sunbury and 600 acres in St John
parish. [TNA.AO13.96.272]

DUNCAN, GEORGE, wine merchant in Charleston 1763-
1778, Loyalist. [TNA.AO13.127.42]

DUNLOP, WILLIAM, in Charleston, sent letter on 21
Nov.1686 to Sir James Montgomerie of Skelmorlie for
delivery to Mr James Foulis, a merchant in London.
[NRS.GD3.5.776-8]

FARQUHARSON, JOHN, a physician in Charleston 1755-
1780, Loyalist, died in Aberdeen 1790, probate 1791
PCC [GM.60.1053][TNA.AO12.47.415]

FISHER, JOHN, emigrated in 1760, merchant and planter in
Orangeburg , a Loyalist militia officer in Charleston
1780, moved to Jamaica, estate worth £4905, 2800
acres. [TNA.AO12.50.1]

FORDYCE, JOHN, a missionary in Prince Frederick parish,
Craven County, SC, by 1742, probate 1751 SC
[NRS.NRAS#0508, drawer 6]

FRASER Dr JAMES, a physician in Beaufort, Port Royal,
1765-1779, Loyalist army physician, moved to UK,
claim for 600 acres at Port Royal, 500 acres on Wando
River, 4 slaves, 2 schooners, medical instruments,
books and medicine. [TNA.AO12.51.174]

FRASER, JOHN, from Wigton, settled in SC ca1700, an
Indian trader with the Yemassees 1715, possibly vice-

president of the St Andrew's Society in 1730, settled in
Coosawhatchie, SC, died in Charleston in 1754
[SCHM.5.56]

FULLARTON, GEORGE, from Ayrshire, a merchant in
Charleston, probate 1709 SC

FYFFE, Dr CHARLES, settled SC 1748, Deputy Naval Officer
for Winyaw in 1757, a JP in 1780, resident of
Georgetown, Loyalist, returned to Scotland; claim for
2 houses in Georgetown, 750 acres, 200 acres and a
house on Black River, 500 acres in Berkeley County,
plus medical equipment and medicine.
[TNA.AO13.83.136]

GARDEN, Rev. ALEXANDER, born 1685 in Edinburgh,
minister of St Philip's, Charleston, from 1719 to 1753,
and Bishop's Commissary from 1726 to 1748,
graduated DD from Marischal College in 1726, died
1756, probate 1756 SC. [SO][CCVC]

GARDEN, ALEXANDER, born 1730, graduated MD from
MCA 1753 also studied in Edinburgh, a physician in
Charleston, a Loyalist who died 1791 in London;
corresponded with Dr John Hope of the Edinburgh
Botanical Garden around 1767 eg 'an account of the
Indian Pink' [NRS.GD253/145/9]

GARDEN, ALEXANDER, born in Charleston 4 December
1757, son of Dr Alexander Garden the botanist,
graduated MA from Glasgow University in 1779,
officer of the American Army 1780-, graduated MD
from Glasgow in 1785, died in Charleston 29 February
1829. [RGG#211]

GARDEN, FRANCIS, brother of Alexander Garden, graduated
MD from Edinburgh University in 1768, died in
Charleston during 1770. [SM.XXXIII.53]

GEEKIE, WILLIAM, from Arbroath, former RN settled Goose
Creek, SC, 1763, as a planter, Loyalist, returned to
Scotland. [TNA.AO12.50.138]

SCOTTISH TRADE WITH
COLONIAL CHARLESTON, 1683-1783

GIBB, Dr ROBERT, born Edinburgh, a physician, emigrated
to Georgetown, SC, in 1754, planter on the Pedee
River, died there 1777, property on Bay Street and
Prince's Street, Charleston, Loyalist, died in SC during
1777. [TNA.AO12.51.99]

GLEN, JAMES, born during 1701, son of Alexander Glen of
Longcroft, provost of Linlithgow, was appointed
Governor in December 1738, arrived in Charleston
during 1743, Governor 1738 to 1756, died 1777.
[NRS.SH; NRAS#0336]

GORDON, HUGH, a saddler in Charleston, Loyalist, settled in
Cape Breton 1785. [TNA.AO12.100.161]

GORDON, JAMES, merchant in Georgetown, SC, also in
Augusta, Georgia, a Loyalist with land in Charleston,
moved to West Indies, claimed for 500 acres, 2 houses
and a wharf in Charleston, 2500 acres in Georgia.
[TNA.AO12.5.38]

GORDON, JOHN, arrived in the 1740s, the major exporter of
deerskins from 1759 to 1773, a merchant in
Charleston, and Jesse Fish, a merchant in St Augustine,
bought land in East Florida in 1763.
[NRS.GD172.2548]; Loyalist, died Bordeaux during
1778. [AJ#1578][TNA.AO12.100.11]

GRANT, LUDOVICK, a Jacobite transportee in 1716, a trader
among the Cherokee from 1724. [Charleston Probate
Courtbook, 1754-1758, p.301]

GRINDLAY, JAMES, an attorney in Charleston, probate 1765
SC

GUILD, THOMAS, probably from Glamis, a planter in
Colleton County, SC, probate 1737 SC

HAMILTON, JOHN, a merchant in 96 District, a Loyalist
merchant, owned land in NC and SC, Major of
Loyalist Militia, moved to New Brunswick in 1782.
[TNA.AO12.47.92]

SCOTTISH TRADE WITH
COLONIAL CHARLESTON, 1683-1783

HAY, JOHN, a merchant, probate 1733 SC

HERIOT, GEORGE, a planter in SC, about 1771.
[NRS.CS16.1.146/192]

HEWAT, Rev. ALEXANDER, born 1733, educated at
Edinburgh University, to Charleston 1763 from
Edinburgh, minister of the Scots Presbyterian Church,
author of a history of SC published in London during
1779, Loyalist, died 1829. [Journal of Southern
History#20.50] [F.7.663][TNA.AO12.47.428]

HOGG, ROBERT, of Hogg and Clayton merchants in
Charleston, SC with a store in Wilmington NC. [UNC,
Chapel Hill, ms. Invoice book]

HUTCHISON, ROBERT, from Clackmannan, settled in SC
1769 -1781, house in King Street, Loyalist, settled in
Kincardine on Forth. [TNA.AO13.96.606]

IMRIE, DUNCAN, son of John Imrie, formerly a ships
carpenter in Dundee then in Carolina, later in East
Florida, died at sea, testament confirmed 1782 in
Edinburgh. [NRS.CC8.8.-]

IMRIE, JOHN, to Charleston 1761, a shipbuilder, a Loyalist
with a claim for a lot on Dutch Church Street,
Charleston, a wharf in Charleston, 1000 acres on the
Edisto River, 350 acres on Little Lynch's Creek, 500
acres near St Augustine.
[TNA.AO12.3.252][NRS.CS17.1.12]

INGLIS, GEORGE, a merchant in Charleston, died 1775
[TNA.AO12.99.325]

INGLIS, THOMAS, a merchant in Charleston ca1765-1776,
partner in Inglis Lloyd and Co, in the Guinea trade [ie
slavery], Loyalist, officer in militia, moved to Jamaica
by 1784, claim for 817 acres on Wando River, 2500
acres on Broad River, 500 acres on Sandy River, 1000
acres at Thickety Meadow; 500 acres on Altamaha
River, Georgia, etc. [TNA.AO12.52.259]

IRVING, ALEXANDER, a planter in SC 1767-1777, brother

of Thomas Irving former Receiver General for SC,
Loyalist. [TNA.AO13.70B.298]

IRVING, THOMAS, Inspector General of Imports and Exports
1767-1774, Member of the Council of SC 1774,
Loyalist, moved to London.
[TNA.AO12.51.304][NRS.CS16.1.161/182]

IRVING, WINIFRED, daughter of William Irving of Gribton,
and relict of Archibald Baird of Georgetown, SC,
1778. [NRS.RS.Dumfries#xxii.154]

JAMIESON, JOHN, a merchant in Charleston, 1771.
[TNA.CS16.1.146]

JOHNSTON, Dr GEORGE MILLIGAN, surgeon in
Charleston and an army surgeon in SC, Loyalist, claim
for 5000 acres and a lot in Beaufort town, died in
Dumfries 1799. [AJ#2671] [TNA.AO12.50.239]

JOHNSTON, JAMES, a solicitor in the Supreme Court of
Justice in SC, was appointed a Notary Public of SC in
1769, [Charleston Misc. Rec. 1769/22]; a Loyalist who
was banished from Charleston in 1777, returned in
1780, Attorney General in 1781, moved to Jamaica,
claimed for 200 acres in Craven County.
[TNA.AO12.46.408]

JOHNSTON, JOHN, a merchant in Charleston, whose will
reveals that he was the son of Mrs Giles Gowan;
brother of Andrew, Thomas and Archibald, Jane,
Giles, and Janet; connected with George Seaman and
Alex Robertson merchants in Charleston, and John
Gowan a merchant in London; his executors were
George Seaman and Alexander Robertson, probate
1739 SC

JOHNSTON, ROBERT, to SC 1772, attorney in the Supreme
Courts of Justice, Loyalist, moved to Bahamas.
[TNA.AO13.130.129]

KEIR, PATRICK, a Presbyterian minister of James Island, SC,
around 1758. [NRS.CS16.1.107; B65.8.10]

KEITH, JAMES, emigrated to SC in 1751, accumulated a
fortune as a planter, later a shoemaker in Charleston,
Loyalist, returned to Banff, claim for 300 acres in
Craven Co, 3 houses in Charleston, and a schooner,
[TNA.AO12.48.306], probate 1788 PCC

KENNEDY, JAMES, a planter in Camden, SC, a Loyalist in
1776. [TNA.AO12.48.277]

KILPATRICK, DAVID, a surgeon in Berkeley County, SC,
probate 1722 SC

KINCAID, GEORGE, a merchant in Charleston from 1757 to
1774, then a planter in Georgia, Loyalist in 1776.
[TNA.AO12.72.17]

KINLOCH, ALEXANDER, wrote to Lord Milton in
Edinburgh advising him of his interest in a naval
officer's place; had settled in Wampee, SC January
1728, bought 180 acres, built a house, satisfied his
creditors except for Alexander Nisbet who threatened
to have him arrested, etc 1732. [NRS.GD237/20.10.20]

KINLOCH, JAMES, born 1685, to SC in 1703, settled in
Waccamaw, them at Grove Hall, granted 9,700 acres in
Craven County in 1737-1738, a politician and planter,
died 1757. [SC Genealogist]

LAMB, THOMAS, born 1729 in Fife, a merchant in
Charleston, died 1786. [Old Scots Church gravestone,
Charleston]

LENNOX, JAMES, in partnership as merchants with David
Deas, both in Charleston, 1765, reference to David
Deas deceased merchant in Leith, etc.
[NRS.RD3.224/1.627; CS16.1.170]

LENNOX, WILLIAM, born 1752, a merchant in Charleston,
1776, then HM Commissioner for Prisoners, died
1781. [NRS.CS16.1.170][Old Scots Church
gravestone, Charleston]

LINN, DAVID, a shipwright in SC, a Loyalist.
[TNA.AO13.95.374]

SCOTTISH TRADE WITH
COLONIAL CHARLESTON, 1683-1783

LINN, WILLIAM, in Charleston, probate 1735 PCC
LINING, JOHN, born 1708 in Dundee, a physician who settled
in SC, died 1760. Correspondent of the Royal Society
of London. [SA]
LIVIE, ALEXANDER, a merchant in Charleston, probate
1756 SC
LOGAN, WILLIAM, was appointed Registrar of the Court of
Vice Admiralty of SC in 1769. [Charleston Misc.
Records 1769/125]
MACAULAY, Rev. ANGUS, minister of the Church of
Scotland, in Charleston 1771-1777, Loyalist.
[TNA.AO12.30.207]
MACBETH, ALEXANDER, a merchant on Elliott Street,
Charleston, a Loyalist. [TNA.AO12.92.1B]
MCCALL, JOHN, a merchant and the treasurer of the SC
Society, 1771. [Charleston Misc. Records, 1771,
fo.544]
MCCLELLAN, DAVID, a carpenter in Charleston, probate
1739 SC
MCCREDIE, DAVID, born 1754 in Galloway, a merchant in
Charleston by 1774, died 1811. [Old Scots Church
gravestone, Charleston]
MCDONALD, PETER, a planter in Charleston, a Loyalist who
moved to Jamaica in 1783. [TNA.AO13.91.210]
MCGILLIVRAY, ALEXANDER, a merchant in Charleston,
by 1743. [NRS.CS16.1.72; RS38.X.88]
MCGILLIVRAY, LAUCHLAN, from Drumnaglash, a
merchant in Charleston by 1755. [NRS.CS16.1.95]
MCGREGOR, DANIEL, a planter on the Santee River, SC,
probate 1724 SC
MCINTOSH, LACHLAN, a merchant in Charleston, a
Loyalist who moved to Jamaica, probate 1789 PCC
MACKENZIE, ANDREW, from Leith to Charleston as clerk
to John Simpson and Co., later a merchant there,

Loyalist militia captain, 1000 acres on Saluda River, Loyalist. [TNA.AO12.51.273]

MACKENZIE, ROBERT, to SC 1753, a merchant in Charleston, partner of John Tunno, a Loyalist, in Edinburgh by 1780. [TNA.AO12.51.273; CS16.17.1/61.123](cf Robert Irons in Montrose, was apprenticed to Robert McKenzie shipmaster in Charlestown, in Leith on 13 May 1752, as a navigator for 3 years. [NRS.RD2.1178/2.104])

MACLAURIN, EUAN, born in Appin, Argyll, a merchant in western SC, Loyalist, died Charleston 1782. [TNA.AO12.47.266]

MCQUEEN, DUNCAN, a gentleman in Pon Pon, SC, probate 1736 SC

MANSON, DANIEL, a shipbuilder in Charleston in partnership with William Begbie from 1763, Loyalist with a plantation in Berkeley County. [TNA.AO.12.50.213]

MARSHALL, JAMES, possibly from Aberdeen, then in St Philips, Charleston, probate 1767 PCC

MARSHALL, PATRICK, a merchant of Charleston, SC, now resident in New Providence, Bahamas, his will, subscribed 9 August 1760, refers to mother Janet Marshall in Dundee, brother William Marshall a merchant in Dundee, brother Alexander Marshall a shipmaster, sister Margaret Marshall in Dundee, brother Charles; executor his partner Charles Dewar of Charleston and the Marshall brothers, probate 1760 the Bahamas

MAXWELL, Sir WILLIAM, of Monreith, to SC with a detachment from Jamaica in 1742/1743 [NRS.GD219/290]

MICHIE, JAMES, in Charleston, Hugh Swinton wrote on 13 September 1746 to James Michie re the disposal of lands and slaves belonging to Mr Abercrombie; the writer was giving up his estate to his creditors; re production of indigo; etc. [NRS.GD237/20/17/9]; probate 1760 SC

MICHIE, KENNETH, a merchant in Charleston by 1745, probate 1749 SC. [NRS.CS16.1.73]

MICHIE, WILLIAM, born 1716 in Strathdon, educated at Aberdeen University, a merchant in Charleston, died 1771, probate 1772 SC, [NRS.NRAS#771, bundle 552]

MIRRYLEES, ALEXANDER, a brewer in Leith then in SC, 1779. [NRS.CS16.1.175]

MONCRIEFF, JOHN, from Perthshire, to SC 1772, a merchant in Charleston, Loyalist, died in Charleston 1821. [Old Scots Church gravestone, Charleston]

MORRISON, PHILIP, in Charleston 1759. [NRS.GD77.200/6]

MOULTRIE, JOHN, settled in SC 1728; a member of the St Andrew's Society of Charleston in 1730; graduated MD from Edinburgh University in 1749. [EMG#4]

MURRAY, ALEXANDER, a merchant in Charleston by 1737, then Naval Officer of Charleston, dead by 1750, son of Charles Murray, clerk of the bailliary of Lauderdale. [NRS.SH; RD3.210.491]

MURRAY, GEORGE, of the Secretary's Office in SC, 1761. [NRS.9.314]; 1769. [Charleston Misc. Rec.1769/232]; died 1772. [Old Scots Church gravestone, Charleston]

MURRAY, JOHN and JAMES, merchants in Charleston, goods from the British Linen Company in 1757, letter book, [NRS.GD219.290]

MURRAY, Dr JOHN, a student in Edinburgh 1737-1742, a physician in Charleston 1747 to 1763, in practice with his cousin Dr William Murray. [NRS.GD219.284-7]

MURRAY, JOHN, of Philiphaugh, purchased a plantation in SC 1757 [NRS.GD219/289]

SCOTTISH TRADE WITH
COLONIAL CHARLESTON, 1683-1783

MURRAY, JOHN, of Murraythwaite, in Charleston 1756-
1758, purchased the office of Secretary of SC.
[NRS.GD219/288, 290]

MURRAY, PETER, a physician in Dorchester, SC, probate
1733 SC

MURRAY, Dr WILLIAM, to SC in 1749, a physician in
Georgetown later in Charleston, in practice with his
cousin Dr John Murray, returned from SC 1765.
[NRS.GD219/284, 288]

NAIRN, THOMAS, to SC by 1698, an Indian Agent in SC,
died 1715, wife Elizabeth Edward died 1721.[SCLW]

NAPIER, WILLIAM, a surgeon in Colleton County, died
1732, younger brother of John Napier of Napierston;
links with Glasgow merchants Thomas Youll and
William Crawford, probate 1732 SC

NICHOLSON, FRANCIS, the Governor of SC, was admitted
as a burgess and guilds-brother of Glasgow in 1724.
[GBR]

NISBET, ALEXANDER, [later Sir Andrew Nisbet of Dean],
was indentured to Alexander Nisbet a storekeeper at
Redbank, SC, in 1721, then settled in Charleston in
1725 as a merchant, land grant in Craven County in
1737, planter of Dean Hall, married Mary, daughter of
Sir John Rutherford, in 1742, died in 1753, probate
1753 SC – his executors were George Seaman
merchant and Robert Hume planter.
[NRS.RD4.116.1084; GD237.1.153.9] [GM.24.48]

NISBET, ALEXANDER, storekeeper at Redbank, SC, ca
1720s. [NRS.GD237.box 10, bundle 4/1]

NISBET, ROBERT, brother of Sir John Nisbet of Dean, a
merchant in Charleston 1721-1740 [NRS.GD237, box
10, bundle 4/1]

OGILVIE, CHARLES, [brother of Alexander Ogilvie], via
London to Charleston 1750, unsuccessful trading
ventures to the West Indies, considered going as a

supercargo on a slaver to Guinea but abandoned the idea in 1752, then considered a partnership with a local ship-owner to collect slaves, moved to London in 1761, married Mary, the daughter and heiress of James Michie, thus acquired much property; Loyalist, in Nantes 1779 routing goods from France to SC or via Bermuda or the Bahamas; in London 1783 selling best two estates in SC, died in London 2.1788. [AUL.MS2740/3]; merchant in London, probate 1788 PCC

OGILVIE, GEORGE, [1748-1801]. Son of Alexander Ogilvie of Auchiries, Aberdeenshire, and Mary Cumine or Ogilvie, educated in London during 1760s – lived there with his uncle Charles Ogilvie, by 1773 managing a plantation in SC and later bought one, a Loyalist in 1776, returned to Scotland in 1779, briefly in SC 1785/86, inherited Auchiries, customs controller of Aberdeen, died Scotland 1801. [AUL.MS2740]

OGILVY, HENRY, a skipper in Charleston, son of Henry Ogilvy of Templehall, Angus, a Loyalist who died in Pensacola 1779. [NRS.CC8.8.126/1]

OGILVIE, JAMES, to Charleston 1743/44, died 1750. [brother of William and Alexander Ogilvie] [AUL.MS2740/1,2,3,4]

OGILVY, WILLIAM, from Angus, settled SC 1764, Secretary to the Superintendent of Indian Affairs for the Southern District 1765-1785, property in Ninety-six County, Loyalist, returned to Newtonmill, Forfar. [TNA.AO.12.47.141]

OLIPHANT, Dr DAVID, born 1720, medical student at Edinburgh ca1741, Jacobite, fled to America after 1746, settled in SC, a physician in partnership with John Murray and later John Linning, a Loyalist. [TNA.AO13.88.96][NRS.CS16.1.165/40;

CS17.1.2.204; NRAS#0627, box 10, bundle 3;
RD3.235.265]
PANTON, WILLIAM, a planter in 96th District, Loyalist who
moved to St Augustine, East Florida, by 1783.
[TNA.AO12.109.246]
PARK, RICHARD, a merchant in SC, 1715.
[NRS.RD2.104.490]
PENMAN, EDWARD, a merchant in Charleston, and
Alexander Penman a coachmaker, sons of George
Penman deceased in Edinburgh, 1786.
[NRS.RD3.245.725], the former naturalised in
Charleston in 1784 while his brother became a burgess
and guildsbrother of Glasgow. [GBR]
PENMAN, HUGH, a merchant in Charleston in 1783.
[NRS.CS17.1.2/343]
PITTIGREW, JAMES, born 1746, a merchant from Glasgow,
to Charleston in 1774. [TNA.T47.12]
POLLOCK, HUGH, a saddler in Charleston, Loyalist, died
Jamaica 1782. [TNA.AO12.99.336]
PRINGLE, ROBERT, born 1702, second son of Robert, and
grandson of Thomas, both merchant burgesses of
Edinburgh, and linked to the Hoppringills of that Ilk, to
Charleston 1725, a merchant on Tradd Street, his
house dated 1742 was built after the Great Fore and
demolished about 1930, he married Mrs Judith Bull a
widow [sister in law of the Lieutenant Governor], died
1776. [see The Letter Book of Robert Pringle, SC,
1972]
RAE, JOHN, born 1716, ordained 1742 in Dundee, a
Presbyterian minister in SC 1743-1761, died in
Williamsburg, SC, 1761, probate 1761 SC. [CCVC]
RAE, ROBERT, to America, teacher in Dorchester, SC, house
in Charleston, Loyalist, returned to Moray by 1781.
[TNA.AO12.51.133]

SCOTTISH TRADE WITH
COLONIAL CHARLESTON, 1683-1783

RAMSAY, JOHN, from Fife, a shopkeeper in Charleston,
        probate 1734 SC, [Caledonian Mercury#2326]

RATTRAY, JOHN, born 1716, judge of the Vice Admiralty
        Court of SC, died Charleston 1761, probate 1761 SC
        [Old Scots Church gravestone, Charleston]
        [SM.13.671]

REID, ANDREW, a gentleman in Charleston, probate 1784
        PCC

REID, JAMES, master of the Charles of Charleston, admitted
        as a burgess and guilds-brother of Edinburgh 1737.
        [EBR] (possibly the partner of Robert Pringle sr. in a
        slaving venture ca1741)

REOCH, ALEXANDER, a merchant in Georgetown, SC, a
        Loyalist who died by 1779. [TNA.AO13.80.408]

RHIND, DAVID, from Aberdeen, a teacher at the Academy of
        Charleston in 1765. [Aberdeen Burgh Archives:
        Proprinquity Book]

RIGG, ALEXANDER, a gentleman in Charleston, probate
        1771 SC

RISK, HUGH, a shopkeeper in Charleston, a Loyalist who
        returned to Glasgow in 1782. [see
        TNA.AO12.122/299]

ROBERTSON, ALEXANDER, a victualler in Charleston,
        probate 1724 SC

ROBERTSON, ANDREW, to America in 1756, in partnership
        in Charleston with John Jamieson and George Baillie
        but in 1773 moved to Savannah, bought a plantation
        180 miles up river in Georgia 1775, Loyalist.
        [TNA.AO12.51.111]

ROBERTSON, FRANCIS, born 1747 in Aberdeenshire, settled
        in SC as a lawyer in 1770, died in Charleston in 1819.
        [S.4.193][GM.90.281][AJ.3795]

ROSE, DAVID, a skipper from Inverness, bought land in
        Craven County during 1743. [SC Deeds, #V2, p.72]

ROSE, Dr HUGH, a physician and surgeon in St John's parish, Berkely County, SC, for 18 years, Loyalist, by 1789 in Stonehaven, Scotland. [TNA.AO12.3.156]

ROSE, JOHN, from Moray, trained in RN yards on Thames, developed a shipyard at Hobcaw Creek on the Wando River, in 1753, active there until 1769 in partnership with James Stewart, business disposed of to William Begbie and Daniel Manson another couple of Scots; possibly the John Rose of Bees Creek, Cooswhatchie Bridge, Loyalist, substantial land, father of Hugh, Loyalist. [TNA.AO12.47.198]

RUSSELL, ALEXANDER, born 1719, a shipwright in Charleston, see deposition of 1768 re loss of the ship Unity, formerly the Eleanor, off the coast of NC in 1764. [Charleston County Misc. Records, 1768]

RUTHERFORD, JAMES, from Edinburgh, a gold and silversmith in Charleston 1751. [SCGaz#914]

RYMER, JAMES, from St Andrews, a Presbyterian minister in SC 1754, died 1755 in Walterborough, SC. [CCVC][SCGaz.10.7.1755]

SANDS, JAMES, a merchant, died Charleston 1767. [AJ#1133][SM.31.502]

SCOTT, WILLIAM, Dumfries, a merchant in Charleston, probate 1765 SC

SEAMAN, GEORGE, Leith, merchant in Charleston, 1750, probate 1769 SC/PCC. [NRS.RD3.210.491; CS16.1.59] married in 1750 to widow of William Allen and thus became stepfather of Elizabeth Allen who married John Deas in 1759. Deas was born Leith during 1735, to SC 1749][a long will includes £500 sterling to Edinburgh Infirmary and £500 to needy and honest housekeepers in Leith]

SEYMOUR, JOHN, from Aberdeenshire, a planter in St Stephen's parish, SC, probate 1775 SC

SCOTTISH TRADE WITH
COLONIAL CHARLESTON, 1683-1783

SHAW, LACHLAN, Lieutenant of an Independent Company
in SC, died Prince William County in 1761, testament
confirmed 1762 in Edinburgh. [NRS.CC8.8.-]

SIMPSON, JAMES, in SC 1763-1779, Attorney General and
Clerk of the Council of SC, Loyalist; appointed Judge
of the Admiralty Court of SC on 5 May 1769.
[Charleston County Misc. Rec. 1769/64]; presumably
the James Simpson who with John Simpson,
gentlemen in Charleston, and grandsons of James
Simpson of Tibbers, appointed attornies in Dumfries-
shire in 1764 [NAS.SC15.55.2]; Loyalist in 1776.
[TNA.AO12.48.142]

SIMPSON, WILLIAM, to America 1766, a merchant and
planter in SC, Loyalist who returned to Edinburgh by
1784. [TNA.AO12.92.2]

SINCLAIR, RICHARD, merchant in Charleston, probate 1733
SC

SKENE, GEORGE, son of Andrew Skene, a minister in Prince
Frederick parish, probate 1766 SC

SKENE, Dr JAMES, studied in Edinburgh ca1765, physician
in SC 1767-1778, Loyalist, settled in Kingston,
Jamaica, graduated MD from Marischal College 1766.
[TNA.AO12.52.163][NRS.CS16.1.165/42]

SKENE, THOMAS, from Angus, settled Granville County,
probate 1760 SC

SMITH, ALEXANDER, from Angus, a tailor in Charleston,
received a land grant in Berkley County during 1737,
probate 1745 SC

SMITH, THOMAS LOUGHTON, from SC, admitted as a
burgess and guilds-brother of Edinburgh in 1769.
[EBR]

SQUYRE, JOHN, a minister in James Island, SC, from 1715 to
1725. [NRS.CH1/2.35, 189; 51, 99]

STEPHEN, JAMES, from Peterculter, a cooper in Charleston,
died 1766. [Aberdeen Archives; Proprinquity Book]

SCOTTISH TRADE WITH
COLONIAL CHARLESTON, 1683-1783

STEWART, ALEXANDER, born 1691, Registrar of the Court of Chancery, Charleston, died there 1763, probate 1763 SC

STEWART, ALEXANDER, to America in 1771, settled as a planter at Monk's Corner, SC, 40 miles from Charleston, Loyalist. [TNA.AO12.100.90]

STEWART, JAMES, from Dunkeld, via Gravesend to Charlesxton in 1749, shipwright at Hobcaw Creek, Wando River, in partnership with John Rose from 1753 to 1769, sold out to another two Scots – William Begbie and Daniel Manson. [NRS.GD38.2.8.24]

STOBIE, JAMES, a merchant in Charleston ca1773, father of James who was apprenticed in Edinburgh to a locksmith. [ERA]

STOBO, Rev. ARCHIBALD, born 1674, graduated MA at Edinburgh University in 1697, married Elizabeth Jean Park 1699, to Darien 1699, settled in Charleston 1700, established the Scots Presbyterian church in Charleston, allocated a land grant on Savanna River 1737, died 1740.
[F.VII.665][SHR.1.416][NRS.CH1.2.24.2.224; RD2.104.490, 1008]

STUART, FRANCIS, merchant in Beaufort County, 1752. [St Helen's Marriage Register, 28.12.1752]

STUART, JOHN, Edinburgh, merchant in Carolina, wife Henrietta Burnett, father of John and Charles both merchants early 1700s. [see Henrietta Burnett's testament, NRS.CC8.8.67]

STUART, JOHN, Superintendent of Indian Affairs in the Southern District, in Charleston 1768, a planter in Charleston, a Loyalist who died in West Florida 1778. [TNA.AO12.51.146]

SWINTON, HUGH, wrote to James Michie in Charleston 13 September 1746, re disposal of lands and slaves

belonging to Mr Abercrombie, etc.
[NRS.GD237.20.17.9]

SWINTON, WILLIAM, planter in Craven County, probate 1742 SC

TAILFER, Dr PATRICK, a physician and surgeon from Edinburgh, to Georgia 1734, moved to SC 1740. [ESG#98]

TAYLOR, ALEXANDER, late of Charleston, SC, then in Caltonhill, Edinburgh, 1776, 1778. [NRS.RS27.229/231, etc]

TENNANT, WILLIAM, from Stirlingshire, an Indian trader in SC, probate 1734 SC

THOMSON, JOHN, from Edinburgh, a merchant in Charleston, probate 1763 SC

THORNSON, ANDREW, born 1754 in Glasgow, a merchant, to Charleston in 1774. [TNA.T47/12]

TURNBULL, Dr ANDREW, from Annan, educated in London, to Florida in 1768, a physician in SC 1781 when he took over Alexander Garden's practice, died in Charleston in 1792. [SM.LIV.309]

TWEED, WILLIAM, a shipbuilder in Charleston, a Loyalist who was hanged after 1778. [TNA.AO12.48.227]

URQUHART, LENNARD, from Edinburgh, a carpenter in SC, probate 1758 SC

WACHOPE, JOHN, a merchant in Charleston, who according to his will he was son of John Wachope in Cameston, his executor was his cousin John Hume a merchant in Charleston, witnesses were Robert Hay, Charles Dewar and John Rattray, probate 1739 SC

WALKER, JOHN, a merchant in Charleston 1760-1775, Loyalist; admitted as a burgess of St Andrews on 13 June 1775. [TNA.AO13.132.262]

WALLACE, WILLIAM, a merchant in Charleston, in his will he refers to his brother John Biggar Wallace, his late friend John Cleland, his widow Mrs Mary Cleland, and their daughter Anna, 1741, probate 1765 the Bahamas

303

SCOTTISH TRADE WITH
COLONIAL CHARLESTON, 1683-1783

WATSON, DAVID, from Leith, a wigmaker in Charleston,
    probate 1732 SC

WATSON, JOHN, jr., a merchant in Charleston, testament
    confirmed 1756 in Edinburgh [NRS.CC8.8.116/1]; his
    widow had a claim on the estate of Robert Watson a
    merchant in the Luckenbooths, Edinburgh, his father.
    [NRS.GD219/290/53]

WEDDERBURN, JAMES, Fife, to SC 1733, Clerk of the
    Common Pleas, land grants in SC 1737-1738.
    [CSPAWI.]

WILKIE, JOHN, a cooper in Charleston, 1769.
    [NRS.CS16.1.138/231]

WILSON, ROBERT, born 1736, apprenticed to Dr Martin
    Eccles RCPE, then studied in London, in army also,
    later in Charleston, died there 1815. [Old Scots Church
    gravestone, Charleston]

WILSON, WILLIAM, trader and merchant in Charleston
    1769-1779, died there 1779, Loyalist.
    [TNA.AO12.48.363]

WOOD, ANDREW, Collector of Beaufort, died 1755. [St
    Helen's burial register, 9.12.1755]

WOODROP, WILLIAM, a merchant in Charleston in 1745.
    [Charleston Misc. Records,
    1769/142][NRS.CS16.1.73]

APPENDIX 3

Scottish Emigrants
bound for South Carolina,
from the
Register of Emigrants, 1773-1774[420]

In 1773 the British Government, alarmed by the high level of emigration to America that was occurring, ordered the English and Scottish Boards of Customs to record various the issues surround this fact. Customs officials at every port in Great Britain were to note the names of those who were leaving, their ages, occupations, place of residence in the United Kingdom, destinations and the reasons they had for leaving. The resulting records, collectively known as the Register of Emigrants 1773-1774, represents a nearly comprehensive passenger list for this two-year period, and is the only available list of emigrants from the colonial era.

The following two ships carried passengers from Scotland the Charleston during the period 1773-1774, and details of their passengers are listed below.

Countess of Dumfries, master Robert Eason, from Greenock to Charleston in October 1774

420. TNA.T47.12

SCOTTISH TRADE WITH COLONIAL CHARLESTON, 1683-1783

Name	Age	Occupation	Residence	Reason
Francis Beattie	22	Farmer	Dumfriesshire	'Want of business'
William Blacklock	23	Farmer	Dumfriesshire	'Want of business'
Andrew Johnston	30	Farmer	Dumfriesshire	'Want of business'
John Cearl	40	Farmer	Dumfriesshire	'Want of business'
William Rodeak	35	Farmer	Dumfriesshire	'Want of business'
John Brown	18	Joiner	Dumfriesshire	'Want of business'
John Paisley	28	Weaver	Dumfriesshire	'Want of business'
Mrs Paisley	26		Dumfriesshire	
Mrs Cearl	50		Dumfriesshire	
John Heastie	30	Shoemaker	Perthshire,	'Want of business'
David Campbell	30	Tailor	Perthshire	'Want of business'
James Pittegrew	26	Merchant	Glasgow,	'Want of business'
Andrew Thornson	20	Merchant	Glasgow	'Want of business'
Edward Corbett	20	Merchant	Edinburgh,	'Want of business'
James Carson	12		Dumfries	'Want of business'

SCOTTISH TRADE WITH
COLONIAL CHARLESTON, 1683-1783

James Fife	35	Merchant
Renfrewshire		'Want of business'
James Paisley	26	Farmer
Dumfries-shire		'Want of business'

Jamaica Packet of Burntisland, master Thomas Smith, from Kirkcaldy to Charleston, June 1775

Name	Age	Occupation	Place of Residence	Reason
Miss Elizabeth Mills			Dundee	
Servant of Miss Mills			Dundee	
John Douglas		Laborer	Dundee	
John Mills		Joiner	Dundee	
Thomas Hill		Joiner	Dundee	

Of the 20 passengers on this ship, the others sailed on to Brunswick, North Carolina.

[Source: TNA.T47.12]

APPENDIX 4

South Carolina Land Grants 1737

Scottish surnames only

Name	Grant	Location
Allston, William	129 acres	Craven County
Baxter, John	1100 acres	Craven County
Buckhannon, Wm.	500 acres	Craven County
Campbell, Hugh	470 acres	Saltcatcher R.
Christie, Henry	300 acres	Craven County
Cleland, John	3290 acres	Craven County
Cochran, John	300 acres	Craven County
Copeland, Hugh	300 acres	Craven County
Crauford, Daniel	776 acres	Granville Co.
Dick, John	400 acres	Craven County
Finley, Francis	500 acres	Craven County
Fleming, Thomas	650 acres	Craven County
Hunter, George	800 acres	Granvill
Kinloch, James	5642 acres	Craven Co. S
Livingston, Wm.	440 acres	Craven County
McCaw, John	299 acres	Colleton River
McClelland, And.	750 acres	Craven County
McGers, James	150 acres	Craven County
McGilveray Martha	400 acres	Savannah River
McKay, Patrick	4050 acres	Granville Co.

SCOTTISH TRADE WITH
COLONIAL CHARLESTON, 1683-1783

McMullen, Wm.	200 acres	Savannah River
Maxwell, James	510 acres	Peedee River
Moultrie, John	400 acres	Berkley County
Neal, Francis	300 acres	Craven County
Nesbett, Alex.	180 acres	Craven County
Skene, Alexander	10000 acres	Peedee/Craven
Stobo, Archibald	900 acres	Savannah River
Wedderburn, James	1000 acres	Craven County

[Source:TNA.CO5.398]

SCOTTISH TRADE WITH
COLONIAL CHARLESTON, 1683-1783

APPENDIX 5

MEMBERS OF THE ST ANDREW'S SOCIETY OF CHARLESTON, 1732 - 1776

Name	Date	Occupation
Abercrombie, James	1731	Attorney General
Abercromby, John	1773/75	
Adam, Thomas	1758	
Aiken, James	1731	
Aiken, James, jr	1731	
Alexander, Alexander	1768	Shipmaster
Alexander, Robert	1768	Shipmaster
Allan, Eleazer [Alexander?]	1731	Merchant
Allan, John	1731	
Anderson, David	1729/30	
Anderson, Hugh	1738/39	Gentleman
Anderson, John	1740s	
Anderson, John	1768	
Angus, Hercules	1764	Shipmaster
Arnot, Thomas	1750	
Atchison, John	1729/30	
Ayton, Philip	1729/30	
Bacot, Peter	1762	
Baillie, Ensign Alexander	1757	Soldier
Baillie, George	1757	
Bampfield, George	1731	
Bannatyne, Francis	1758	
Barclay, William	1733	
Baron, Rev. Alexander	1749	Minister
Baron, Alexander, MD	1770	Physician
Bayne, Lt. Duncan	1757	Soldier

SCOTTISH TRADE WITH
COLONIAL CHARLESTON, 1683-1783

Beale, Othneil	1762		
Beattie, Robert	1765	Shipmaster	
Bell, Thomas	1758		
Bell, Thomas	1763		
Berrie, James	1729/30	Merchant	
Berenger de Beaufain, Hector	1740s		
Blakie, Rev George	1740s	Minister	
Blakie, George	1764		
Blakie, John	1769		
Bogg, Peter	1749		
Bonar, William	1750		
Bower, William	1771		
Boyd, Robert	1757		
Brazier, William	1767		
Bremar, John	1771		
Brisbane, James	1764		
Brisbane, Robert	1740s	Physician	
Brisbane, William, jr	1772		
Brown, Malcolm	1765		3?
Brown, Robert	1754/56		
Brown, Samuel	1731		
Buchanan, James	1729/30		
Bulloch, James	1729/30		
Butler, John	1758		
Burn, John	1757	H.M.Councillor	
Cameron, Alexander	1767		
Cameron, John	1773/75		
Campbell, Lt Col. Alexander	1757	Soldier	
Campbell, Lt. Colin	1757	Soldier	
Campbell, Colin	1769	Shipmaster	
Campbell, Lt. Donald	1757	Soldier	
Campbell, Duncan	1729/30		
Campbell, Hugh	1731	Planter	
Carruthers, John	1733		
Cargill, John	1765		
Carson, James	1768		

SCOTTISH TRADE WITH
COLONIAL CHARLESTON, 1683-1783

Carson, William	1766	Planter
Cartmell, Robert	1735	
Cathcart, Andrew	1763	
Cassels, James	1763	Planter
Caw, David	1740s	
Chiene, William	1765	
Chisholm, Alexander	1768	Planter
Clark, John	1729/30	Shipmaster
Cleland, John	1734	HM Councillor
Cleland, William	1729/30	Physician
Clitherall, Dr James	1764	Physician
Clow, Patrick	1736/37	
Cooper, James	1758	
Cooper, John	1749	
Corbett, Edward	1773/75	Receiver General
Cowan, Andrew	1751/53	Shipmaster
Cowan, James	1769	
Cowie, James	1740s	
Cowper, Basil	1764	
Cozens, Edmond	1740s	
Craig, Robert	1765	
Cramahe, Alexander	1740s	
Crawford, Archibald	1768	
Crawford, Daniel	1729/30	
Crawford, David	1731	SC Postmaster
Creighton, James	1764	
Crokatt, Charles	1729/30	
Crokatt, David	1731	
Crokatt, James	1729/30	Merchant
Crokatt, James	1751/53	Physician
Crokatt, John	1729/30	Merchant
Crokatt, John, jr	1738/39	Merchant
Crooke, R. Cunningham	1762	
Cruickshanks, John	1735	
Cuming, Sir Alexander	1758/30	
Cunningham, Andrew	1758	336

SCOTTISH TRADE WITH
COLONIAL CHARLESTON, 1683-1783

Curry, Henry	1729/30	
Cuthbert, George	1740s	
Dallas, Walter	1729/30	Merchant
Dalrymple, Captain Robert	1770	Soldier
Deans, Robert	1758	Joiner
Deas, David	1740s	Merchant
Deas, John	1758	Merchant
De Lancey, Peter	1767	
Demere, Captain Raymond	1754/56	Soldier
Denniston, John	1769	Shipmaster
Dering, John	1766	
Dick, Alexander	1735	
Dick, James	1765	
Dick, Robert	1769	
Dickson, David	1769	
Dickson, James	1729/30	
Dishington, James	1768	
Dillon, Robert	1765	
Donaldson, James	1770	
Douglas, David	1773/75	
Douglas, James	1732	
Douglas, William	1733	
Drummond, James	1767	
Ducat, George	1729/30	Merchant
Duff, Captain James	1757	Soldier
Dunbar, Simon	1740s	
Duthie, James	1767	
Dysart, George	1731	
Elliott, Charles	1763	Merchant, NC
Eson, Robert	1769	Shipmaster
Fair, William	1762	
Falconer, James	1763	
Farquharson, Capt. Charles	1757	Soldier
Fleming, James	1762	
Fleming, William	1735	
Forbes, George	1751/53	

SCOTTISH TRADE WITH
COLONIAL CHARLESTON, 1683-1783

Forest, Commodore A.	1740s	Naval Officer	
Fotheringham, Alexander	1765		
Franklin, Thomas	1749	Admiral	
Franks, David	1740s		
Fraser, Alexander	1740s	Merchant	
Fraser, John	1758		
Freeman, William George	1738/39		
Fyffe, James	1729/30		
Gamble, Captain Thomas	1769		
Garden, Rev. Alexander	1738/39	Minister	
Glen, James	1754/56	ex Gov of SC	
Goldie, John	1769		
Gordon, Lord Adam	1765		
Gordon, Alexander	1740s		
Gordon, Hugh	1731		
Gordon, Lt. Hugh	1757	Soldier	
Gordon, James	1736/37		
Gordon, Lt. James	1766	Soldier	337
Gordon, Captain John	1757	Soldier	
Gordon, John	1768		
Gordon, William	1729/30		
Graeme, David	1750		
Graeme, William	1758		
Graham, Mungo	1740s		
Graham, William	1773/75		
Grant, Andrew	1734	Merchant in GA	
Grant, Ensign James	1757	Soldier	
Grant, Capt. James	1757	Soldier	
Grant, James	1757	Gov East Florida	
Grant, Lt. Joseph	1757	Soldier	
Grant, Lt. Robert	1757	Soldier	
Grant, Ensign William	1757	Soldier	
Grant, Lt. William	1757	Soldier	
Gregory, William	1740s		
Griffin, Thomas,	1732		
Grindlay, James	1740s	Attorney	

SCOTTISH TRADE WITH
COLONIAL CHARLESTON, 1683-1783

Grindlay, Robert	1769	Shipmaster
Gunn, Henry	1762	
Haggart, Ensign William	1757	Soldier
Haig, George	1772	
Haig, John	1729/30	
Hamilton, William	1757	Shipmaster
Hammerton, John	1740s	
Hannay, William	1735	
Harris, Valentine	1751/53	
Hay, John	1731	Merchant
Hay, John	1751/53	Shipmaster
Hay, Lt. W.	1757	Soldier
Henderson, James	1770	
Heron, Lt Col. Alexander	1750	Soldier
Hewat, Rev. Alexander	1763	Minister
Hodge, John	1736/37	
Holiday, William	1771	Planter
Home, Sir James	1740s	
Hope, Charles	1733	
Hope, Lord Charles	1766	
Houstoun, Ensign Lewis	1757	Soldier
Hume, John	1738/39	
Hunter, Andrew	1764	
Hunter, David	1729/30	
Hunter, George	1749	Surveyor
Hunter, James	1762	General, SC
Hutchison, James	1729/30	
Hyndman, Donald	1758	Shipmaster
Inglis, Alexander	1769	
Irving, Joseph	1767	
Irving, Thomas	1773/75	Merchant
Irwin, James	1740s	
Jamieson, James	1768	

SCOTTISH TRADE WITH
COLONIAL CHARLESTON, 1683-1783

Jamieson, John	1754/56	
Jamieson, Neil	1758	Shipmaster
Jamieson, Robert	1751/53	
Johnston, Archibald	1763	Planter
Johnston, Augustus	1769	
Johnston, Charles	1758	
Johnston, Charles	1763	
Johnston, James	1770	Supreme Ct Clerk
Johnston, John	1736/37	Merchant
Johnston, John	1764	
Johnston, Robert	1731	Governor of SC
Johnston, Thomas	1740s	
Johnston, William	1738/39	
Keir, Rev. Patrick	1763	Minister
Keith, Rev. Alexander	1750	Minister
Keith, William	1765	Surgeon
Kellie, Andrew	1770	
Keltie, William	1763	
Kennedy, Thomas	1740s	
Kerr, James	1733	
Kincaid, George	1763	Merchant
King, James	1762	
Kinloch, Francis	1750	
Kinloch, James	1735	Merchant
Kinsley, Zephaniah	1772	
Kirkwood, John	1765	
Ladson, Robert	1773/75	
Lawson, Lt John	1757	Soldier
Learmonth, Alexander	1764	Merchant
Larmonth, John	1770	
Leigh, Sir Egerton	1754/56	
Lind, Thomas	1766	
Lindsay, Robert	1772	Shipmaster
Lining, John	1731	Merchant/Physician
Lining, Thomas	1740s	Physician
Littleton, William Henry	1758	Governor of SC

SCOTTISH TRADE WITH
COLONIAL CHARLESTON, 1683-1783

Livie, Alexander	1740s	
Livie, Robert	1772	
Lorimer, Rev. Charles	1750	Minister
Lloyd, James,	1732	Merchant
Lundberry, Andrew	1765	
McAlpine, Col.	1764	Soldier
MacAulay, Alexander	1760	
McCloud, Patrick	1767	
McDonald, Adam	1740s	
McDonald, Lt. Alexander	1757	Soldier
McDonald, Capt. Alexander	1757	Soldier
McDonald, Lt. Donald	1757	Soldier
McDonald, Ensign John	1757	Soldier
McDonald. Captain William	1757	Soldier
McEuan, William	1767	
McGilchrist, William	1740s	Minister
McGillivray, Alexander	1732	Merchant
McGillivray, Archibald	1732	
McGillivray, John	1729/30	
McGillivray, John	1768	
McGillivray, Lachlan	1733	Merchant
McGillivray, Lachlan	1758	
McGillivray, William	1773/75	
McIntosh, Capt. Alexander	1757	Soldier
McIver, David	1729/30	
Mackay, Captain James	1751/53	
Mackay, Patrick	1733	Merchant in GA
Mackay, William	1738/39	
Mackewn, Robert	1763	
Mackie, Patrick	1749	
McKenzie, Major Alexander	1757	Soldier
McKenzie, Ensign Alexander	1757	Soldier
Mckenzie, Ensign Alexander, {2]	1757	Soldier
McKenzie, Captain Hugh	1757	Soldier
McKenzie, James	1763	

McKenzie, John	1732	Merchant
McKenzie, John	1740s	Shipmaster
McKenzie, Kenneth	1751/53	
McKenzie, Robert, jr	1763	
McKenzie, Capt. Roderick	1757	Soldier
Mckenzie, Lt Roderick	1757	Soldier
McKenzie, William	1729/30	Planter
McKenzie, Lt. William	1757	Soldier
McKinlay, Patrick	1766	Shipmaster
Mackintosh, Duncan	1740s	
McLarty, Angus	1766	Shipmaster
McLean, James	1740s	
McLean, John	1732	
McLean, John	1749	
McLean, Ensign William	1757	Soldier
McLellan, James	1733	Cabinetmaker
McMartin, Lt. Cosmo	1757	Soldier
MacMurchy, Hugh	1764	
McNab, Lt John	1757	Soldier
McNabney, James	1729/30	
McNeill, Archibald	1765	
McNeill, John	1765	
McQueen, John	1757	Shipmaster
McRae, George	1757	
Marshall, Alexander	1758	
Marshall, James	1763	Merchant
Marshall, Patrick	1758	Merchant
Marshall, William	1768	
Mason, William	1763	
Matthews, John	1766	
Maxwell, Rev. William	1729/30	Minister
Maxwell, William	1762	
Mayne, Charles	1751/53	
Menzies, James	1734	
Michie, Alexander	1763	
Michie, Benjamin	1740s	Merchant

SCOTTISH TRADE WITH
COLONIAL CHARLESTON, 1683-1783

Michie, John	1732	Merchant
Michie, Kenneth	1738/39	
Michie, William,	1757	
Middleton, William	1762	
Milligan, George	1751/1753	
Milne, James	1757	
Milne, John	1740s	
Mitchell, David	1757	
Mitchell, George	1734	Physician
Mitchell, Robert	1749	
Monteith, John	1731	
Montgomerie, Adam	1738/39	
Montgomery, Alexander	1757	
Montgomerie, Arch, EarlEglinton	1757	Soldier
Montgomerie, William	1749	
Moodie, Thomas	1757	
Morgan, William	1770	
Morison, Rev. Phillip	1757	Minister
Morrice, Hugh	1766	Shipmaster
Moultrie, Alexander	1772	
Moultrie, John	1729/30	Physician
Moultrie, John	1750	Lt Gov of E. Floria
Moultrie, Thomas	1762	
Moultrie, General William	1758	Soldier
Moultrie, William, jr	1773/75	
Muir, John	1771	
Muir, William	1750	Shipmaster
Munro, Captain George	1757	Soldier
Munro, Rev. Henry	1757	Minister
Murray, Alexander	173/39	Merchant
Murray, James	1735	Merchant
Murray, John	1740s	Merchant
Murray, John	1757	Physician
Murray, Peter	1729/30	Physician
Napier, John	1758	
Netherclift, Thomas	1771	
Nicholas, George	1740s	

SCOTTISH TRADE WITH
COLONIAL CHARLESTON, 1683-1783

Nisbet, Sir Alexander	1732	
Nisbet, Robert	1729/30	Merchant
Oucconnastotah	1773/75	Cherokee Chief
Ogilvie, Charles	1751/53	Merchant
Ogilvie, William	1767	Sec Indian Affairs
Oliphant, David	1749	Physician
Orme, James	1735	
Oswald, William	1738/39	
Paine, James	1731	
Paine, Robert	1733	
Parish, George	1750	
Parsons, James	1758	
Patterson, Hugh	1740s	Shipmaster
Petrie, Alexander	1740s	
Petrie, Edmund	1772	
Phillip, George	1740s	
Philp, Robert	1757	
Pickerman, Robert	1740s	
Pitcairn, John	1751/53	
Preston, James	1767	
Porter, Hugh	1762	
Pringle, Robert	1736/37	Merchant
Ramsay, John	1765	
Rattray, John	1738/39	Judge
Reid, Daniel	1733	
Reid, James	1734	Shipmaster
Reid, James	1749	
Reid, Patrick	1740s	
Rhind, David	1754/56	Teacher
Rhind, William	1740s	
Rigg, Alexander	1731	Gentleman
Rigg, John	1731	
Robertson, Capt. Archibald	1757	Soldier
Robertson, James	1772	
Robertson, Peter	1734	
Robertson, Robert	1734	
Robertson, Robert	1771	

SCOTTISH TRADE WITH
COLONIAL CHARLESTON, 1683-1783

Rogers, James	1750	Shopkeeper
Rose, Alexander	1754/56	
Rose, Lt Alexander	1763	Soldier
Rose, James	1765	
Rose, John	1765	Shipwright
Rose, Lewis	1764	
Ross, Thomas	1764	
Ross, William	1740s	
Roupell, George	1740s	
Rowand, Robert	1758	
Rowand, William	1765	Saddler
Russell, James	1740s	
Russell, Robert	1763	
Rutledge, Andrew	1749	
St John, James	1732	
Sampson, Ralph	1765	
Sandilands, Charles	1731	
Sands, James	1763	Merchant
Sarrazin, Jonathan	1769	
Saxby, William	1731	
Scott, Patrick	1740s	
Scott, William	1729/30	Merchsant
Seaman, George	1734	Merchant
Seton, James	1733	
Shaw, Lt. Lachlan	1757	Soldier
Shepherd, Charles	1740s	
Simpson, Edward	1740s	
Simpson, James	1763	Judge
Simpson, John	1763	
Simpson, William	1754/56	
Simpson, William	1768	
Sinclair, George	1729/30	
Sinclair, John	1740s	
Sinclair, Captain John	1757	Soldier
Sinclair, Richard	1732	Merchant
Skene, John	1729/30	Physician
Smart, John	1729/30	

SCOTTISH TRADE WITH
COLONIAL CHARLESTON, 1683-1783

Smith, Alexander	1729/30	Tailor
Smith, Charles	1762	Shipmaster
Smith, James	1763	
Smith, Robert	1732	
Smith, Thomas Loughton	1762	
Smith, Thomas Stitt	1731	
Solomans, Moses	1740s	
Somerville, Tweedie	1731	
Steel, Hugh	1749	
Steel, Robert	1740s	
Stephen, Lt Col. Adam	1757	Soldier
Stephenson, Hugh	1764	
Stephenson, John	1767	
Stevenson, John	1773/75	
Stewart, Alexander	1729/30	Registrar
Stewart, James	1731	
Stewart, James	1766	Shipwright
Stewart, John	1740s	
Stewart, Peter	1772	
Stirling, Robert	1758	Shipmaster
Stobo, Archibald	1732	Minister
Stobo, James	1731	
Stobo, William	1732	
Strachan, James	1751/53	Shipmaster
Strickland, James	1772	
Stuart, Allan	1757	
Stuart, Charles	1763	
Stuart, Adjutant Donald	1757	Soldier
Stuart, Francis	1751/53	Merchant
Stuart, James	1729/30	
Stuart, John	1750	
Stuart, John	1765	Superntendant, Indian Affairs
Sutherland, John	1735	
Sutherland, Major N.	1757	Soldier
Swinton. Hugh	1733	
Swinton, William	1732	Planter
Taylor, James	1768	

Tennant, William	1729/30	Indian Trader
Thompson, James	1740s	
Thompson, John	1763	
Thompson, William	1731	
Tollemache, John	1769	
Trail, James	1772	
Trail, Robert	1772	
Tran, Arthur	1751/53	
Troup, John	1757	
Tunno, John	1768	Merchant
Tweed, Alexander	1764	Merchant
Tweed, James	1764	
Urquhart, Alexander	1768	Shipmaster
Utting, Captain Ashby	1740s	
Valton, Peter	1768	
Van Der Dussen, Alexander	1729/30	
Walker, James	1729/30	
Wallace, Captain James	1763	
Wallace, William	1735	Merchant
Walter, William	1738/39	
Watson, John	1733	
Watson, John, jr	1740s	Merchant
Watson, Magnus	1767	
Watson, William	1736/37	
Watson, William	1751/53	Shipmaster
Wedderburn, Alexander	1740s	
Wedderburn, James	1733	Clerk of Court
Weir, Thomas	1732	
Welch, Mungo	1729/30	
Wells, John, jr	1767	
Wells, John, jr	1758	
Wells, Robert	1754/56	
Wells, William Charles, MD	1773/75	Physician
Welshuysen, Daniel	1732	
Whytlaw, Thomas	1767	
Williams, William	1765	

SCOTTISH TRADE WITH
COLONIAL CHARLESTON, 1683-1783

Williamson, William	1729/30	
Wilson, Dr Robert	1758	Physician
Wilson, William	1770	Merchant
Witherspoon, John	1732	Minister
Wood, Adam	1758	
Woodrup, William	1738/39	Merchant
Wright, James	1738/39	Governor of Georgia
Wyllie, Hugh	1751/53	Shipmaster
Young, Andrew	1729/30	
Young, Henry, jr	1767	
Young, Thomas	1758	

BIBLIOGRAPHY

Primary Sources

ABERDEEN BURGH ARCHIVES
    Proprinquity Book Volume III
ABERDEEN UNIVERSITY, Special Collections,
    MSS997/2740
ANGUS ARCHIVES, Montrose Burgess Roll ms
ARCHIVO GENERAL DE INDIAS, Seville
    De Montiano Auto, fo.8
CHARLESTON PUBLIC LIBRARY, South Carolina
    Charleston Probate Court Book, 1754-1758
    Charleston County Miscellaneous Records, 1727-
    1729
    Charleston County, Wills, Inventories and
    Miscellaneous Documents
    South Carolina Probate Court Records, 1736-1739
    South Carolina Probate Court Book, 1754-1758
DUNDEE CITY ARCHIVES
    Customs and Excise, CE70
    The Lockit Book of the Burgesses of Dundee,
    1513-1981, ms
    Dundee Shipping Register ms
GLASGOW ARCHIVES, TD301/6
GUILDHALL, LONDON, RECORD OFFICE, MRE/93
INDIA OFFICE, London, O series

SCOTTISH TRADE WITH
COLONIAL CHARLESTON, 1683-1783

NATIONAL ARCHIVES, London
    Audit Office AO12; AO 13
    Colonial Office, CO5.363; CO5.366; CO.387;
    CO5.398; CO5.401; CO5.508-511; CO5.670
    Customs, 14/1; 14/2; 14/4; 36/1
    Exchequer, E190
    High Court of the Admiralty, HCA
    Prerogative Court of Canterbury, PCC probate
    records
    Treasury, T47/12
NATIONAL ARCHIVES OF SCOTLAND, Edinburgh
    Admiralty Court, AC7, AC9, AC10
    Church Records, CH1
    Commissary Court, CC8/8/-
    Court of Session, CS17; CS96; CS238
    Exchequer Records, E72, E504
    Gifts and Deposits, GD1, GD3, GD18, GD30,
    GD45, GD76, GD112, GD172, GD176, GD205,
    GD215, GD219, GD237, GD345
    National Register of Archives, Scotland
    Register of Deeds, RD2, RD3, RD4
    Register House, RH15
    Sheriff Court, SC9
NATIONAL LIBRARY OF SCOTLAND, Edinburgh,
    MSS6682; 7003; 87993/4
NORTH CAROLINA STATE ARCHIVES, Raleigh,
    SS978
PUBLIC ARCHIVES OF CANADA, Ottawa,
    R/G4.C2.Volume I.
RECORDS OF THE SCOTS CHURCH IN
    ROTTERDAM, MS I/60

SCOTTISH TRADE WITH
COLONIAL CHARLESTON, 1683-1783

SOUTH CAROLINA HISTORICAL SOCIETY,
  Charleston
  Pringle Garden family papers, 1701-1882,
  MS275.01.01
  Fraser Collection, Correspondence 1774-1784,
  MS11.135
  Cleland Kinloch papers, 1784- MS1168.03.0102
  Fraser Family papers, 1755-1872, MS1029.00
  Isabella MacLaurin memorial, 1784, MS34.468
  Alexander Garden papers, 1758-1767,
  MS1138.03.01
  Ships' Registers in South Carolina Archives, 1734-
  1780, MS052S.1973
  Ships to South Carolina, 1774-1781, MS43.493
  Minerva Ship's log, 1771. MS43.340, MS275
SOUTH CAROLINA STATE ARCHIVES, Columbia
  Records of the Secretary of the Province of South
  Carolina, 1692-1721
W. C. CLEMENTS LIBRARY, University of Michigan
  Miscellaneous Bound Collections

Printed Primary Sources

Acts of the British Parliament Relating to North America,
  Volume II, L. F. Stock, Washington, DC, 1924
Acts of Parliament of Scotland, series, Edinburgh,
  Scotland, 1824
Calendar of State Papers, America and the West Indies,
  1661-1732, London, England, 1880-1969, series
Calendar of Treasury Books, 1660-1718, London,
  England, 1868-1957, series

SCOTTISH TRADE WITH
COLONIAL CHARLESTON, 1683-1783

Calendar of Virginia State Papers, Volume I, Richmond, Virginia, 1875

Journal of the Committee for Trade and the Plantations, London, England, 1925-1937, series

Journal of the House of Commons, Volume XVI, London, England

Journal of the South Carolina House of Assembly, Columbia, South Carolina, 1951

Monumental Inscriptions in the British West Indies, V. L. Oliver, Dorchester, England, 1927

Parish of Holyroodhouse or Canongate Marriage Register, 1564-1800, Edinburgh, Scotland, 1915

Register of Marriages for the Parish of Edinburgh, 1595-1700,
H. Paton, Edinburgh, Scotland, 1905

Register of Marriages for the Parish of Edinburgh, 1701-1750,
H. Paton, Edinburgh, Scotland, 1908

Register of Marriages for the parish of Edinburgh, 1751-1800,
F. J. Grant, Edinburgh, Scotland, 1922

Register of Edinburgh Apprentices, 1701-1755, C. B. Boog-Watson, Edinburgh, Scotland, 1929

Register of the Privy Council of Scotland, 2nd series, 1625-1660; 3rd series, 1661-1691, P. Hume Brown and H. Paton, (eds), Edinburgh, 1899-1970

Roll of Edinburgh Burgesses and Guildbrethren, 1701-1841, C.B. Boog-Watson, Edinburgh, Scotland, 1930

The Burgesses and Gild-Brethren of Glasgow, 1573-1750, J. R. Anderson, Edinburgh, Scotland, 1925

The Letter Book of Eliza Lucas Pinckney, 1739-1762, E.
Pinckney, South Carolina, 1972
The Letter Book of Robert Pringle, 1737-1745, W. B.
Edgar (ed), South Carolina, 1972

Contemporary Newspapers and Journals

Aberdeen Journal, 1747-1786
Belfast News Letter, 1737-1786
Caledonian Mercury, 1722-1786
Edinburgh Evening Courant, 1718-1786
Georgia Gazette, 1763-1776
Glasgow Mercury, 1778-1786
Maryland Gazette, 1727-1786
Scots Magazine, 1739-1786
South Carolina Gazette, 1732-1786

Secondary Sources

(a) Books

Agnew, J., Belfast Merchant Families in the Seventeenth
Century, Dublin, Ireland, 1996
Anderson, P. J., (ed), The Officers and Graduates of
King's College, Aberdeen, Aberdeen, Scotland,
1893

SCOTTISH TRADE WITH
COLONIAL CHARLESTON, 1683-1783

Andrews, E. W., (ed), Journal of a Lady of Quality: Being
    the Narrative of a Journey from Scotland to the
    West Indies, North Carolina, and Portugal in the
    years 1774 to 1776, New Haven, Connecticut,
    1922

Bailyn, B., Voyagers to the West. A Passage in the
    Peopling of America on the Eve of the Revolution,
    New York, New York, 1986

Bailyn, B., and P. D. Morgan, (eds), Strangers within the
    Realm. Cultural Margins of the First British
    Empire, Chapel Hill, North Carolina, 1991

Baker, E.M., 'Indian Traders, Charles Town, and
    London's Vital Links to the Interior of North
    America, 1717-1755', J. P. Greene, R. Brana-
    Shute, and R. J. Sparks, (eds), Money, Trade, and
    Power. The Evolution of Colonial South Carolina's
    Plantation Society, Columbia, South Carolina,
    2001

Blackburn, R., The Making of New World Slavery from
    the Baroque to the Modern, 1492-1800, London,
    England, 1997

Brock, W. R., Scotus Americanus. A survey of the sources
    for links between Scotland and America in the
    eighteenth century, Edinburgh, Scotland, 1982

Burnett, G., History of My Own Time, Edinburgh,
    Scotland, 1833

Butel, P., The Atlantic, London, England, 1999

Butel, P., and L. M. Cullen, Cities and Merchants: French
    and Irish Perspectives on Urban Development,
    1500-1900, Dublin, Ireland, 1986

332

SCOTTISH TRADE WITH
COLONIAL CHARLESTON, 1683-1783

Cage, R. A., The Scots Abroad: Labour, Capital and
    Enterprise, 1750-1914, London, England, 1985
Calder, A., Revolutionary Empire, the Rise of the English
    Speaking Empires from the Fifteenth century to the
    1780s, London, England, 1981
Cameron, A., The Bank of Scotland, 1695-1995,
    Edinburgh, Scotland, 1995
Campbell, R. H., The Carron Company, Edinburgh,
    Scotland, 1961
Canny, N., The Origins of Empire. British Overseas
    Enterprise to the Close of the Seventeenth Century,
    Oxford, England, 2001
Canny, N., and A. Pagden, Colonial Identity in the
    Atlantic World, 1500-1800, Princeton, New Jersey,
    1987
Chambers, R., The Domestic Annals of Scotland,
    Edinburgh, Scotland, 1861
Chaplin, J. E., An Anxious Pursuit, Agricultural
    Innovation and Modernity in the Lower South,
    1730-1815, Chapel Hill, North Carolina, 1995
Clowse, C.C., Economic Beginnings in Colonial South
    Carolina, 1670-1730, Columbia, South Carolina,
    1971
Cochran, L. E., Scottish Trade with Ireland in the
    Eighteenth Century, Edinburgh, Scotland, 1985
Coker, P. C., III, Charleston's Maritime Heritage, 1670-
    1865, Charleston, South Carolina, 1987
Coker, W. S. and T. D.Watson, Indian Traders of the
    South East Spanish Borderlands, Gainesville,
    Florida, 1986

Coldham, P. W., Emigrants in Chains. A Social History of
Forced Emigration to the Americas of Felons,
Destitute Children, Political and Religious Non-
Conformists, Vagabonds, Beggars and other
Undesirables, 1607-1776, Baltimore, Maryland,
1992

Coldham, P. W., American Migrations, 1765-1799,
Baltimore, Maryland, 2000

Coldham, P. W., British Emigrants in Bondage, 1614-
1788, Baltimore, Maryland, 2004

Coulter, E.M., and A. B. Saye, A List of Early Settlers of
Georgia, Baltimore, Maryland, 1983

De Alberti, J. and A. B. Wallis-Chapman, English
Merchants and the Spanish Inquisition in the
Canaries, London, England, 1912

Devine, T. M., The Tobacco Lords, A Study of the
Tobacco Merchants of Glasgow and their Trading
Activities c.1740-90, Edinburgh, Scotland, 1975

Devine, T. M., "The English Connection and Irish-
Scottish Development in the Eighteenth Century",
T. M. Devine and D. Dickson, (eds), Ireland and
Scotland, 1600-1850, Edinburgh, Scotland, 1983

Devine, T. M., Exploring the Scottish Past, East Linton,
Scotland, 1995

Devine, T. M., Scotland's Empire, 1600-1815, London,
England, 2003

Devine, T. M., and G. J. Jackson, Glasgow, Volume I,
Beginnings to 1830, Manchester, England, 1995

De Wolfe, B., Discoveries of America, Cambridge,
England, 1997

Dickson, R. J., Ulster Emigration to Colonial America,
    1718-1775, Belfast, Ireland, 1976
Dobson, D., A Directory of Scots Banished to the
    American Plantations, 1650-1775, Baltimore,
    Maryland, 1983
Dobson, D., The Original Scots Colonists of Early
    America, 1612-1783, Baltimore, Maryland, 1989
Dobson, D., Jacobites of the '15, Aberdeen, Scotland,
    1993
Dobson, D., American Data from the Records of the High
    Court of the Admiralty of Scotland, 1675-1800,
    Baltimore, Maryland, 2000
Dobson, D., Scots in the Carolinas, 1680-1830, Volume 1,
    Baltimore, Maryland, 1986
Dobson, D., Scots in the Carolinas, 1680-1830, Volume II,
    Baltimore, Maryland, 2003
Dobson, D., Scottish Emigration to Colonial America,
    1607-1785, Athens, Georgia, 1994
Dobson, D., Ships from Scotland to America, 1628-1828,
    Volumes I, II, and III, Baltimore, Maryland, 1998,
    2002, and 2004
Dobson, D., Scots in Georgia and the Deep South, 1735-
    1845, Baltimore, Maryland, 2000
Dobson, D., Transatlantic Voyages, 1600-1699,
    Baltimore, Maryland, 2004
Dobson, D., 'Seventeenth Scottish Communities in the
    Americas', in A.Grosjean and S. Murdoch, (eds),
    Scottish Communities Abroad in the Early Modern
    Period, Leiden, The Netherlands, 2005
Donnachie, I., A History of the Brewing Industry in
    Scotland, Edinburgh, Scotland, 1979

Donnan. E., Documents Illustrative of the Slave Trade to
America, Volume IV, Washington, DC, 1935

Duckham, B. F., A History of the Scottish Coal Industry,
Volume I, 1700-1815, Newton Abbot, England,
1970

Duncan, T.B., Atlantic Islands, Madeira, The Azores and
the Cape Verde Islands in Seventeenth Century
Commerce and Navigation, Chicago, Illinois, 1972

Dunlop, J. G., Letters and Journals, 1663-1889, London,
England, 1953

Durie, A. J., The Scottish Linen Industry in the Eighteenth
Century, Edinburgh, Scotland, 1979

Equino, O., The Interesting Narrative of the Life of
Olaudah Vassa, the African, London, England,
1789

Gilhooley, J., A Directory of Edinburgh in 1752,
Edinburgh, Scotland, 1988

Graham, E. J., A Maritime History of Scotland, 1650-
1790, East Linton, Scotland, 2002

Gray, M., The Fishing Industries of Scotland, 1790-1914,
Oxford, England, 1978

Greene, Jack P., Selling a New World, Columbia, South
Carolina, 1989

Greene, Jack P., Rosemary Brana-Shute, and Randy J.
Sparks, (eds.), Money, Trade, and Power. The
Evolution of Colonial South Carolina's Plantation
Society, Columbia, South Carolina, 2001

Griffin, P., The People with No Name. Ireland's Ulster
Scots, America's Scots Irish, and the Creation of a
British Atlantic World, 1689-1764, Princeton, New
Jersey, 2001

Grosjean, A., and S. Murdoch, (eds), Scottish
Communities Abroad in the Early Modern Period,
Leiden, The Netherlands, 2005

Gow, I., 'The Eighteenth Century Interior in Scotland', W.
Caplan, (ed), Scotland Creates. 5000 years of Art
and Design, London, 1990

Hair, P. E., and R. Law, "The English in West Africa to
1700", in N. Canny, (ed), The Origins of Empire,
Oxford, England, 2001

Hallen, A. W. Cornelius, The Scottish Antiquary, Volume
X, Alloa, Scotland,1896

Hamilton, H., Life and Labour on a Aberdeenshire Estate,
1735-1750, Aberdeen, Scotland, 1946

Hamilton, H., The Industrial Revolution in Scotland,
London, England, 1966

Hancock, D., Citizens of the World, London Merchants
and the Integration of the British Atlantic
Community, 1735-1785, Cambridge, England,
1995

Hancock, D., The Early Modern Atlantic Economy,
Cambridge, England, 2000

Hatfield, A. L., Atlantic Virginia, Intercolonial Relations
in the Seventeenth Century, Philadelphia,
Pennsylvania, 2004

Hewison, J. K., The Covenanters, Glasgow, Scotland,
1908

Hewitt, G. L., 'The State in Planters' Service', J. P.
Greene, R. Brana-Shute, and R. J. Sparks, (eds),
Money, Trade, and Power. The Evolution of
Colonial South Carolina's Plantation Society,
Columbia, South Carolina, 2001

SCOTTISH TRADE WITH
COLONIAL CHARLESTON, 1683-1783

Hoffman, R., The Economy of Early America, the
      Revolutionary Period, 1763-1790, Virginia, 1988

Holcomb, B. H., South Carolina Naturalizations, 1783-
      1850, Baltimore, Maryland, 1985

Holland-Braund, K. A., Deerskins and Duffels, the Creek
      Indian Trade with Anglo-America, 1685-1815,
      Nebraska, 1996

Hotten, J. C., Original Lists of Persons of Quality and
      Others who went from Great Britain to the
      American Plantations, 1600-1700, London,
      England, 1874

Howe, George, History of the Presbyterian Church in
      South Carolina, Columbia, South Carolina, 1870

Hume, J. R., The Industrial Archaeology of Glasgow,
      Glasgow, Scotland, 1974

Hurst, R., and J. Prown, Southern Furniture, 1680-1830,
      Williamsburg, Virginia, 1997

Karras, A. L., Sojourners in the Sun, Ithica, New York,
      1992

Kupperman, K. O., Major Problems in American Colonial
      History, second edition, Boston, Massachusetts,
      2000

Lavery, B., Maritime Scotland, London, England, 2001

Lesser, C. H., South Carolina Begins, the Records of a
      Proprietary Colony, 1663-1721, Columbia, South
      Carolina, 1995

Littlefield, D. C., Rice and Slaves, Champaign, Illinois,
      1991

Lynch, M., The Oxford Companion to Scottish History,
      Oxford, England, 2005

Marshall, J. M., The Life and Times of Leith, Edinburgh,
      Scotland, 1986

SCOTTISH TRADE WITH
COLONIAL CHARLESTON, 1683-1783

Meining, D. W., The Shaping of America, Volume I,
    Yale, Connecticut, 1986
Meriwether, R. L., The Expansion of South Carolina,
    1729-1765, Kingsport, Tennessee, 1940
Meyer, D., The Highland Scots of North Carolina, 1732-
    1776, Chapel Hill, North Carolina,1978
Middleton, R., Colonial America, a History, 1607-1760,
    Cambridge, England, 1992
Minchinton, W., C. White, and P. Waite, (eds), The
    Virginia Slave Trade Statistics, 1698-1775,
    Richmond, Virginia, 1984
Montgomerie, R., a Discourse Concerning the Designed
    Establishment of a New Colony to the South of
    Carolina in the Most Delightful Country of the
    Universe, London, England, 1717
Morgan, K., Bristol and the Atlantic Trade in the
    Eighteenth Century, Cambridge, England, 1993
Morgan, P. D., Slave Counterpoint, Black Culture in the
    Eighteenth Century Chesapeake and Low Country,
    Chapel Hill, North Carolina, 1998
Mowat, S., The Port of Leith, Its History and People,
    Edinburgh, Scotland, 1994
Murdoch, A., British Emigration, 1603-1914, Basingstoke,
    England, 2004
McCusker, J., and R. R. Menard, The Economy of British
    America, 1607-1789, Chapel Hill, North Carolina,
    1985
McCusker, J., and R. R. Menard, 'The Centrality of
    Trade', in The Atlantic Staple Trade, Volume II :
    The Economics of Trade, Aldershot, England,
    1996

SCOTTISH TRADE WITH
COLONIAL CHARLESTON, 1683-1783

McCusker, J., and K. Morgan, The Early Modern Atlantic
Economy, Cambridge, England, 2000

McFarlane, Anthony, The British in the Americas, 1480-
1815, London, England, 1994

McInnes, A. I., (ed), Scotland and the Americas, c1650-
c1939, Edinburgh, Scotland, 2002

Mackay, W., (ed.),The Letterbook of Baillie John Steuart
of Inverness, 1715-1752, Edinburgh, Scotland,
1915

McLeod, W., (ed), Journal of the Hon. John Erskine of
Carnock, 1683-1687, Edinburgh, Scotland, 1893

McMillan, B. C., Captive Passage, the Transatlantic Slave
Trade and the Making of the Americas,
Washington, DC, 2002

McNeill, W. A., Papers of a Dundee Shipping Dispute, in
Miscellany X of the Scottish
History Society, Edinburgh, Scotland, 1965

MacPherson, D., Annals of Commerce, Manufactures,
Fisheries and Navigation, Edinburgh, Scotland,
1805

McVeagh, P., The Creamware Potter, East of Scotland,
1750-1840, Edinburgh, Scotland, 1980

Nairne, T., "A Letter from South Carolina, London,
1710", in J. P. Greene, (ed), Selling a New World,
Columbia, South Carolina, 1989

Nash, R. C., 'South Carolina and the Atlantic Economy on
the late Seventeenth and Eighteenth Centuries', in
The Atlantic Staple Trade, Volume II: The
Economics of Trade, Aldershot, England, 1996

Nash, R. C., The Organization of Trade Finance in the
Atlantic Economy, Britain and South Carolina,

SCOTTISH TRADE WITH
COLONIAL CHARLESTON, 1683-1783

1670-1775, in J. P. Greene, R. Brana-Shute, and R. J. Sparks, (eds), Money, Trade and Power, The Evolution of Colonial South Carolina's Plantation Society, Columbia, South Carolina, 2001

Nesbitt, R. C., Nisbets of that Ilk, London, England, 1941

Nisbet, J. A., Nisbets of Carfin, London, England, 1916

Olmert, M., The Official Guide to Colonial Williamsburg, Williamsburg, Virginia, 1997

Ormiston, T., The Ormistons of Teviotdale, Exeter, England, 1951

Parker, A. W., Scottish Highlanders in Colonial Georgia, Athens, Georgia, 1997

Pearson, Edward, 'Planters Full of Money. The Self-Fashioning of the Eighteenth-Century South Carolina Elite', J. P. Greene, R. Brana-Shute, and R. J. Sparks, (eds), Money, Trade and Power. The Evolution of Colonial South Carolina's Plantation Society, Columbia, South Carolina, 2001

Ramsey, W. L., "All and Singular the Slaves", J. P. Greene, R. Brana-Shute, and R. J.Sparks, (eds), Money, Trade, and Power, The Evolution of Colonial South Carolina's Plantation Society, Columbia, South Carolina, 2001

Rauschenberg, B. L., and J. Bivins jr., The Furniture of Charleston, 1680-1820, 3 volumes, Winston Salem, North Carolina, 2003

Richardson, D., 'British Empire and the Atlantic Slave Trade, 1660-1807' in The Eighteenth Century, P. J. Marshall, Oxford, England, 2001

Ripley, W., Charles Towne, Birth of a City, Charleston, South Carolina, 1998

SCOTTISH TRADE WITH
COLONIAL CHARLESTON, 1683-1783

Roberts, F., and I. M. M. McPhail, Dunbarton Common
  Good Accounts, 1614-1660, Dunbarton, Scotland,
  1972

Robinson, W. S., The Southern Colonial Frontier, 1607-
  1763, Albuquerque, New Mexico, 1979

Salley, A. S., jr., Warrants for land in South Carolina,
  1672-1711, Baltimore, Maryland, 1998

Scott, H., (comp.), Fasti Ecclesiae Scoticanae, Edinburgh,
  Scotland, 1925-1928

Scott-Moncreiff, R., (ed.), The Household Book of Lady
  Grizell Baillie, 1692-1733, Edinburgh, Scotland,
  1911

Sellers, L., Charleston Businesses on the Eve of the
  American Revolution, Chapel Hill, North Carolina,
  1934

Smout, T. C., Scottish Trade on Eve of Union, Edinburgh,
  Scotland, 1963

Snapp, J. Russell, John Stuart and the Struggle for Empire
  on the Southern Frontier, Baton Rouge, Louisiana,
  1990

Solow, B. L., Slavery and the Rise of the Atlantic System,
  Cambridge, England, 1991

Taylor, A., American Colonies. The Settlement of North
  America to 1800, London, England, 2001

Thomas, H., The Slave Trade, the History of the Atlantic
  Slave Trade, 1440-1870, London, England, 1997

Thomson, A. G., The Paper Industry in Scotland, 1590-
  1861, Edinburgh, Scotland, 1974

Truxes, T. M., Irish American Trade, 1660-1783,
  Cambridge, England, 2000

Turnbull, J., The Scottish Glass Industry, 1610-1750,
  Edinburgh, Scotland, 2001

SCOTTISH TRADE WITH
COLONIAL CHARLESTON, 1683-1783

Vickers, D, A Companion to Colonial America, Oxford,
        England, 2003
Walvin, J., Black Ivory, a History of British Slavery,
        London, England, 1993
Weis, F. L., Colonial Clergy of Virginia and the Carolinas,
        Baltimore, Maryland, 1976
Whatley, C. A., The Salt Industry and its Trade in Fife and
        Tayside, c.1570-1850, Dundee, Scotland, 1984
Whatley, C. A., The Scottish Salt Industry, 1570-1850,
        Aberdeen, Scotland, 1987
Whatley, C. A., The Industrial Revolution in Scotland,
        Cambridge, England, 1997
Whatley, C. A., Scottish Society, 1707-1830, Manchester,
        England, 2000
Whyte, D., Scottish Clock and Watchmakers, 1453-1900,
        Edinburgh, Scotland, 1966
Whyte, I. D., Scotland before the Industrial Revolution,
        An Economic and Social History c1050-c1750,
        London, England, 1995
Wokeck, M. S., Trade in Strangers: The Beginning of
        Mass Migration to North America, Pennsylvania,
        1999
Wood, P., Black Majority, New York, New York, 1974
Worth, John E., The Struggle for the Georgia Coast,
        Athens, Georgia, 1995
Yeoman, P. (ed), The Salt and Coal Industries at St
        Monans, Fife, in the 18th and 19th Centuries,
        Glenrothes, Scotland, 1999
Southern Furniture, 1640-1820, New York, New York,
        1952
Shipping, Maritime Trade and Economic Growth of
        Colonial North America, Cambridge, England,
        1972
343

INDEX

SCOTTISH TRADE WITH
COLONIAL CHARLESTON, 1683-1783

346

348

SCOTTISH TRADE WITH
COLONIAL CHARLESTON, 1683-1783

352

354

355

357

358

363

365